THE OXLEY PARKER PAPERS

Printed by Benham and Company Limited
Colchester, England

THE
OXLEY PARKER
PAPERS

FROM THE LETTERS AND DIARIES
OF AN ESSEX FAMILY OF LAND AGENTS
IN THE NINETEENTH CENTURY

by J. Oxley Parker

BENHAM AND COMPANY LIMITED

COLCHESTER

Woodham Mortimer Place

CONTENTS

LIST OF ILLUSTRATIONS

PREFACE

This book deals with the lives of two men, and some brief remarks about them may be of interest to readers. Nothing is recorded of the education and youth of Christopher Comyns Parker. He was the eldest son of the first John Oxley Parker, a well-known attorney of Chelmsford, but after a short time in his father's office he decided he had no wish to devote his life to the law. An outdoor life of farming was what appealed to him, and he had the strength of mind to break away from an established business career at the age of twenty-two, and to devote his life to one of which he was ignorant—farming. To this he soon added estate management, and it was not long before his reputation for integrity and hard work brought him clients. It is evident that his name was known outside Essex, for within a year of the foundation of the Surveyors' Club in 1835 he was elected a member of that select body which was, and still is, limited to thirty-nine members for all England.

Though farming and land agency absorbed most of his time and energy, he also took an active part in local affairs—as Mayor of Maldon, Chairman of the Guardians, and a Deputy Lieutenant of the County; and he always took a keen interest in political elections. We have no record of any recreations or amusements.

Much more is known of his son, John Oxley Parker. From early days he had a great zest for life, and a great love of his fellow-men; and clearly he was popular wherever he went. He had inherited his father's tireless energy, carried on his work as farmer and estate agent, and modelled his business life on that of his father.

He was the typical country squire, taking a deep interest in all that occurred in his county, clearly a man to whom people turned for advice and welcomed on committees. But recreation too played an important part in his life. He was very fond of shooting, hunting, and dancing, and enjoyed all social occasions, attending archery meetings and village fêtes; and, when cricket started, at once provided a ground and took an interest in the game, though he never played.

This book is compiled from the letters and diaries of Christopher Comyns Parker and John Oxley Parker, records which have preserved a clear picture of life in a country district in the nineteenth century. C.C.P. filed all correspondence under the name of his client and the letters were tied together with red tape; and, in the case of the estates he managed, the number of letters and receipts increased year by year. Nothing was destroyed. There was a large book-case at his home, Woodham Mortimer Place, with numerous pigeon-holes, where all correspondence was stored away, and this system was carried on by his son J.O.P.

On the death of J.O.P. his two daughters lived on at the Place and the letters remained untouched until after the death of the surviving daughter at the age of ninety, when the house was sold. I did not know of the existence of the letters until I discovered them one day by accident, with a large number of maps and account books. I filled several trunks with neat bundles of letters, and spent evening after evening reading them, tearing up hundreds that seemed of no permanent interest. I handed many to the Essex Record Office, and retained those that took my fancy.

This book is the result. Although my name appears as author, most of the work was done by that well-known historian, Dr. H. E. Priestley, and I am at a loss to express the immense debt I owe him for many, many hours of work, and for his knowledge and experience in deciding the form and material for the chapters.

I should like to add my thanks to Mr. F. G. Emmison and Miss Hilda Grieve of the Essex Record Office. Without their encouragement and advice the book would not have been attempted.

At Mr. Emmison's request, I decided shortly before this book was published to place all the remaining family records, with the exception of the diaries, on loan in the Record Office.

J. OXLEY PARKER

The Old Rectory
Faulkbourne
Essex

The Parker family from 1694

Charles George
b. 1780
d. 1847

n

Oxley   Elizabeth O.

7
uisa Durant
322
393

pher W.   Oxley Durant   Eva C.   Charles A.
                   b. 1854   *b.* 1856   *b.* 1858
                   d. 1932   *d.* 1936   *d.* 1935
n C. Farrer   *m.* G. Gambier Parry *m.* G. T. Brunwin Hales   *m.* Agnes Durant
57   *b.* 1857   *b.* 1859   *b.* 1859
52   *d.* 1943   *d.* 1932   *d.* 1933

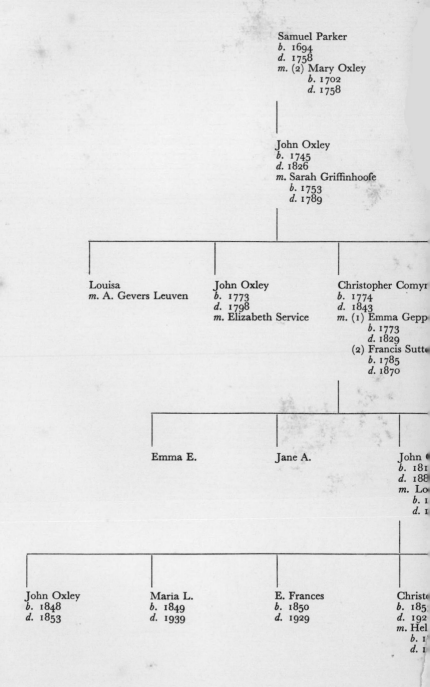

Samuel Parker
b. 1694
d. 1758
m. (2) Mary Oxley
    b. 1702
    d. 1758

John Oxley
b. 1745
d. 1826
m. Sarah Griffinhoofe
    b. 1753
    d. 1789

Louisa	John Oxley	Christopher Comyn
m. A. Gevers Leuven	*b.* 1773	*b.* 1774
	d. 1798	*d.* 1843
	m. Elizabeth Service	*m.* (1) Emma Gepp
		b. 1773
		d. 1829
		(2) Francis Sutt
		b. 1785
		d. 1870

Emma E.	Jane A.	John
		b. 181
		d. 188
		m. Lo
		b. 1
		d. 1

John Oxley	Maria L.	E. Frances	Christe
b. 1848	*b.* 1849	*b.* 1850	*b.* 185
d. 1853	*d.* 1939	*d.* 1929	*d.* 192
			m. Hel
			b. 1
			d. 1

CHAPTER I

FAMILY AND ESTATE

ON 4 DECEMBER 1735 Samuel Parker of Ipswich married Mary, the eldest daughter of Dr. Christopher Oxley of Southwark. Samuel was a widower whose first wife, Margaret, had died two years previously, leaving him with one surviving daughter, Elizabeth. Her marriage in September 1735 to Jonathan Abbott had left her father alone. At forty-one, Samuel Parker was young enough, and his various properties in Suffolk gave him income sufficient, to marry again and raise a second family.

In the ten years which followed the family duly arrived: Samuel, born in 1736, Mary in 1738, Jane in 1741, Christopher in 1743, and John Oxley in 1745. Samuel at the age of fifteen went to sea and was a lieutenant at twenty-one, but before any of the other children either took up careers or married, both Samuel the elder and his wife died, she on 2 May and he on 10 October 1758.

The family property, Samuel's in Suffolk, and Mary's inherited from her father in Southwark, was left to the children. The latter estate, known as the Bermondsey property, became divided amongst various members of the family, but was bought back at a later date from his cousins by John Oxley Parker the Younger (1812–87). Oxley Durant Parker, in his book *The Oxley Parker Family*, writes of the marriage and the Bermondsey property:

The marriage of Samuel Parker with Mary Oxley therefore proved an important event in our family, and as our father used to say with truth, it [the Bermondsey property] was the best farm he had, and maintained the family in bad times; and its rent roll has materially improved since his death in 1887, being worth some thousands a year.

I

The four youngest children, after the deaths of their father and mother, were taken to live with their uncle, John Oxley, who lived at Springfield, near Chelmsford, in Essex. Of these, Christopher later went into business in London and the two sisters to Kent. Only John Oxley, the youngest, remained in Essex.

Oxley Durant Parker also gives as detailed a history as has yet been found of these four children of Samuel and Mary Parker. Of the youngest brother, John Oxley, he says:

His uncle, John Oxley, was now advancing in years, and one can readily understand how anxious he must have been to find an opening for his young nephew. Luckily he had a great friend and neighbour, John Comyns, afterwards Lord Chief Baron of the Exchequer, who lived near by at Hylands, two miles from Chelmsford, and it was probably at his suggestion that he should become an Attorney-at-Law, and from the 'Record Office', on the Roll of persons articled to Solicitors, we find 'in 1760 John Oxley Parker, of Springfield, was articled to Mr. Maplesdon Bound of Chelmsford for 5 years'.

The profession of Attorney-at-Law in those days was different from what it is to-day. Country banks had not grown into the importance that they have to-day, and in the matter of advances of a pecuniary nature, the countryside looked to a good firm of solicitors for assistance, and therefore they acted in the capacity of Bankers to a great many people.

Probably before his uncle, John Oxley, of Springfield, died on July 8, 1770, he [John Oxley Parker] decided to start on his own account, and for some time we know that he resided in lodgings in Chelmsford, but by the turn of the year he evidently felt so firmly established in his business, that on February 23, 1771 he married Miss Sarah Griffenhoofe, the only child of Dr. Christopher Griffenhoofe and Priscilla, his wife, of Chelmsford at St. Mary's Church, now the Cathedral of the Essex diocese. She was born at Chelmsford in 1752, and had been baptised in the same church on January 21, 1753.

. . . The *Chelmsford and Colchester Chronicle* of March 1, 1771, announces the wedding: 'On Saturday was married Mr. John Oxley-Parker, an eminent Attorney-at-Law in this Town, to Miss Griffenhoofe, an agreeable young lady of the same place.'

We are left to contemplate what strange events create and dissolve families. A late second marriage in 1735 with children, the untimely deaths of both parents in 1758 which turned the children's lives in entirely different directions, the inheritance of sufficient property, the guardianship of a kind uncle, the counsel of a learned and able lawyer, the enterprise of a younger son and his sons—not one, but all these happenings have gone to create this family which rightly keeps in memory the name 'Oxley' and the Christian names its members have borne for generations.

John Oxley Parker and his bride went to live at The Friars, Moulsham, on the spot where the Dominican, or Black Friars, had once had a house. As a solicitor in Chelmsford, John Oxley Parker prospered. His great-grandson says of him:

So far as one can judge, John Oxley Parker was gaining the confidence of all around him, and his business was rapidly increasing; he had been appointed Deputy Registrar of the Archdeaconries of Essex, Middlesex and Colchester, within the counties of Essex and Herts, also of the peculiar jurisdiction of Writtle with Roxwell annexed, and of Good Easter in the County of Essex, and this appointment probably threw him a good deal with Sir John Comyns of Hylands; in addition he was acting as professional agent of the respective Wardens and Fellows of New College and Wadham College for their estates in Essex. 'He enjoyed likewise for upwards of 50 years the appointment of Steward of the Manor and Estates belonging to the ancient family of the Mildmays, the duties of which (I am quoting now much from the obituary in the *Chelmsford Chronicle* at his death years afterwards) situation he uniformly discharged with the utmost fidelity, assiduity and zeal.'
. . . His wife died comparatively young on February 12, 1789, at the Friars, and was buried in the family vault in the St. Mary's, Chelmsford, Churchyard on February 19th. It is outside the West End of the Cathedral and surrounded with high iron railings. She was 'universally lamented'.

They had four children: Louisa, who in 1793 married Arnout Gevers Leuven, a young man attached to the court of William III of Holland, then in exile in this country, about which we shall read later; John Oxley, born in 1773, who went into his father's business and died without issue in 1801; Charles George (1780–1847), who also went into the family business and in time became a prosperous Chelmsford solicitor, and Christopher Comyns (1774–1843), of whom, with his son John Oxley (1812–87), this study principally treats.

Christopher had the opportunity of going with his brothers into his father's business, but, after trying it, decided that a life in the open air was much more to his liking. At Michaelmas, 1796, therefore, at the age of twenty-two, he took Woodham Mortimer Place and some land around it, to farm, leasing it from the then Lord of the Manor of Woodham Mortimer, Samuel Wegg. The house remained the family home during almost the whole of the following century, the lease being renewed from time to time.

It seems that Christopher did well in his chosen vocation, for he spared no expense in bringing his home up to date. A letter of 1817 from Robert L. Appleyard of Lincoln's Inn, solicitor to the Lord of the Manor, says:

By the memoranda I made when we met in Brook Street, the whole of the land in Woodham Mortimer is held by you except the Manor and the Wood.

He went on to ask C.C.P.'s opinion of its value. The reply ran:

The farm I occupy is most of it naturally of very bad quality and is necessarily obliged to be farmed at great expense to keep it in a high state of cultivation. . . . The rent . . . was full its value and really higher than most farms in the neighbourhood, but I have since expended about £1000 on this House and otherwise much improved the appearance of the place by dressing it with Plantations, that I have no doubt as a 'residence' it might, now the prospects of farming have revived, let at an advance of from £30 to £50 a year; but such a letting must depend upon some person like myself having large occupations on the Marshes wanting a residence where his family may be tolerably secure from Essex Agues.

He goes on to say that the wood is worth £3000, the manor £26 15s. a year, the tithes £400 a year, and the parson's house and glebe £70 to £75 a year.

It appears from the above that in 1817 C.C.P. was farming extensively in Woodham Mortimer and that he also had land in Bradwell under cultivation and as marsh pasture, probably the farms in Bradwell owned by his father. In 1826, when John Oxley Parker died, he expressed a wish that his property at Bradwell and Danbury should be offered to his son Christopher at the prices of £7500 and £1200 respectively. Christopher gave notice that he would purchase these on 30 June 1826. The Bradwell estate, which was the larger, included Eastlands, Dunbirds Farm, and Munkins Farm, and the old Saxon church of St. Peter's-on-the-Wall.

Extracts from the Woodham Mortimer Manor Rolls show something of the way in which C.C.P. established himself during the early years of the nineteenth century. In a court of 9 August 1806 he received his first grant of land from the manorial waste, an unspecified quantity, probably only a few roods 'upon which a cottage now occupied by William Deadman and Obadiah Baker has since been built'. At a court of 25 July 1812 he received, by the surrender of three owners, 30½ acres of land containing three tenements. For the three tenements and 7½ acres of the land he paid £350 to the former owner, William Martin. In addition to this he received in grants from the waste more than 10 acres which were added to the fields he already held. In 1814 he added a further 4 acres, and in 1821 a total of 42 acres bought from various persons and confirmed by transfer in the Manor Court on 14 February of that year.

Enclosures of 'waste' land of the manor such as have been mentioned above were occurring all over England at this time on a large scale. In this connection it is worth recording an incident which occurred about 1933.

It concerned a small wood of just over 3 acres bordering the main road, of hot gravelly soil, which was habitually used as a camping-ground by gipsies and such-like. It became customary for lorries to dump tins and rubbish there, and these of course looked unsightly and gave an uncared-for look to the village. So

I [J.O.P., who owned it then] had the rubbish cleared away, put barbed wire across the entrance to prevent further dumping, and put up a notice in the Post Office asking for the co-operation of the village in my efforts to prevent further dumping.

Next time I passed, the wire was cut, the stakes removed, and further dumping of rubbish had occurred. I consulted a leading farmer and expressed my disappointment at the lack of support from the village. His reply was most interesting. 'I am afraid you must desist from your efforts, Mr. Parker. The villagers believe that this land is Common Land, and by fencing it they suspect that you have plans to do something with it, and deprive them of it.' So I consulted an old manor map and a study of that led me to the conclusion that the village tradition, handed down from father to son, was correct; the land was in fact Common Land and I had no genuine title to it, although it had been sold to my father as freehold. The reason it had never been enclosed was the poor quality of the soil!

But to return to the nineteenth century. Whilst all this was happening, C.C.P., who was developing his business as a land agent, was in the best position to know the value of land which was up for sale. On 20 October 1818 he was present at Garraway's coffee-house in 'Change Alley when various farms in Danbury, Woodham Mortimer, and Hazeleigh were put up for auction. He seems to have bought at the auction Lot III, a 52-acre farm called Judges, for £1710, two copyhold plots totalling 4 acres for £118 (Lots VI and VII), and Lot VIII, a 58-acre farm called Potkilns for £1750. On the back of another copy of the same sale bill occurs the following memo signed by the two contracting parties:

John Wiggins of Tyndalls Esqr hereby agrees to sell and Christopher Comyns Parker Esqr hereby agrees to purchase Lots 2 and 5 described in the within Particulars for the sum of Two Hundred Pounds subject to the conditions within mentioned. . . . Witness our hands this day.

C. Comyns Parker
John Wiggins

6

Lot II was a 10-acre field in Danbury and Lot V a copyhold plot of three-quarters of an acre adjoining his own land east of Woodham Mortimer Church. Another sale bill of 7 July 1819 shows a purchase of 7½ acres on the Danbury–Maldon road. In addition, he was, from 1816, occupying Oak Farm, Woodham Walter, at a rent of £84 4s. a year and his son J.O.P. continued to lease until 1863 when he bought it from the Duke of St. Albans.

Before C.C.P. was enabled by the terms of his father's will to purchase the main Bradwell and Danbury lands, he already possessed some 450 acres in Woodham Mortimer and nearby parishes, with a total rental value of £532:

Particulars of Lands and Premises belonging to C. Comyns Parker, situate in Woodham Mortimer, Hazeleigh, Purleigh, Latchingdon and Bradwell, taken December 27th, 1818.

The Grange in Woodham Mortimer consists of a good substantial brick-built House with a large wheat Barn, cart Stable for eight Horses, Riding Stable for six Horses, Cow House, Cart Lodges and other convenient outbuildings all in very good repair, large gardens and Orchard well planted with fruit trees, and arable and pasture Land making together 118 acres, on which are also two Tenements, with another Barn in tolerable repair, near the Farm House and four other Tenements situate in . . . all let at low rents to Labourers amounting to . . . . 90½ acres are Freehold, 17½ acres Copyhold of the Manor of Woodham Mortimer and 10 Acres copyhold of the Manor of Waltons in Purleigh; there is a valuable Clay pit on the Farm; the whole is remarkably well timbered. Lease for 52 years at £100 a year with Rent. Land Tax redeemed, 4 years of Lease from last Mic[as] unexpired. Quit Rent £1 1s. 1d.

Copyhold Lands and Premises in Woodham Mortimer in hand— Two new brick-built Tenements, with good Garden well planted with fruit and other Trees, and 20 acres in enclosures. Quit Rent 10s.

Copyhold lands in hand in Purleigh and Hazeleigh late Matthew Halls, containing 18 acres in three enclosures, quit Rent 3s. 6d.

Farm in occupation of William Martin upon Lease for 14 years from Mic[as] last, of which 12 acres are Freehold on which is a small Farm House, Barn, Stable, Cow House and Cart and other Sheds all in good repair. Also 6½ acres copyhold of Woodham Mortimer on which there are three substantial Tenements underlet at £10 a year Rent during the life of Mary Bonner aged 72 yrs to whom an anny of £15 a year is payable, £42 after the decease of Mary Bonner —£35 a year.

Marsh House. Copyhold of the Manor of Waltons in Purleigh, consists of good substantial timber and tiled Farm House, good double Barn, half new built this year, Stables for eight horses, Cow House, new Cart Lodge and several other Cattle Sheds, Hen House, Piggeries etc, all in very good repair with 150 acres of arable and Pasture land in 14 enclosures well timbered. Rent £200 a year by agreement of 7 years made 25th Sept, 1813. Land Tax £7 9s. 6d., Quit Rent £1 15s. 8d.

Two newly erected Tenements adjoining the above let at £10 a year.

Two tenements erected 20 years since on the Manor of Lawling Hall. Rent £10 a year. Fine on death or alienation 5s. Quit Rent 1s.

Two new erected Tenements on the Manor of Bradwell Hall. Rent £10, Quit Rent 1s.

Miss Wegg, who was Lord of the Manor of Woodham Mortimer during the greater part of C.C.P.'s occupation of the Place, had an agent named John Webb. Between landlord and tenant relations were easy and friendly. When times were difficult the landlord was accommodating:

She [Miss Wegg] desires me to say that she does not entertain the least doubt of your paying the remainder of the rent, and does not wish to press for an immediate payment if inconvenient to you, only requests you to remit the money when it suits you. . . . (23 June 1822.)

In the same month C.C.P. asked for an abatement, but the agent very politely put him off:

I hardly know how I can mention the question of Reduction to her as she has had only one application on that subject from a poor Tenant whose rent was raised . . . only two years ago.

He was delighted, therefore, without asking for it, to get an abatement of 25 per cent in the following December 'on account of the depress'd state of the Agriculture of the County'. In the following year there was another reduction of half the percentage, i.e. 12½ per cent.

Miss Wegg died in 1842 and in August of that year C.C.P. received a letter from his friend C. G. Round.

If you have not already been introduced to your new Landlord I must introduce him to you in the person of my brother Mr. James Round to whom it has pleased Miss Wegg to devise her property at Woodham Mortimer. Her other farms in Essex she has left to me, but her Woodham Mortimer property to James. Long may it remain in doubt whether you are more pleased with him as your landlord or her with you as his tenant.

A letter from James Round arrived at Woodham Mortimer Place the following day:

You will be as much surprised to learn as I was that our old friend Miss Wegg has left me by her will her estate, manor and advowson at Woodham Mortimer. For your own sake I could have wished you a better landlord. But you must bear with me and I will endeavour with God's help to do my duty, and I trust that you and yours will ever find me not unready to give my best consideration to whatever may contribute to the comfort of my tenants.

The pleasure was mutual:

. . . most sincerely do I congratulate you upon the acquisition and I assure you it will give Mrs. Parker and myself much pleasure to see you and Mrs. James Round at Woodham Mortimer Place where I may show you the whole of your property in this Parish.

Having been tenant since Mic^as, 1796, and made the Place what it is, you may imagine I have felt anxious to learn who was to be my landlord. I now feel happy that there is little probability of any circumstance occurring to prevent my passing the remainder of my days here.

His remaining days were not many, for on 1 August 1843 he died as the result of a fall from his horse. His will, dated 15 July 1836, was proved in the Prerogative Court of the Archbishop of Canterbury on 20 March 1844.

I give and bequeath all my messuages lands tenements and real estate whatever and wheresoever situate and of what nature and

9

quality soever whether in possession reversion, remainder or expect-
ancy or whether at law or equity or over which I have any disposing
power And also my ready money and monies in the public stocks or
funds or securities And all and singular other my goods chattels and
personal estate whatsoever and wheresoever not hereinbefore by me
otherwise disposed of unto the use of my s^d son John Oxley Parker
his heirs executors etc., subject to the payment of legacies of £200
and £4000 all debts paid.

At a manor court of James Round on 25 June 1845 John
Oxley Parker was admitted to all his late father's copyhold
lands within the parish of Woodham Mortimer.

From 1842 onwards, relations with the Round family became
more intimate:

Amongst other property left to me [wrote C. G. Round] are the
houses and land at Acton and Ealing, between one hundred and
forty and one hundred and fifty acres of land. I believe that this land
is in hand. I should be extremely desirous of having the benefit of
your advice on putting it off. I have no inclination to hold an offhand
farm fifty-five miles away. . . . (12 September 1842.)

—and from James Round (20 January 1850):

Mrs. Joseph Round has not forgotten that she is indebted to you
for examining and advising on her farm at St. Osyth.

This happy landlord–tenant relationship eventually brought
into the agency the lands owned by the whole Round family, at
Birch, Layer Marney, St. Osyth, Bergholt, Clacton, and the
castle at Colchester, owned by C. G. Round:

September 19th, 1857. Early to Birch and afterwards to Colchester
with Mr. Round for the purpose of inspecting the ground around the
Castle etc, the Corporation having applied for the Castle Bailey as
a cattle market. Afterwards consulting with Mr. Round and preparing letter offering the ground on south and west sides provided that
20 feet space in front of outer walls on those sides should be enclosed
and the ground on the east and north sides thrown into Mr. James
Round's garden—C. G. Round esq.

The letters which passed between James Round and J.O.P.
with regard to reductions in rent are surely almost without

precedent in the history of landlord and tenant relationships, at least in the nineteenth century. In 1850 the tenant charged only a part of the sums due for bricks and tiles when making improvements, and these partial charges were repeated time and again, whereas under the usual terms of any lease it was the obligation of the landlord to provide them all. On one occasion, in 1850, the landlord offered to reduce the rent of Woodham Mortimer Place, but J.O.P. insisted on paying it in full. On 14 February 1851, James Round wrote:

If the experience of another year of Free Trade has led you to change your mind as to my proposal for reducing your rent, I am quite willing to have it acted upon.

J.O.P., who was at that time engaged in extensive repairs to the Woodham Mortimer property, replied:

As to my rent, I am extremely indebted to you for your kind consideration. Should the times require it I know that you will be ready to meet them by reasonable reduction, but for the present, or rather the past year, I must be content to regard your liberal acquiescence in my request to supply the materials for my new laundry in the light of an abatement. (15 February 1851.)

The cost of the materials for the laundry was £36. J.O.P. charged his landlord £30.

In the following month his account showed a larger expenditure than the landlord had expected, on a couple of cottages. James Round's gentle reproof was followed by a confession which must have put him quite at his ease:

I imagine the outlay on Barnard's must have come upon you gradually, or you would never have thought it right to expend so much of *my* money without first letting me know the extent to which it might be necessary to go. You must *never* do the like again. In the meantime I am goodnatured enough to tell you that in consequence of the receipt of an unexpected sum of money, the defalcation in the annual remittance has not been *seriously* inconvenient. . . . (14 March 1851.)

After this time James Round seems to have employed an agent named John Freeland of Gray's Inn, to whom his methods of dealing with his friendly tenant must have appeared strange. Freeland's businesslike attitude, and possibly his lack of realisation of the amount of money the Parker family had put into Woodham Mortimer Place during the previous half-century, led to a difference of opinion in which Mr. Round was unhappily involved.

The lease on the Place was renewed, sometimes at seven, sometimes at fourteen, and sometimes at twenty-one years, and the security which such an arrangement afforded made it worth while for the tenant to improve the premises he occupied, obtaining payment for certain materials from the landlord. In 1857 there were some difficulties about getting an allowance for paint for Woodham Mortimer Place, and J.O.P. reminded Mr. Round's agent that he had gone to great expense.

With regard to the paint for outside work which has usually been granted, I considered that I was asking what is a reasonable allowance. I allow it to my own tenants, and also in cases in which I act for other people, and think it desirable. A tenant may sometimes hesitate to incur the double expense of paint and labour, and the premises suffer from the delay, but where the allowance of material shares the cost, the thing is done at the proper intervals. I do not like to have to call attention to my own acts, but I could point to innumerable cases in which I have waived my charges upon my landlord in bricks, lime etc etc; gravel carried into roads, in the woods etc., and recent alterations of stables, brewhouse etc., new alterations of sewers from the house costing not less than £500. The only allowance I have been granted was £50 whereas the sewerage etc, undertaken *at Mr. Round's suggestion*, alone, cost £120. (1 May 1857.)

J.O.P. signed the new lease, and was not reimbursed for the paint he had bought. A week later, he closed the correspondence with:

'I don't mean to say that I am not satisfied or that I consider that Mr. Round has failed to meet my views in a kind and friendly manner, but there is something to be said on the other side, and my mode of treating the place may fairly deserve some consideration.' (8 May 1857.)

Before the end of his life, J.O.P. owned considerable lands in Woodham Mortimer, Purleigh, Danbury, Bradwell, and Hazeleigh. In 1853 he extended his interests in Woodham Mortimer where a tenant of the manor died, leaving Nursery Farm vacant. He took the farm at a rental of £84 per annum and the lease continued till 1873 when he bought the farm at a sale owing to the death of the owner and Lord of the Manor, Mrs. Agnis, though what he paid for it is not quite clear. A letter from his solicitor, Walter V. Gepp, in July 1873 mentions the payment of 'the balance of purchase money', which came to £2700.

In 1863 the Duke of St. Albans decided to sell off part of his land in Woodham Walter and at a sale in July of that year J.O.P. bought Oak Farm.

Thus, partly through inheritance, partly through judicious purchases, the family estate was built up. Many changes have taken place since 1887, when J.O.P. died, but small parts of this large and scattered estate still remain in the hands of the family.

CHAPTER II

LOUISA

IN JULY 1793 Louisa Elizabeth, the only daughter of John Oxley Parker and elder sister of Christopher, married Arnout Johannes Gevers Leuven in St. Mary's Church, Chelmsford. The bridegroom was a young Dutchman of good family. He was, says his grand-daughter, writing a century later, 'secretary and book-holder of M. Schimmelpenninck v. Myenhuis, father of the Earl Schimmelpenninck v. Myenhuis, later Chamberlain of King William III of Holland'. He had met Louisa at various parties in London and they had become attached to each other. At that time it probably seemed to Louisa's father that a young Dutchman, likely to reside all or at least most of his lifetime in England was, if his character, background, and fortune were satisfactory, a good match for his daughter.

Unhappily neither English nor Dutch took full account in 1793 of the fierce storm that was blowing up in Europe. The whole continent was already at war with the Revolution, the French king had perished under the guillotine. The resounding victory of the French at Valmy the previous year had turned back the invader and saved France. Now in 1793 Great Britain had added her arms to the rest of the monarchies, and nobody seemed to doubt that the Jacobins would soon be vanquished and the Revolution brought to nought. Had John Oxley Parker foreseen the rise of a military dictator and a grim war of twenty-two years' duration he might have hesitated before consenting to the marriage of his daughter to a Dutchman.

At the time of the wedding, however, things were looking promising. The French were in full flight from the Netherlands and the Rhine, and Holland seemed safe. A year later, disaster

14

struck. The new Jacobin armies carried the tricolor to the banks of the Rhine and in December 1794 Pichegru crossed the frozen rivers of Holland and occupied the whole country, capturing the fleet as it lay ice-bound at Texel. Stadhouder William and his family fled to England. It is said that when he was in London Arnout and Louisa were very kind to him and that he lived with them a good deal. They were certainly very friendly, for twenty years later when Napoleon was a prisoner on Elba and the Stadhouder was on the point of being restored as King of Holland and Belgium, Arnout wrote to John Oxley Parker:

My brother we expect in the course of a fortnight; he is now at the Hague where the States-General are assembled; last Tuesday he dined with the Sovereign whom I see to-day in the Times is to be King of Belgium. What a change for this man in one twelf month, when I used to see him in Harley Street daily in a little bit of a house, when he told me that he would accept a Colonel's place in Foreign service on the Continent, when I told him that he should have patience and should be King of Holland if he liked it in less than 6 months, this conversation passed between us. He has promised great things to my Brother who seems still upon very easy and good terms with him, to do something for me here. I wish to see it con-firm'd, than Princes often make promises and soon forget them again. (5 November 1814.)

On Arnout's part there was no reason to fear bankruptcy merely because of war, for he was in England, and in England fortunes may be made in war-time by British and foreigners alike. There was transport to be found, military equipment to be bought and a thousand other incidentals that go with war-time expenses. For twenty-one years Arnout seems to have been reasonably prosperous in some kind of business in which he was closely connected with his brother Peter.

Then, on 26 February 1815, Napoleon escaped from Elba and set sail for France. Throughout March he made the long triumphal march up the Rhône, gathering forces as he pro-gressed, and by the 17th of the month he was advancing on Paris. Arnout's brother Dick Gevers Leuven, the one who had been at the States-General, was now a minister of the Dutch Crown, and was able to get information. This was transmitted through Arnout to Woodham Mortimer and Springfield Place:

The accounts from France are not so gloomy to-day as they have been for the last two or three days. Bonaparte does not seem to get so many adherents as was expected and there seems no doubt that there will soon be a foreign Armie of great strength in that country [France] to assist Louis the 18th and his Court—in the meantime it is dreadfull that so much blood will be spilled again. (17 March 1815.)

I am happy to say the French Mail just arrived brings Paris papers of the 15th stating the French funds had risen from 6 pr. ct. to 10½ pr. ct., that there was much more confidence as to the Troops, Paris very quiet, and that Boney had not gone from Lion, this shows plainly that he does not see his way so clear yet, besides there are a great body of Troops marching against him and adresses of all parts of France are coming in to assure Louis the 18th of their loiatly [loyalty] and fidelity to his person. God gives it may all turn out well. My Brother has no news.

On the 20th Napoleon entered Paris. On the 27th Gevers wrote:

What continual bad news from France, what an immasing [amazing] alteration in everything.

Those hundred days between February and June 1815 were the ruin of Arnout's business. 'In 1815', wrote his granddaughter Julia van Arkel,

my grandfather lost his fortune, Napoleon taken all his shipps with their contents, and so he came to Holland with his family and settled themselves at Voorburg where they both died.

The story of Arnout's bankruptcy, the flight to Holland and Louisa's struggles to restore her husband's fortunes is told in a series of letters. First there are those of Arnout himself commenting on affairs abroad.

War seems inevitable, and the sooner it begins I think the better, but I am afraid it will be a terrible slaughter. (14 April 1815.)

Shortly afterwards Napoleon was defeated at Waterloo but there was no compensation for Gevers Leuven for the loss of his property, and his son Arnout found himself bankrupt and compelled to flee the country to escape his creditors. In fact it was C.G.P., brother of Louisa, who arranged with a Burnham boat-owner for his conveyance to Dunkirk. Louisa had to leave the house at Hackney where they had been living and the children were boarded out with friends.

Arnout managed to arrange with his brother Dick, who was in the service of the Dutch king and clearly well-to-do, for a cottage on his estate at Endegeest, and Louisa and the children arrived in Holland. But Louisa did not easily adjust herself to the altered circumstances and humbler standard of living, and in a few months' time was complaining about Dick. Probably he found poor relations a burden to him, and the presence of a bankrupt brother and his family an embarrassment. Hence he gave them notice to quit, said he could do no more for them; the allowance of T.400 (thalers) ceased as well as supplies of vegetables, milk, etc., in spite of undignified requests from Louisa. The cottage does not seem to have been a very desirable residence as the woman who came each Saturday to clean had to scrape shovelfuls of fungi off the skirting-boards!

However, they did stay on a few months, until August 1817, when another brother, Peter, found them a house at Voorburg and helped them with furniture. And brother Dick relented and renewed his T.400 a year, and this was supplemented with help from England. But Louisa continued to maintain that life was impossible, and having been advised that if her husband Arnout came to England he would in all probability be arrested, came over to England herself. She hoped to persuade the creditors to relent and accept a small composition, but the general opinion was that Arnout had behaved too badly, and her efforts proved unavailing.

Between 1817 and 1821 there is a gap in the correspondence, but it seems reasonable to assume that circumstances had

17

somewhat improved, and early in 1821 we learn of the marriage of their daughter Maria to Baron van Heerdt, nephew of Count van Strum, Governor of the Hague. Clearly this was a most advantageous match, all the Gevers family attended, and Uncle Dick, who had been mentioned in the letters mainly to expatiate on his meanness, entertained the bride and bridegroom at Endegeest Castle and supplied horses for their honeymoon. Louisa poured out her feelings on this occasion with a wonderful letter to her father:

I must now inform you as I was going to do last Tuesday that Maria was married on Wednesday the 24th to Baron van Heerdt; his uncle, Count van Strum . . . and Captn Trent of the Navy, his uncle, were his witnesses. Admiral Capelle and Mr. D. Gevers [were] Maria's. All the parties met by 10 o'clock to breakfast. Mrs D. G. came likewise. At a $\frac{1}{4}$ to 11 Gevers and myself went to Dick's coach with the Bride and Bridegroom to the Town Hall; as it is very near, the witnesses walked, all in full uniform, the Count and Ad^1 C. with their stars. Dick's uniform was very handsome, dark green with a great deal of gold about it and two full epaulettes with white carramere [?] waistcoat and breeches. His servants were in their dress liverys. After the ceremony we returned as we went, only that Gevers walked. They were then sufficiently married according to the Dutch law, as it now is, which is in fact the french law, for the Code Napoléon still exists. In about half an hour the new married couple went in Gen^1 Strum's carriage with him and myself, Mrs. D. G., Ad^1 C, Capt. T. and G in Dick's, he with Louisa and Isabella [Louisa's two youngest daughters] in his Barouche and Theodore, Charles and Tom [Louisa's three youngest sons] in Heerdt's travelling carriage; we all went to the English Embassador's where his Chaplain married them. We after all went to the Trent's where there we sat down to table, three and twenty. The bride looked as everybody said, extremely well, indeed they all said they never saw her look so handsome and tried to make me allow I thought so as they said I never would say she was handsome. The little girls looked very neat and were much admired for they had muslin frocks very nicely trimmed which Heerdt sent them in the morning and with which they were much delighted. At half past 2 o'clock the new married pair set off as every one that [thought?] for Utrecht, but it was agreed upon with her Uncle and Aunt that they should stop at Endegeest as the road between Leyden and Utrecht is very bad and they would have to pass it in the dark. . . . The next morning Dick let them have four horses to take them forward one stage and on Friday they arrived at 5 o'clock at his seat at Overysel where Maria writes me word they were received with great kindness and distinction and all the peasants for some miles around assembled to welcome them with firing of guns. . . . They talk very much of the wedding, they say there never was such a one in Voorburg and they don't suppose there ever will be again. (1 February 1821.)

Five years later, in 1826, her husband Arnout died at the age of fifty-nine, leaving the impression that his bankruptcy had overwhelmed him; and that it was beyond his capacity to recover from the problems and difficulties that resulted.

Louisa survived him only six years, dying at the age of sixty. She wrote so many grumbling and begging letters that it is refreshing to read one to her father in reply to his offer of financial help at the time of her husband's death, in which she says: 'You are most kind, my dear father, in the offer that you make, but as I have paid all that is immediately necessary I need not trouble you.' And she ends up, 'in everything that was possible for him to help me, he did: never had anyone a more kind and attentive husband'.

CHAPTER III

FRIENDSHIP

IN THE SUMMER OF 1815 the Rev. Charles Fanshawe was appointed to a curacy at Kimpton near Andover. There was a big rambling house attached to it where he hoped to run a private school for gentlemen's sons. He was married and had at that time a growing family. But a big problem faced him. He was a very worried and harassed debtor.

Some time before the series of letters between him and C.C.P. begin, he had done a great deal of borrowing. Interest was paid on the large amounts he had borrowed in the form of annuities: (1) £500 per annum on £4000 from the executors of B. Bridges, and payable to John Bridges of Maldon (12½ per cent); (2) a mortgage of £2000 on Dengie Rectory to the same; (3) £280 per annum on £2100 from the Rev. J. Richards of Walworth (13⅓ per cent); and (4) £78 per annum on £600 from a man named Reynolds (13 per cent). The annuities on the first were to have priority over the second and third. Bridges also had compelled him to insure his life for £4000, for which he paid annually out of his annuities £140.

In addition, Mr. Fanshawe had a number of debts at Andover, London, and various places in Essex, mainly in Maldon and district. These 'simple contract creditors', as they were called, included milliners, nurserymen, hatters, booksellers, innkeepers, oilmen, shirtmakers, collarmakers and other tradesmen. In London and Essex alone they amounted to over £2500. His total indebtedness could not have been less than £10,000.

His assets and securities were the income from the family property in Dengie Parish, the tithes of that parish, of which he was Rector and Patron (£650 per annum), the income from

Rectorial tithes at Morton, Norfolk (£120 per annum), and whatever small personal income he had from his curacy. He also at this time collected fees at the rate of £50 a year from the parents of each of the boys he boarded, but his school was more a liability than an asset. He had two sources of considerable income in prospect, the first arising from the estate of his deceased mother at Morton, which was to be divided between her three sons and would probably bring him in about £3700. This, however, depended on the sale of this estate, and at the time the first of this series of letters appears, an agent named Chapman is negotiating its sale to Mr. Trench Berney. There was another more distant prospect of money when the death of his aunt, Mrs. Althea Fanshawe, would make him rich enough to pay off all his creditors. The trouble was that, having borrowed and spent so much money, the sums he had to pay in interest were more than he could afford. At the same time, his simple contract creditors were pressing him on all sides for settlement of their long-overdue bills.

The trustees of Fanshawe's estate were his father-in-law, the Rev. John Faithfull, Rector of Warfield, and his friend Christopher Comyns Parker. The letters between C.C.P. and Fanshawe give every indication of a family or personal friendship of long standing. They address each other informally by surname only, and the word 'friend' is used by Fanshawe in many a note of gratitude running through them.

I do not hesitate to say how from my heart I thank you and your excellent wife for your kindness on this trying occasion which is the touchstone of friendship. (14 May 1815.)

For all his services during the whole ten years of Fanshawe's embroilments C.C.P. seems, from what accounts we have, to have taken no payment beyond expenses, and in one place, Fanshawe, acknowledging his indebtedness, says:

I am as much gratified by your kindness and persevering trouble in my affairs as ashamed of my inability to pay you as I ought in any coin but thanks.

His father, General Fanshawe, and his two brothers, Frederick and Henry, were in Russia, and the possibility of joining them there to escape his creditors was always present in his mind. In a letter of 22 October 1815, to C.C.P., he put forward the plan of threatening flight to persuade his creditors to reduce their high rates of interest:

My father . . . strongly urges my coming immediately to Petersburg; . . . he says that had he known last year what my situation was he would have obtained for me the Chaplaincy in the Factory at St. Petersburg and that now he has a scheme in agitation which if it succeed may enable me to come there in an advantageous situation. Now if I accept of his offers and leave England, the Annuities are not worth a pinch of snuff. I can resign the living to which my father can present any other person who may pay me for the resignation and I shall be safe in Russia—could not the prospect of this induce the parties to take legal interest and the annual premium they pay for the insurance on my life instead of the present enormous interest? Do you think you and Mr. Faithfull as trustees could make such an offer to the annuitants?

In writing this, Fanshawe seems to have taken no account of the feelings of the two men who were acting as his trustees. The Rev. John Faithfull was very dubious about it. C.C.P. not only flatly condemned it as inexpedient, but also as the kind of action which furnished grounds for creditors asking such high rates of interest.

I must beg you will excuse my attacking your annuitants unless armed with better weapons than I am at present aware of being able to be furnished with. I can but allow you are paying enormous Interest and I am well convinced there are Harpyes who live upon the distresses of the thoughtless, the imprudent and the unfortunate borrower, but I likewise know they make their advances, at times, when it is essentially necessary, and generally with very great risk as the contents of your letter very evidently prove. Had these Annuities been contracted while under age and afterwards ratified or even had you procured the Loans immediately upon coming of Age, before you might have been presumed to have arrived at years of discretion I then might have been inclined to have urged the abatement but under the present circumstances I must confess I should feel myself at a loss for either rational or honorable argument to enforce.

The sensible counsel which followed is an example of C.C.P.'s inflexibility and sound judgment when confronted with this, the first of a long series of doubtful propositions which Fanshawe put to him to get out of his difficulties:

Should you really have the offer of an advantageous situation abroad, there may be a reasonable plea to propose to your annuitants terms which might furnish you with an Income to induce you to remain in England, but even then I should deem it necessary to be prepared to say your Brother and Father-in-law or some two responsible Persons should be bound to immediately redeem the Annuities if you should quit England or do any Act respecting your Preferment which might be detrimental to their Interest—for having once opened their Eyes (if you can fancy them ever shut) to a probable chance of your quitting this Country, what security would they have, after receiving only simple Interest for a few years, that you might not should more advantageous offers occur, ultimately leave them in the lurch?

Meanwhile, there was no money to be had. The assigning of the legacy from father to sons necessitated much going and coming, sometimes across Europe. There were difficulties too about the title to the Norfolk estate. 'I do not think I shall be in England much longer,' wrote Fanshawe, '. . . Mr. Chapman shuffles most wickedly.' Then, in another place he goes on to say, 'I would rather have bread and cheese here than turtle and venison abroad'. On 24 July 1816, he seemed on the point of departure. His two brothers had come to England and in an interview with Chapman had been told that payment might be expected in a fortnight, but:

I do . . . believe that it was all a tale to impose on a careless sailor and a foreigner ignorant of our customs. I am therefore making preparations to quit the kingdom, as Mr. Chapman's promises begin to be a by-word and my creditors here will wait no longer. I know there is enough to pay everybody and I do not intend to withdraw my money with my person, but to leave a good name though an imprudent one: thus has the infamous supineness of one man blasted all my prospects which were growing good—God grant they may not quite close in darkness; my father is eager to have us come and did not my wife's situation preclude the possibility of it I should set out immediately with my whole family—she I fear cannot come till the Spring and my only doubt is how to support her during my absence and until she can follow me. If I could stay on till then with the same pupils it might be more advantageous, but I must quit this curacy at Mich⁵ and cannot leave the neighbourhood without paying my bills unless I abscond.

A week later he had quite changed his mind about going:

My prospects here are such as I will not relinquish. I have an offer of S⁰ Henry Wellesley's sons for the holidays for I believe the next four years during which he is to be at Madrid; the confinement will be great but the connexion with such a family is of great importance.

At the same time he wrote personally to Berney, the purchaser of the Norfolk estate, asking him why payment was being held up. The reply he received was wordy, over-polite and completely non-committal, 'a deal too civil, periods too rounded, and plaguey flummery'. By this time Berney had become the tenant of the estate. He had offered the purchase money as early as 1815 but the title had not then been made out so he had been allowed to take over the lease of the Hall Farm from the previous tenant and was living there. (29 September 1816.)

Mr. Berney generally we believe is at Morton Hall where he has got deep into bricks and mortar. . . . I fear he has planted extensively, which will of course pay no Tithe.

Fanshawe's inclination to go off to Russia varied at this time in direct proportion with his depression at the state of his affairs.

My fate is, I fear, fixed for a frozen clime where however I have hopes of a warm reception; nothing but the death of my Aunt can avert this and I do not much expect that, though after three paralytic strokes it would not be quite unexpected, she herself certainly looks forward to it as at no very great distance but so she has for twenty years last past to my certain knowledge.

Thus, in spite of C.C.P.'s sound advice against running away from his creditors, the possibility of taking such a step was always in his mind.

Unless my Aunt dies before next Spring we shall certainly all go to Petersburg, and when once there though I hope nothing can induce me to act dishonourably, the annuitants are completely in my power, and if they will not take simple interest and the annual sum sufficient to keep up insurances they may perhaps get nothing. (18 October 1816.)

A letter from Bridges and Quilter, Attorneys, of Red Lion Square, on 30 October 1816, makes Fanshawe's position very clear. In a statement demanding nine months' annuity payments (£350) and interest (£95), they state:

... it is the bounden duty of the Executors to require payment at least half-yearly, for the benefit of the persons who may be entitled for the time being, because the securities they hold authorise them to enter into the receipts and profits of the Farm (in Dengie) and to collect the Tythes or sequester the living in case of non-payment of one quarterly annuity 30 days after it becomes due. The advowson is included in their securities as well as the lease of the Farm.

Chapman, in Norfolk, made delaying promises, first, that payment for the estate would be made in January 1817, then in April of that year he gave hopes for Midsummer. Fanshawe wrote again to Berney requesting an advance of payment but with no effect. Simple contract creditors pestered him. One, who had put in his kitchen range, had him arrested and he was only saved from gaol by the timely intervention of a neighbour who lent him twenty pounds. Even his school, for which he had hoped for a profit, had put him a further £700 in debt:

My family including pupils has amounted to sixteen in number ever since last September year [September 1815]; to support which and furnish this house I received eight hundred pounds: the sum I owe is the excess of expenditure above income and I cannot accuse myself of any extravagance nor do I hope you will when you consider what it costs to furnish a house capable of containing the above number of persons in the plainest way and what it costs to maintain them in the cheapest manner for a year and a quarter, for I have calculated in the seven hundred pounds what will maintain them till the year is up. (10 December 1816.)

The summer of 1817 arrived, and yet there was no settlement of the Norfolk sale, nor could Chapman arrange an advance of purchase money. Increased numbers of creditors pressed for payment and in July of that year Fanshawe assigned the payment of his debts to his trustees C.C.P. and John Faithfull while he went on the Continent to see his father. His letter of 4 July seems to envisage the sale of his effects in England, school and all, and a possible long stay abroad:

If you the Assignees are to pay 20 shillings in the pound to *all* my creditors in *all* parts, our furniture here and everything which would enable us to go on taking pupils must be sold also: the Norfolk money has been so long delayed and I have consequently been so long in doubt as to the possibility of my staying in England that I have been obliged to refuse many pupils and nobody has been able to recommend me effectually. I have consequently been receiving for two years and more not half enough annually to meet the expenses of my house and the bills down here have mounted up to a frightful height at the same time. I do not know what my share will come to exactly and now I must determine whether I accept any offer of my father's when we meet or not.

He sailed for Ostend. His wife was anxiously awaiting news at home, not knowing what was to be the fate of her and her young family:

My husband informed me that he met you in London and he promised me that he would get you to write to Mr. Chapman desiring to be informed when the day of payment for the Norfolk estate was fixed; if you and Mr. Chapman write to my husband it will be near a month before I can hear and it is of consequence for me to know something about it to form plans and indeed it will be some relief to my mind to know even the worst. If the Norfolk money is not paid it will be impossible for my husband to return to England and therefore on that hangs a great deal of our fate.

From Ostend Fanshawe made his way to Spa where his father was staying. The latter had no offer to make.

26

Nothing can exceed the kindness with which my father has received me—he offers me anything and everything that I can wish for in the shape of an asylum but he does not seem inclined to give up my share of the Norfolk money unless my creditors will come to some terms—he says that fatal experience has taught him the advantage which is taken of unwary debtors and that if they will take fifteen shillings in the Pound he has then no objection to fulfill his promise. I have written this to Mr. Faithfull and hope he and you may be able to effect my stay in England on these terms. . . . If I do not succeed with my creditors I shall go to Petersburg without returning to England. (7 August 1817.)

The idea of paying fifteen shillings in the pound on the debts of a man who was bound in the long run to inherit a great deal of money shocked C.C.P.

I was much surprized by the receipt of your letter of the 7th August, as the impression on my mind is that when Mr. Faithfull and myself met the Creditors at Chelmsford to solicit the indulgence of a Letter of Licence for your personal protection, the inducement we held out to them to comply with our request was the certainty of their ultimately receiving the whole of their demands. . . . Now I am fearful after so many impediments to cause delay and repeated assurances that the whole would ultimately be paid, few would consent to accede to your proposition. . . . Fatal experience may have taught your father the advantages that are taken of unwary Debtors but yours now owing were but few of them accumulated at a period which ought to allow of that denomination. . . . I must confess I am astonished at your proposal. (17 August 1817.)

He wrote in like terms to his co-trustee Faithfull and a week later he replied to Mrs. Fanshawe. Speaking of the proposal to pay fifteen shillings he wrote:

. . . this proposition . . . I am of opinion could not be offer'd without just irritation and the certainty of being told that the promise of General Fanshawe by letter ought to be held as sacred as his bond. If it is necessary for Mr. Fanshawe to have what the five shillings upon his debts will yield, surely some of his and/or your relations should unite in making the advance upon the security offer'd to the Creditors. I trust that you are convinced by what I have done that I would willingly do any thing in my power to assist you and Mr. F.

27

in your difficulties that can be done without a sacrifice of my own integrity. (25 August 1817.)

Possibly Fanshawe was not entirely to blame. In his desperation he was only too ready to fall in with any suggestion another person might make. This could have been specially the case with his father to whom he owed so much and who looked at the matter from afar and rather unimaginatively. His own ideas of right and wrong were by now clouded by the urgent desire to free himself from his creditors whom he considered greedy and inconsiderate. Indeed he was beginning to consider it even a virtue to deprive them of the interest he had agreed to pay. In this as in all his doings there was a lack of stability. His letters show an inability to look at a situation squarely and to reason his way calmly out of his difficulties. He was imprudent, reckless, vacillating and devoid of that moral stamina which C.C.P. possessed in such great measure. In his next letter, of 15 September 1817, we find him back in Warfield at the home of his father-in-law, and heartened by the news that £24,000 of the purchase money for the Norfolk estate had been paid over. Now he readily gives way on his former proposal to pay only fifteen shillings. He was quite willing to pay twenty but would like to delay paying five of them until his father's death:

There are confident hopes that the whole will be settled before Michˢ. Still I trust you will not object to asking the creditors to take 15 shillings in the pound now and an undertaking to be paid the remaining 5 at my father's death. . . . Things are now got to that crisis that delay is fatal, for if I am obliged to go to Russia this voyage cannot be put off beyond the 5th or 6th of October.

Fanshawe was utterly inconsistent. In this same letter in which he threatened to go off to Russia he put forward a second scheme for paying off his debts which involved his remaining in England. This was a complicated transfer of livings which he hoped would result in thousands of pounds being put into Bridges's pocket so that every debt could be paid off. It involved the removal of Fanshawe from his curacy at Kimpton to the Rectory of Fawley in Oxfordshire. This would leave the living of Dengie vacant as pluralities were no longer possible. He hoped that ultimately he would be able to present one of Bridges's sons to this but until then it could be held by his father-in-law, Robert, son of the Rev. John Faithfull, reserving some of the revenue to pay the annuities. A further part of the scheme involved a presentation to Grantham which was said to be worth £1200 a year.

The first part of the scheme came to fruition. Bridges was informed that Fanshawe was likely to be offered the living of Fawley, and on 19 September 1817 the three men met in Chelmsford and no objection was raised by Bridges. A change of fortune, if it had not already arrived, seemed at least to be in prospect, provided the simple contract creditors could be satisfied within a few days.

Unfortunately, though Chapman had part of the purchase money, he did not pay any of it over, and the Rev. John Faithfull, on 27 October, sent to C.C.P. a most urgent and despairing letter:

I have received a letter from Fanshawe this morning, and he desired me to write to you and Mr. Chapman. His prospects of life will be blasted and he will be in a prison if his share of the money arising from the Norfolk estate is not paid within a week. I have assisted him to stop the most clamorous creditors in full confidence that we should have received the money before this time.

Next day, in a moving appeal to Chapman, C.C.P. expressed more plainly his opinion of the Bridges–Richards–Reynolds type of person than ever he had ventured to do in his letters to Fanshawe:

. . . this day I have received a letter from Mr. John Faithfull begging me if possible to expedite the business as he has only prevented the most clamorous creditors from sending Fanshaw to prison on an assurance that his debts would be paid in the course of a week or two. Your candor and apparent wish to render every assistance when I had the pleasure of seeing you at Norwich gave me every reason

THE OXLEY PARKER PAPERS

to hope when the business rested with you no delay would be caused
which could possibly be avoided, therefore I must confess I was
much surprized and disappointed when I saw your letter to my
Brother (C. G. Parker, Attorney of Chelmsford) starting so many
queries which were to be satisfied before the money was to be paid,
which certainly might well have been answered months or almost
years since. Mr. Fanshawe has just been or is about to be presented
to a living near Henley upon Thames with a good House fit for the
Purpose of receiving Pupils with every prospect of success if this
Business could be settled—all which must be blasted by delay; do
pray Sir let the distresses of so large and respectable a Family
stimulate you to give assistance rather than throw unnecessary
impediments in the way of parting with the Money. I can have no
other motive for my interference in this Business than that of reliev-
ing the distresses of a Family of a good-tempered imprudent Friend
and acquaintance. Never having been a Creditor for a shilling I
certainly should not have undertaken the Trust but to rescue him
from the fangs of a merciless Moneylender.

A few days later he heard from Fanshawe, who had not even
enough money to pay for the institution into his new living:

What can be the matter now—how can Chapman now evade payment when we know he has the money in his hands and my father's
consent; my uncle Laton who is joint trustee with him wrote me word
on the 7th that he was ready and only waited for Chapman's
preparing the deductions etc. Mr. Faithfull is very ill as the scarlet
fever has appeared amongst the scholars at Warfield and he is
agitated about my business. Pray write to him instantly to ease his
anxious mind and let me hear from you in London on Monday. . . . I
am called upon to take institution at Fawley and have not money
sufficient; the fees . . . are £35 besides the journey can you let me
have £50 to meet me there?

C.C.P. stated frankly his position as Trustee:

I must candidly confess I had resolved not to allow myself to become
a Creditor in your concerns well knowing the opinion of the World
is materially biassed by the actions of an interested or disinterested
party—but the present application induces me to swerve from my
intentions, well satisfied as soon as you receive any emolument from
your preferment you will place me in the same independent situation

in which I have always acted. I have written to Messrs Dixons to advance you Fifty Pounds upon your giving them a Note of hand for the same.

In November, therefore, Fanshawe was inducted to Fawley and the Rev. John Faithfull's son Robert became prospective incumbent of Dengie with the idea that he would be non-resident and employ a curate.

The debt now pursued the debtor to Fawley, and on 29 December Fanshawe received a letter pointing out that there were arrears of interest amounting to £700 and asking for particulars of the new Fawley living, so that a charge on that might be obtained.

The first three months of 1818 passed, and still no payment from Chapman in respect of the Norfolk estate, and the ordinary creditors were becoming very restive, especially Mrs. Collins who had a carpenter's business at Tillingham and was owed £476 3s. 4d. The attorney Joseph Day was very insistent, and Faithfull and C.C.P. had to go bail for Fanshawe to save him from prison. At the same time Fanshawe was so pressed by his Andover creditors that he left home, parish, and school, and his wife did not know his whereabouts, and had to correspond through C.C.P.

In May 6s. 8d. in the £1 was paid to ordinary creditors in London and Essex, and a lull occurred till November when C.C.P. again found himself in difficulties, with only £940 to meet interest and other bills of £1121. But on 11 December came a letter from Chapman to say that 28 December was fixed for payment of the Norfolk estate.

The colossal task of dealing with the debts of Charles Fanshawe was taken on by C.C.P. in addition to his own exacting business affairs. The volume of work he got through at that time is amazing. He paid £1000 off the principal of Bridges's annuity, £500 off Richards's and cleared off Reynolds's altogether, making a total outlay of £2100. The relief thus afforded to Fanshawe in annual payments was £239 6s.

(Bridges £110, Richards £51 6s., and Reynolds £78). The rest of the Norfolk money was more than swallowed up in payment of arrears, law expenses, and the temporary satisfaction of simple contract creditors. The smaller details of the work he must have had little time for.

The business of cutting down the annuity payments was hardly concluded before Fanshawe was again building his castles in the air. He was still hoping that his old aunt would come to his rescue and take over the principal of the Bridges annuity for 5 per cent interest, that is £150 a year instead of the £390 that was being paid to Bridges. But evidently Fanshawe's aunt was as wide awake as everybody else to his improvidence, for he says:

I do not think we ought to ask more of her . . . as she ordered me never to mention the matter again since she had put all her stock into trustees' hands that she might not be worried about what she did not understand or wish to enter into. (13 May 1819.)

The actual amount to be received by him from the Norfolk estate turned out to be £3856 (21 May 1819), but of this £468 11s. was paid in costs by C.C.P. for Fanshawe's share alone. The total costs for the sale were £1405 12s. 11d. 'It has been hinted that this is enormous', he wrote. Out of the proceeds C.C.P. received the £50 which, sadly against his better judgment, he had lent some time previously, and Fanshawe claimed the £78 that his father-in-law had paid out in November 1818 to shut the mouth of Reynolds's attorney Finnis.

Knowing Fanshawe as he did, C.C.P. was alert to the minutest indication that the acquisition of money, even at second-hand, had precipitated him into another bout of extravagance. An unfortunate passage in a letter of 25 May 1819 shows this up clearly:

On Wednesday, 2nd June [wrote Fanshawe], we have a ticket from the Duke of Marlborough to see his gardens near Reading between three and five. They are the finest in the world and will never be shown after this year. Can you come down for that, and then come

to Henley on that day by some Oxford coach and we will pick you
up as we pass through?

C.C.P. replied promptly, on the day of receipt:

I do not like your expression 'pick you up as we pass thro'', as I am
fearful you are keeping a carriage which prudence ought not to
allow. I know you will excuse my observation well knowing I have
but one motive—a full conviction that your happiness will be materially increased when you are able to live within your income.

The answer was a humble statement of Fanshawe's economies
and his hopes:

I do not keep a carriage but as Lord Archibald Hamilton has sent
his son a ticket for all of us to be admitted we form a party and should
have so contrived as to bring you back. Still, I have a vehicle. Mr.
Faithfull *lent* his daughter a horse (you understand why it is not
given) and I have a neat taxed cart, in which we go about much
happier than ever I did in my carriage. I hope to be able soon to live
within my income but the positively necessary expenses of repairing
this great old house and getting rooms ready for young men at
present keep my nose to the grindstone. If it shall please God to let
me keep up the pupils I now have for two or three years I shall get
clear of the world.

The pressure was now relaxed, but difficulties were by no
means at an end, and Fanshawe was constantly producing
schemes to alleviate the financial position. The most promising
one was the sale of the next presentation, or better still the sale
of the advowson to the Dengie living, and it was thought that
the latter might bring in £5000. Fanshawe was full of enthusiasm. But a question arose as to his title, and C. G. Parker,
attorney and brother of C.C.P., was consulted. He advised that
Fanshawe's title to three-fifths was unquestioned, but his title
to the other two-fifths was in doubt, and might well deter a
purchaser. Poor Fanshawe was being pressed by his Andover
creditors, and owing to bad times for farmers, concessions had
to be made in the tithe payments due to Fanshawe from his
Dengie living. At the same time Richards, to whom he owed
£2100, wrote that he was in urgent need of money to purchase

property offered to him, and that he was willing to accept £850 for half his debt, and £1600 for the whole. Fanshawe fought hard for his plan, pointing out that for many years he had been in undisputed receipt of the whole income of the living, but no sale was achieved.

Unhappily, financial worries were only part of the tribulations Fanshawe now had to endure, for by this time his wife had become very ill. The beginning and development of her illness may be traced in her letters, which are full of family affection and gratitude. The cares and physical strain of a large family, a school, a lovable but demanding husband, damp inconvenient houses, insufficient staff and, above all, financial worries which, being a sensitive person, she probably took more to heart than Fanshawe did, sapped her physical resources. There were long periods of pregnancy, coughs and colds. Then in February 1820 came indications of something more serious. 'My wife has been very ill and is now hardly able to leave her room.' In June 1822: 'My wife is gone to Cheltenham in search of relief from some very disagreeable complaints.' There was no progress towards recovery, and in November: 'My wife has been very seriously ill but thank God recovering; she was out yesterday for the first time for five weeks.'

In January 1823 she was worse and had been paying weekly visits to a London doctor.

My wife is going back to town again next week and will be at 6 Clarges Street for some time to benefit, I trust, by the attendance of an eminent surgeon who has discovered the cause of her complaint which is a very dangerous one if neglected but at present capable of cure. It is called constriction of the rectum.

In March 1823 Fanshawe was still hoping:

My wife is I trust likely to do well; this day week she was certainly at death's door.

The end of the month brought a serious repetition of her trouble and Fanshawe wrote in distress:

. . . My poor wife causes me the most serious alarm, another attack similar to the former occurred on Saturday and although the abscess broke in time to allow the bowels to be relieved yet as this stoppage has happened twice in three weeks and she is more and more weakened, I dread another which it seems medical skill cannot prevent or indeed hardly cure. She is so thin that her wedding ring goes on her middle finger with ease. If therefore I seem importunate pray attribute it to her great anxiety to see affairs a little arranged as she thinks herself dying.

He continued to be anxious about his wife. In May she had seemed somewhat improved but 'the good amounts to no more than being carried downstairs and wheeled out for an hour . . . and carried up again'. On 16 May he wrote:

Pray come down if you can to Fawley. Seeing you might perhaps raise the spirits of my poor wife. She has an odd idea in her head that she shall go off suddenly and when the circumstances of——'s death were told her, exclaimed That is the way you will find me some morning—twice she has alarmed me by a sort of sinking attended with coldness of the extremities which however yielded to hot brandy and water, but she has continual spasms at the stomach and always complains of a tightness about the heart. If she is, what she would call nervous, it is very miserable both to see and I fancy to feel.

Complications were increased by another pregnancy. 'All our hopes are now centred on her delivery' (4 June 1823). The confinement was due in the middle of July but on 19 June Fanshawe wrote:

Wonders will never cease; my wife has been so wrong in her calculations that she has just produced a little boy in such a hurry that an old woman was the only person present—all however is going right and Young (i.e., the doctor) now expects to see an end to all other complaints: she does not but I believe he knows best.

Within a fortnight he had changed his mind. 'I fear . . . that the complaint of which she has so long suffered is inveterate.'

Her depression, too, persisted:

Poor dear woman, she little knows how her head has been affected

35

but is more than ever convinced that she shall die soon. There is not the slightest ground for such a conviction but it is of course very harassing.

In later letters there are indications that Mrs. Fanshawe made no improvement, then, after 7 September, his letters to C.C.P. stop for a period. The first indication of her death appears in a letter of C.C.P. to Richards dated 2 December:

. . . his Father and Brothers are in high situations in Russia and since the death of his wife he may be inclined to cling less to the comforts so universally allowed to be peculiar to England.

The miserable story of debt dragged on. Letters from Richards arrived with painful regularity. C.C.P., tired of repeated explanations, concluded one of his letters:

I am fearful you must place yourself in the situation to which many Creditors are obliged to submit and think yourself tolerably well off if you realise 10s. in the pound upon a debt contracted during the extravagant high price of landed property. (18 October 1823.)

Richards retorted with an indignant letter written by his wife:

I cannot suffer myself and Children to be robbed [sic] of our own property and left to starve.

—to which C.C.P. replied in few words:

I cannot pay Money as a Trustee without Funds From which to take it.

Then, on 23 April 1824, with creditors on the point of enforcing the law and tension on all sides raised almost to breaking-point, C.C.P. received a black-bordered letter from Fanshawe:

My poor old lady was released yesterday from all her sufferings— her affairs will not turn out worse than I expected. I find the stock is 5700/3 Reduced, fourteen hundred 3/Consols, three hundred/ fours Consols. You may therefore make as good terms as you can with Richards and Bridges immediately.

36

The fate of his aunt, the poor lady from whom this bounty descended, was to Fanshawe a secondary matter. Here at last was he, with a sure prospect of being freed at once from all his embarrassments. His outlook and mood changed completely. Even his handwriting became bolder and firmer. Instead of alarm, he received creditors with laughter and enjoyed their discomfiture. C.C.P., who was no man for taking advantage of a situation, could not help putting a sting into the tail of his letter to Bridges (2 May 1824):

I have little doubt you will make good your former professions of Friendship to Mr. Fanshawe by giving every facility to the termination of this business which by this fortuitous completion has been so beneficial to your Family.

Good fortunes, like bad, were not, even in Fanshawe's case, to arrive singly. On 9 February 1825, a buyer was found for Dengie who, such was the force of C.C.P.'s recommendation,

. . . desires me [Fanshawe] to say that he has never been nearer to Dengie than Rochford but takes it solely on your representation as a man takes his wife for better or worse.

Robert Faithfull was now relieved to go to Warfield, Bridges and Richards would receive their dues in full. The intense relief Fanshawe felt shows clearly in his letters which become chatty and full of domestic detail:

How I wish we lived within reach, one such family as yours within a walk would satisfy all my wishes, meanwhile mine is splendid misery —fine dinner-parties and no intimates—my nearest neighbour a cold-blooded *radical*.

My great pupils will, I believe, be quite gone and I am not over-anxious about any more. If little boys offer I will take them or else contract my establishment and vegetate—but the moment I attempt that, all my servants kick up their heels and because I will not keep as many now as when I had six pupils and wife and four more children living at home, give warning. Let them go to the ———.

The clearing-up of details was only a matter of time, and as the months passed by, letters were much less frequent. The Rev.

Charles Fanshawe was, doubtless, freed from encumbrances, fitting himself into a life which embraced more leisure and more pleasure. Then, on 11 December 1825, when the very last transaction was on the point of being concluded, C.C.P. received a letter from Fanshawe addressed as never before: *Dear Sir.*

It instructed C.C.P. to obtain the lease of Dengie which Bridges had relinquished, together with the insurance policy.

But why the formal salutation? The explanation appears in the second paragraph:

I am sorry that I saw nothing of *you* during my stay at Chelmsford, and more so that Mrs. Parker's neglect of my unoffending wife was the cause which prevented any intercourse. Indeed she had better not have called at all than have behaved as she did. I feel it the more as I am ashamed to own again and again that to your active friendship I am indebted for all I now have.

The reply from C.C.P. explains the rest of the story:

After so many years of anxious solicitude for the interest of yourself and Family in no uncommon trials and with an ultimate success that amply awarded every exertion how happy should I have felt that I had undertaken the charge had not strange misconceptions and perverted ideas of charges never uttered and slights never intended totally alter'd the conduct of yourself and the Family with whom you are now allied towards me and mine—for had not such an alteration taken place how can I reconcile your repeated visits to Chelmsford when I was confined to Woodham Mortimer without your once making an effort to call upon us, which neglect Mrs. Parker felt if possible more than myself, but the letter received yesterday astonishes me more than ever, for when I have seen Mrs. Parker with Mrs. Fanshawe previous to your marriage they appeared very sociable and I have a quotation from you on one of her letters to that effect. I am aware Mrs. P has never congratulated either her or you as she has repeatedly observed she could not—her regard for the late Mrs. Fanshawe was very sincere and that regard did not die with the object of her affection. I cannot reconcile your sorrow at not seeing me. I called before and after Marriage but not once have I seen you either at Woodham Mortimer or at Mr. Gepp's where I was to be found almost every Friday—nor can I learn from Mrs. Parker nor those who were with her what you mean by her be-

38

haviour when she called. If in speaking the truth I have given offence I do not regret it as regards myself, having always held it the bounden duty of a sincere friend to express his opinions candidly —but I have never felt offence if those opinions have not been approved nor acceded to. I cannot conclude without doing my wife the justice to say this is the first instance I have experienced of censure upon her conduct for want of attention, and had Mrs Fanshawe made her appearance I have no doubt she would have received it in this instance.

Things were never the same again. On 2 April 1826 C.C.P. lost his father, and in his letter of sympathy Fanshawe used the old form of address.

More months passed, during which Fanshawe, even after being relieved by his inheritance and the sale of the presentation, could not avoid getting into financially embarrassing situations. Again C.C.P., continuing to look after his affairs, wrote letters, settled accounts, paid visits. His second wife, probably younger and more active than his first had been, sought to know the truth about his finances, in the hope that, by her influence in the home, she could help him out. Her letter, the last but one in the long series, sums up the character of Fanshawe, given by one who loved him, and made the last effort at conciliation:

I am writing for what he should have requested long ago, but the dear soul is certainly not a Man of Business—however that is no vice. . . . I am blessed with one of the best husbands and his dear children. I only pray . . . that time, economy and patience may see us free. I shall then envy no earthly being—you know me—and to obtain this wish, *we* shall think no sacrifice too great. Yes, if you knew *half* his present sufferings you would not doubt his *ardent* wishes on what I have said. Our joint prayers have been heard on my late illness, and when Husband and Wife are so united on Religious subjects, and so faithfully perform the same, what may we not humbly hope may through God's Mercy *yet* be our lot?

This letter, though it may not have restored the old relationships, affected some measure of reconciliation. Fanshawe's wife had been seriously ill; his own wife too had met with a bad accident. There, if at all, were grounds for common feeling. C.C.P.'s last letter was characteristic of the generosity he had always shown.

I shall shortly remark on a subject on which I have never before expressed my opinion to you or Mr. Fanshawe. Surely he had known my wife long enough to be satisfied however she might disapprove a Widower with so large a family marrying again and however disinclined she might be to congratulate him or your Family upon the event, yet she too well knew herself to act rudely to him or to any one, and the sincere affection she had for his dear departed wife certainly made her feel uncomfortable when the rules of society rendered it necessary that she should call. I have never expressed what I felt at his hasty observations after that call and I sincerely wish he had curbed his feelings rather than indulged in that sort of language which never can attain any favourable results. Those who know me cannot doubt my disposition cordially to forgive and as much as possible to forget every insult offered to me and mine when those who have given them do feel a wish that the occurrence had never taken place.

However anxious Mr. Fanshawe now is respecting his pecuniary concerns, I continue to assert that he will not find a friend more zealous than myself to relieve him from his difficulties. My own affairs have never caused me half the anxiety or manoeuvring to make small resources answer large demands, and to the time of Mrs. Althea Fanshawe's death I kept all parties tolerably quiet altho' there were at that period very heavy arrears due, some of which I settled for considerably less than could have been legally demanded, and I was amply repaid for all my trouble by his expressions of gratitude for my services.

Thus the *amende honorable* was made from both sides. Whether Fanshawe followed it up with a personal letter and completed the reconciliation we do not know.

CHAPTER IV

OXLEY

GRANDFATHER PARKER had lived all his married life at The Friars, Moulsham. Here his four children had been born, and here his wife had died in 1789. From the house of the ageing widower his children passed one by one: first Louisa in 1793 to marry her Dutchman, then Christopher, who married Emma, the daughter of his friend Edward Gepp, in 1797; then John Oxley who married Elizabeth Service in 1798 and died suddenly eight years later without issue. His death was a severe blow to his father, for he was a promising young lawyer. The third son, Charles, aged twenty-six at his elder brother's death, followed him in the business, and even after his marriage in 1812 lived on with his father at The Friars. There was in the Parker family a long succession of grandchildren. First came Louisa's, born between 1795 and 1812. Though their father was Dutch, his business was carried on largely in London and they lived there until the disasters of the Napoleonic Wars sent Mr. Gevers Leuven back to Holland, a ruined man. Then there were Christopher's three girls and boy, born between 1804 and 1814 at Woodham Mortimer Place, and finally Charles's eight children, all born between 1813 and 1824. The floods on the low-lying land near the Chelmer, and possibly Charles's rapidly growing family, brought about their removal to Springfield Place in the latter year. Here Grandfather John Oxley Parker died in April 1826, at the age of eighty-two.

Oxley, Christopher's son, was then fourteen years old. His father was forced by the needs of his profession as a land agent to spend long periods away from home, and his mother had indifferent health. At the age of five, therefore, the little boy had been sent to a private boarding school run by the Rev. James Hutchinson at Chelmsford. Before Oxley was admitted the schoolmaster sent to his father a note with a rather ominous ring. 'My house is now open', he wrote, 'and am every hour expecting subjects on whom to exercise my scholastic authority.' Here, with his cousin Tom Gepp, Oxley learnt the rudiments of Latin. When he was old enough he was sent to the famous school at Greenwich kept by Dr. J. C. Burney, grandson of the learned and lovable Dr. Burney the musician, and nephew of the famous Fanny. At one time his father had contemplated sending him from there to Winchester but there was said to be so much bullying in that school at the time that the boy implored his mother to persuade his father to let him stay with Dr. Burney. His wish was granted and he remained there until he was past sixteen. The kindly discipline of Burney brought out the best in him and inspired encouraging letters from his father who, in spite of his busy life, always found time to write to his children:

My dear boy,

Your exertions to obtain promotion have afforded me great pleasure and satisfaction and Dr. Burney's letter giving us the information was very gratifying. I trust you will continue to deserve his good opinion by saying now your future studies will be a pleasure to you instead of a toil and vexation and every indulgence we can afford will be granted with readiness when at home while you continue to exert yourself at School. . . . Notwithstanding the cold and dreary weather we have had, the beauties of Spring will make their appearance, our Garden is looking very gay and all the plants pushing forth their buds and bloom. Betty says she takes great care of your Garden and intends having it cropped with radishes by your return to Woodham, when we shall all greet you most cordially,

Believe me, my dear Boy,
Your's most affectionately,
C. Comyns Parker.

That was in 1824. Two years later he could write in the same strain to the author J. T. Rutt who had sent him a presentation copy of a book:

I flatter myself from your observations respecting my son, you had an opportunity of perceiving that Dr. Burney's exertions are not entirely lost upon him; and I shall request he will add to his store of knowledge by an attentive examination of your volume.

The next we see of Oxley is in summer, 1827, when he is fifteen. His little sister Elizabeth has also been at boarding school, at Miss Blaxland's academy in Bromley, Kent, and he is instructed by his father to meet her at the 'Spread Eagle', Gracechurch Street, to catch the coach to Kentish Town where they are expected by their cousins, the Griffenhoofe family. Mama adds a note:

You will I am sure be as much surprised by the contents of Papa's letter as I was when Mrs. G's arrived this morning to request you to accompany Papa and Oxley to Kentish Town next Wednesday, for I never hinted to you that Papa meant to indulge Oxley with a trip to Kentish Town. . . . You had better put on your silk frock and merely the night things, combs, brushes and shoes, for one night you sleep at Mrs. G's and Thursday I hope to see you at dinner. . . . God bless you my sweet girl. We shall meet soon, which will afford real comfort and happiness to your affectionate mother.

In January 1829 Oxley was preparing himself to go to Oxford. C.C.P. was at that time managing the property and collecting the tithes of Purleigh for Oriel College, and he sounded Dr. Hawkins, the Provost, as to his son's admission. In January 1829 he went up but was not accepted.

It grieved me exceedingly to part from you as I did at Oxford, but I hope Oxley met his disappointment as you could desire and that he is now diligently recovering his ground in the exact elementary knowledge of the Greek and Latin languages. Without this he may be quite sure he never could pursue his studies here to real advantage. And he may be doubly sure that he would not become an exact and accurate scholar in this matter *at the University* if he did not come here thoroughly well grounded.

Oxley worked hard preparing for his matriculation. At this time he was probably at home, though it was difficult to find a good private tutor for him.

43

Oxley employs most of his time in endeavouring to prepare himself for College, altho' I have not been able to gain the assistance I wished. (C.C.P. to Dr. Hawkins.)

In January 1830 he was admitted. C.C.P. sent to Dr. Hawkins a present of game and £35 which he had paid for Oxley on his arrival at Oxford.

You mentioned your fears about his having Rooms in college immediately. I hope should those fears be realised that the inconvenience will not be of long duration. (Dr. Hawkins to C.C.P.)

Dr. Hawkins was kindness itself. He found the rooms, and from the time he arrived in Oxford, Oxley's tradesmen's bills are addressed: 'Parker—Oriel'. Among them is one for valuation of furniture, January 1830, from a Mr. Marriott, the previous occupant of his rooms. On the 22nd of the same month Oxley went to Loder & Gunner's and bought household goods to fit up his new quarters; china cups and saucers at 8s. 6d. the half-dozen, coffee-cups at 6s., egg-cups, plates, teapot and cream-jug, decanters, tumblers and a water-jug; a candlestick and snuffers, a washing-set, soap-drainer and brush-tray; hat-, clothes-, nail- and toothbrushes, a shaving-glass and some soap. From Stevens & Son he had a gilt coal-hod (7s. 6d.), a shovel, saucepan, ladles, a 'footman', a copper tea-kettle, a sugar-box and a pair of bellows; from William Cooke a carpet whisk (4s. 6d.), a hearthbrush and mop (5s. 6d.), a deal shirt-horse (3s. 6d.), rope matting and a sofa-cover which cost £1 13s. 8d. for material and making. His washing and cleaning were sent out weekly ('2 pr. gloves cld & mended 1/4; P trousers clnd 1/–, marking 2 cravats 3d.'). At the end of January he bought a dozen bottles of fine old port and sherry (£2 10s.), and two bottles of choice brandy (14s.). There was 5s. 3d. returnable on the fourteen bottles. His expenditure book, neatly and carefully kept, repeats the totals on the bills, and includes many small items such as tips (porter 1s., boots 1s., postman 1s., coalheaver 1s., sweep 6d.), and purchases for which he had no receipts (corkscrew 2s. 6d., straps 6d., for scouring room 3s., Tyrolese minstrels 3s. 6d., concert 4s. 6d., bet lost 2s., Bohemians 4s. 6d.). There were boating excursions (Iffley lock 1s. 6d., boy to steer twice 2s.), skating in the winter (grinding skates and stick 1s. 6d., ferryman, sweepers, etc., 4s.), coach payments to and from London (13s. 6d.), tips to coachman and guard (6s.) and lunch on the road (2s. 4d.). On 18 February the Provost of Oriel wrote to C.C.P.:

If your son is as happy in his new abode as he appears to be when I meet him, he must like it very well. I saw him very well this morning. He has told you probably that I was able to give him rooms after all in the College.

At the end of March he wrote:

I will not close even this hasty letter without giving you the pleasure of knowing that yʳ Son has begun very well—both as to studies and conduct. We must not trust to a First term, but I hope he will really go on well.

The second term passed successfully, and in June the Provost was able to write:

It gives me great pleasure to be able to tell you that your son's conduct and diligence have been very satisfactory to the College during his *second* term; and this second term is a more important test than the first. If the first year is passed well, you may feel pretty secure about him.

C.C.P. must have seen the maturing of his son in the summer of 1830 with great satisfaction. It was a happy time, for, after losing his first wife in 1829, he was approaching his marriage to Frances Sutton. In one of the delightful letters he sent to his youngest daughter Elizabeth, then at school, C.C.P. wrote:

Oxley has been staying at Springfield Place and was to attend the bazaar at Baddow from there—he is quite the young man of pleasure.

At the end of 1830 Oxley was very much at home in his new life. Reports from Dr. Hawkins show complete satisfaction, and the development of that close friendship which was to last so long. Forty-seven years later, when Oxley was sixty-five, he wrote in his diary:

Afternoon to Rochester to stay with the Provost of Oriel. Found him full of life and spirit—in his 91st year.

Dr. Hawkins died in 1882.

Oxley was able to indulge his love of hunting whilst at Oxford. In November 1830, Thomas Barrett sent him a bill:

Oct. 28 Ride	8	o
Nov. 3 Hunter with the Harriers	1 5	o

In December he bought a pair of best gilt spurs at 15s. Later his father allowed him to keep two horses whilst in residence, and he used to hunt regularly, but he did not neglect his studies. Another bill of November is for a mahogany elevating desk (£2 4s.). In April 1831, when his place at Oxford was assured, he seems to have taken measures to increase the comfort of his room. A bill from John Atkin of that date is for a partial refurnishing.

> O ye Spiers of Oxford! your presence overpowers
> The Soberness of reason!

said Charles Larkyns, purposely misquoting Wordsworth to the innocent freshman Verdant Green. Cuthbert Bede's hero could not have been there many years after Oxley who also saw at the corner of Oriel Street the emporium of R. J. Spiers with its spacious range of shop windows 'crowded with a costly and glittering profusion of *papier-maché* articles, statuettes, bronzes, glass, and every kind of "fancy goods" that could be classed as "art-workmanship" '.

Two bills from Spiers' establishment remain in the Oxley Parker collection and one of them is signed by the noted 'R.J.' himself.

Dr. Hawkins kept a friendly eye on his protégé all the time he was at Oriel, and his business letters to C.C.P. end almost invariably with a note such as, 'I have seen Oxley who is quite

46

well but has no message to send besides his regards and duty'
(10 March 1832) or, 'I saw Oxley this morning perfectly well'
(2 November 1831). He came down in 1833 with a good B.A.
degree. His tutors were Hurrell Froude, elder brother of the
historian, and John Henry Newman, later to become a cardinal
of the Church of Rome.

Oxley was now twenty-one, a fine handsome young man who
stood more than six feet high, gifted with a happy and generous
disposition and manners that naturally attracted people to him.
If his father, his sisters, or Dr. Hawkins ever had a harsh word
to say about him it has not been recorded. If the traits of
character that showed themselves in his later life also guided
him as a young man, he cannot be too highly spoken of. His
father jokingly said he was 'quite the young man of pleasure',
but his pleasures were moderate and comparatively innocent.
In days when other youngsters in their 'teens lost hundreds at
the gaming-table, Oxley's florin can mean nothing. In an age
when the fast set, even at Oxford, drank themselves under the
table, Oxley's few bottles of wine and brandy which lasted for
months were the height of moderation. When C.C.P. received
his only son back from Oxford he must have been a happy and
proud man indeed.

In what way Oxley was trained for his profession as farmer
and land agent, we do not know. It is quite probable that he was
sent by his father to one farm after another to learn agriculture,
and that he accompanied some other land surveyor on his
journeys in Essex, for we read nothing about him in his father's
diary during the first years. Only on 1 March 1836 does the
first notice appear:

Oxley went to Bradwell, called at Mott's Farm.

Then, two months later:

Attended Mr. Linsey[?] and looked over his lands in Hazeleigh to
value Tithe due to Mr. Marriott. Oxley wrote to him thereon.

It appears that most of the time during these months of 1836

47

he accompanied his father. Then he was sent out alone, the number of commissions he carried out being gradually increased. On 10 August he went to Boreham House to meet Sir J. Tyrrell. We hear no more about him until May 1837 when, possibly owing to C.C.P.'s illness, increase in business, and preoccupation with tithe, he went to Frame Farm, Tolleshunt D'Arcy once, to Coptfold in Margaretting twice, to Canney Wood, Battles Hall, and to St. Lawrence to inspect the sea-wall there. After that C.C.P. often entered his son's activities separately at the end of each month. Then, in May 1841, we find Oxley keeping a diary of his own which runs for over two years concurrently with his father's. This was the first of thirty-four volumes.

The sentimental and social side of his life is still to be seen in the surviving letters. In 1842, at the age of thirty, we see him in love. Who the Walker family of Edinburgh and Great George Street, London, were, we do not know, but two years previously he had met them and had hoped with some justification for the hand of their daughter Jessie. These hopes, after a bright beginning, were dashed by the news that he was rejected. He wrote to Jessie's sister and to her friend Miss MacDougall, who had previously encouraged him, saying that he would in future avoid meeting Jessie until his feelings were so schooled that he could face such a meeting with composure. Some time later they saw each other again in company, and Jessie's letter to Oxley explains what happened on that occasion:

I know you will be surprised to receive a letter from me when you wrote that you will probably be in Gt. George St. this morning, but I hope it will reach you in time to tell you that I think you had better not come to us to-day for I am now going to give you a final account of my feelings to you. You *must* know that when the conversation began on Wednesday evening I had not the most remote idea how it was to terminate, but only commenced it as I would have done to the most common acquaintance; but certainly when I found that after my conduct to you on two former occasions you still cared for me I was for a short time staggered and fancied that perhaps your

48

constant affection for me might *in time* be returned sufficiently to make my future life happy, but during your week's absence I have examined my own feelings narrowly and am convinced that much as I like and value you as a friend they are not such as would make either you or myself happy. After this I know you will agree *with me*, first in blaming me for yielding on Wednesday from the excitement of a moment, and secondly in agreeing at once to put an end to all suspense. I fear that you have had much reason to blame me for, in the last two years, but believe me that until Wednesday evening I never had the slightest idea of encouraging anything beyond friendship. . . . Hoping that you will soon forget the disagreeable events of the past two years, I remain, dear Oxley,

Very sincerely yours,
Jessie Walker.

His reply to Jessie voices the despair of the rejected lover:

I will still so far do your bidding as to strive to *forget* what has passed. I will blot out at once all that is *disagreeable*, but no more, for to cease from any remembrance of the last two years would be to forget some of the most agreeable, the brightest, the sunniest of those few days of my existence which have had a blessing to gild them. Should your determination be *final* and *conclusive*, I will not annoy you by my presence till my feelings are too well schooled and taught to allow the chance of the escape of such a slight impression as has been the cause of this, to you disagreeable, to me most painful circumstance.

Your name has been mingled with my fondest prayers, and though I may no longer mix with it the idea of mutual blessing, still let me express the fervent, heartfelt prayer, that your future happiness in life may be far greater than ever I could hope to bring you.

Believe me to be with all truth,
Yours, my dear Jessie, most sincerely,
J. Oxley Parker.

Some time later, hearing nothing more from Jessie, he wrote his last long letter to her friend Miss MacDougall. It concludes:

As my happiness was raised to the highest pitch by the renewal of hope so is the depression the greater and the more difficult to overcome, and I feel this the more, and through the day has the thought recurred to me even more frequently than usual in consequence of business taking me to London to-morrow, and the feeling that I cannot bend my steps in that direction whither they have hitherto turned with the greatest readiness weighs heavy on my heart, but I am determined of this, that under present circumstances I will not present myself in George Street while my feelings are unstrung so as to hazard any expression or exhibition of emotion.

To tell you of the weariness and loneliness of heart with which I now look forward to the future were useless—suffice to say that under present feelings no other circumstance will extinguish the last lingering gleam of hope, but the interposition of such a barrier between us as man cannot put asunder.

With every apology for inflicting my scribbling on you, believe me to be . . .

The crisis in this love-affair lasted no longer than two months. The hurt was great while it lasted, but the young spirit was resilient, and C.C.P.'s illness called for extra exertions from his son. At that time he was conducting a difficult arbitration for his father at Horkesley; bargaining with a tenant at Prittlewell about the rental of some cottages there; examining sea-walls and looking after the home farms. This, with his days off at the hunt (15 and 27 February and 5 and 8 March) and family affairs, gave him enough to keep his mind occupied. Probably first love was an experience he never forgot. His actions during the next year or two showed, however, that to him it was a thing that must be endured and could be cured.

Land management in the last ten years of C.C.P.'s life was no sinecure. In 1830 the country was hit by a severe agricultural depression which brought disaster to many. In 1835 the Poor Law Reform Act had a temporarily depressing effect on the conditions of farm labourers and, at the end of the 'thirties it seemed as if agriculture would never recover. Peel and his followers saw no remedy save the repeal of the Corn Laws. C.C.P. steadfastly opposed it. The last years of his life were the hardest and the most uncertain, and his own health was not good. Oxley in 1843 was more than an assistant; he was carrying an equal burden with his father. It was well, for when the end came it came suddenly.

July 15th, 1843. At home, after to Bradwell. C.C.P. met with severe accident by fall from his horse.

He was an immensely large man weighing twenty-one stone and over six feet in height. In his daughter's diary (Elizabeth) I find:

Mr. Whimper would not bleed till Dr. Baker (of Maldon) came in the evening, syncope would have followed from which Papa never could have rallied, had he been bled directly. Papa told Mama this day, 'This will be a very serious accident.'

Oxley carried on with his work. On the 16th he was at Bradwell where his father was lying, on the 18th at the Assizes, on the 19th at Bradwell and Plumborough, on the 20th at Ongar, on the 21st at the laying of the foundation stone of the new Birch Hall, near Colchester (demolished in 1954). On the 22nd C.C.P. was brought home by carriage from Bradwell.

. . . at one o'clock the carriage arrived with Papa and Mama; my dear father had borne the journey—17 miles—without suffering, and on being assisted out, with ease he stood erect and walked unsupported into the house, looked into the Library where the piano was being tuned, and then sat during the afternoon in the dining room, rejoiced to get home. . . .

The full story of C.C.P.'s death is told in Elizabeth's diary, how the doctor came and found fractured ribs. Relatives and friends called. Mr. Morrell, Rector of Woodham Mortimer, came on the 30th and read psalms and prayers.

Papa objected to the door being shut, saying, 'We need not be ashamed of what we are doing.'

Oxley went on with the work, farming and writing letters most of the time, and remaining near home. Occasionally he snatched half a day for a necessary journey, to Great Sampford on the 25th and to Chelmsford on the 28th. His diary records are brief.

July 26th. CCP very ill.
July 29th. At home. CCP very ill.
July 30th (Sunday). CCP so ill that no hopes were entertained of
    recovery.
July 31st.   d⁰   d⁰
August 1st. My much valued Father expired p.m. 8 o'clock—pre-
    sent—my uncle CGP and aunt; James Parker, Peter
    and Isabella Gevers, T. L. Ward, Drs Baker and Miller,
    my [step]mother, sister and myself.
August 7th. My poor Father's remains were this day committed to
    the Grave.

Christopher Comyns Parker died beloved by all. The *Essex County Chronicle* said of him:

He was the owner and occupier of a large breadth of land in the Hundred of Dengie, and in other parts of the County; his spirited outlay in the improvement and cultivation of the soil was allowed to be most judicious, and in his agricultural pursuits, generally, he afforded an excellent example to his neighbours. The numbers of persons he employed in the various occupations of bailiffs and general labourers, was great indeed, to whom, in affliction, he was indulgent, and in wages he was liberal; as regards the latter, he was the first to raise, the last to fall. His practical knowledge of the value of land, in every part of this county in particular, peculiarly fitted him for the important trust of land steward, which he filled with justice to the landlord, without oppressing the tenant. In the commutation of tithe he was extensively engaged, and his decisions were alike satisfactory to the receiver and the payer. Mr. Parker was Chairman of the Maldon Board of Guardians, where his services were duly appreciated.

In his domestic habits he was an excellent husband, a kind parent and a sincere friend. His absence, as a generous benefactor to the poor, will be severely felt.

The funeral was attended by his friends and relatives, proceeding by coach from Woodham Mortimer Place to the church, where the largest concourse of people in those parts for some time—tenants, farmers, labourers, wives, and children—assembled to pay their last respects.

Oxley, at the age of thirty-one, now had on his shoulders the whole weight of the family business, the agencies, the manage-

ment of the farms in hand and the family property in Bermondsey. One of his first tasks was to write to his father's clients asking
them to continue to employ him as their agent. All but one
consented.

Now, little more than a year after his disappointment in love,
he cannot have had much time to indulge in self-pity or remorse,
for every minute of his day was occupied. His diaries show this
clearly. Though labelled 'Business Day Books', they are much
more personal than those of his father. He describes the weather,
the state of the land, the progress of the crops on the many
farms he visited, the attitudes of owners and tenants. During the
latter part of his life he tended to write down the little unusual
things, such as the hearing of the first cuckoo and the nighting-
ale, the first sight of a swallow in spring,the unusual views he
had of the northern lights, and sudden rainstorms. His records
are none-the-less factual, but through them one can see the
working of a rich and lovable nature.

A momentous year for him was 1843. From 7 August
onwards the diaries reveal the determination that, for a while at
least, work and nothing but work should be the rule. He drove
himself. His pleasures were fewer; even his beloved riding to
hounds was cut down, and for some years almost stopped. He
relieved the stress of work with occasional shoots in winter, with
coursing at Bradwell or Southminster, with regular dinners at
the Beefsteak Club in Chelmsford, with family archery meetings
and an occasional ball, for he dearly loved social life and
dancing. In the winter of 1844–5 we see him still working hard,
journeying here and there, enjoying an occasional shoot or
coursing day, still very little hunting, but:

January 22nd. To Rivenhall Place. Ball. Sir John Wood's.
January 23rd. Evening to Bocking. Met Durant and went together
to Ball Sible Hedingham Rectory.
January 24th. Returned to dinner. Maldon Ball.

Then, on the morning of 25 January, the first hunt since the
23rd of November in the previous year.

What was responsible for this extraordinary effort sustained throughout the years 1842 to 1847? Disappointment in love may have had something to do with it in the beginning, the death of his father at a time when business was bad certainly drove him to further exertions, but there may have been something more, even as early as 1844. A letter from Richard Durant to his younger sister Louisa in August 1843 throws some light on the situation:

I sent poor Miss Parker [Elizabeth] her book last week by Wilson [a mutual friend]. I have not seen him since his return but I hear from his brother that Oxley and his sister are tolerably well—it is now ½ past 4—I have seen Wilson who tells me that he did not see Mrs. Parker but heard she was much depressed—have you written? if not I think you should—*begging Miss Parker when the first shock shall have somewhat subsided to let you know how they all are.* . . . Wilson tells me that everything is left to Oxley except 4M to his sister to be invested in the names of trustees—we fear this argues that 'everything' is not over much. Oxley is I hear following the business actively so that he poor fellow will feel less than the two ladies. Wilson seems to think they are much comforted by the presence of the Dutch cousins.

Richard Durant had been a schoolfellow of Oxley's at Dr. Burney's, and they had kept up the friendship. His father Richard Durant was a wealthy London silk merchant who lived at Putney Hill, Surrey. In 1841 he had purchased a large estate, Sharpham, near Totnes. The estate contained 1030 acres, with a large mansion, solidly built of Portland stone in 1760, and 120½ acres of foreshore on the River Dart and its tributary the Harbourne. The price paid for the estate was £71,820 without the timber, which was paid for at valuation. C.C.P. was asked to do the valuing but he was too ill and Oxley went in his stead with his cousin, Mr. Thomas Lay Ward. The work took them from 22 March to 16 April, when they returned to London. On Good Friday they had a pleasant day out on the Dart, on Easter Sunday they went to Totnes, working on Easter Monday. The following Sunday they had a day in Torquay and

PLATE I *John Oxley Parker as a young man*

PLATE II *Louisa, wife of John Oxley Parker*

on Friday, 9 April, Oxley set off on a short excursion. That day he inspected the new lighthouse on the breakwater outside Devonport. On the 11th he called on some timber merchants respecting the valuation and 'had photographic likeness taken'. Later that week he was joined by his father and stepmother, and C.C.P. looked over his valuation lists.

Between 1843 and 1845 Oxley saw a great deal of the Durant family. Before his father's death he and Richard had gone out a great deal dancing together. At the end of August 1843 it seems from a letter of Richard's to his sister that Oxley, 'by way of fulfilling an engagement', was at a ball at Epping Place 'polka-ing to admiration'.

I introduced him to one or two of my best partners—one said he polka-d better than he waltzes—he has got into a bad habit of rolling in his waltz, thinking it effective, but I must tell him it will not do—at least if he does not alter I cannot recommend him.

There is no mention of this engagement in Oxley's diary for 1843, but there seems no other year in which one can place it.

In October 1844 Oxley and his sister spent a week at Sharpham and returned with Richard via Exeter on the 14th. It was probably during this time that Oxley, setting aside all thoughts of Jessie Walker, fixed his affections on Louisa. At certain times they must have been much in each other's company. The story of the eighteen months prior to their marriage is told in a series of delightful letters sent to Oxley by Emily Comyns, who signs herself 'your affectionate adopted sister'. She and her husband Dr. Comyns had just moved from Rivenhall to Cheltenham where the doctor had taken over a new practice. The letters are bright, full of the latest gossip and memories of happy times spent at the various Essex balls:

I often play the Bohemian Polka—it is so very pretty. If you don't come [to Cheltenham] now you must do so some time either before or after Xmas. I should like to introduce you to the beauties, animate and inanimate, of Cheltenham. . . .

I have not had much rest since I came home—on Wednesday

evening we were at a party where there was some dancing and a little Polka but it was a slow affair. Last night was the Master of the Ceremonies Ball. It was well attended—between 5 and 600—a nice Band and beautiful room and we danced till past 2. I had one good Polka and some new Waltzing but nothing very superior—can't expect it out of Essex. Certainly the Dunmow Ball was *nicest*—notwithstanding the bad room. I think you would enjoy a Polka in the Rotunda—such beautiful boards, but painfully slippery. (26 September, 1845.)

On 5 December Oxley went to Ogbourne St. George in Wiltshire to go over a farm belonging to J. Round. This was forty miles from Cheltenham which he visited on Saturday and stayed until Monday.

December 7th (Sunday) At Cheltenham (stayed with Dr. Comyns. Mrs. Smith there)
December 8th. At Cheltenham. Remained to dinner and returned to Town by mail train.

He had a thoroughly enjoyable time, playing with the children, who loved him. Little Willie, just learning to talk, prattled continually of 'Occe Parker'. While he was there he sang favourite songs to Emily's accompaniment:

I have had great pleasure in copying out 'I'm Afloat' for you and have endeavoured to make it very legible that you may have no difficulty in learning it, and I hope, when next we meet, to hear you sing it *very splendidly*. I can hardly express the pleasure your little visit gave me, and can now with little difficulty believe you have really been here, as I had been looking forward for so long a time to the thought of your coming, and now it is remembered with past events. (Emily to Oxley, 12 December 1845.)

During this short stay Oxley had the chance to tell her quite confidentially of his attachment to Louisa. She was delighted and could not help expressing her delight in writing:

I could not half express the feelings I experienced of sincere congratulation to yourself on one subject you so kindly told me about. I trust you may be *very very happy*, and I'm sure (*if you try to make her so*) your wife cannot fail of being one of the happiest women in the world, for you possess (and it is a dangerous though a delightful quality) the power of making yourself loved; often indeed where you care not for the affection bestowed. Perhaps you'll think me very impertinent for speaking such home truths, but remember, we are to be dear friends now and for ever, and as you are engaged and I married there can be no harm in cherishing a brotherly and sisterly affection. . . . I suppose you will soon be paying another flying visit to Putney; how *she* can live between times without writing I cannot imagine, but I hope for both your sakes that the necessity for concealment will soon be over as I consider the 1ᵈ post the greatest boon to lovers. . . . I was very glad to hear you sing again—and really you can sing and some of your notes are very sweet. I hope Mrs. Oxley will encourage the latent talent. (12 December, 1845.)

Oxley went again to Cheltenham on 16 February and this time stayed four days. In her next letter Emily wrote:

I send you the song 'Love and Courage', as you seemed to like it so much.

In March she hoped that his engagement to Louisa would be known by August, and perhaps even his wedding-day fixed. There is a hint in one letter about the disappointment of another young maiden at the rumour of Oxley's attachment to Louisa:

I am very glad to hear that Miss Round has now quite recovered her health and spirits. I used to think she was to be your wife and many people think so now: but you have other intentions.

On 7 June Emily wrote in great excitement. She had heard from a friend of a notice in the Chelmsford newspaper of the wedding of John Oxley Parker and was mystified, first that she had known nothing about it previously, and secondly that the name of the bride was Caroline and not Louisa.

. . . still I cannot allow one post to leave without conveying you my best wishes and congratulations on the auspicious event. . . . I beg you (when you can snatch five minutes from Cupid) send me a few lines and tell me *all about it.*

The happy bridegroom was not Oxley but his cousin John Oxley, son of Charles George, of Springfield Place. Oxley had already written to explain this to Emily and their letters had crossed:

Your note was quite a blessing to receive, and I now congratulate you very much on *not* being married. I could hardly believe it was you. . . . (8 June.)

In July Emily was at Rivenhall Place and on the 27th Oxley went to see her. The course of love was not running quite as smoothly as had been hoped, and no announcement of an engagement could yet be made:

I shall be very glad when I can congratulate you openly on the subject—for the poor girl's sake you really ought to have it all explained as soon as possible that she may not be subjected to such painful *blushing matches* as those you described. (28 July.)

A letter of November shows why, at least officially, the question of Oxley's and Louisa's engagement could not yet be recognised publicly:

My dear Mr. Parker,
The arrival of your kind letter of yesterday gave me *very very* great pleasure. I had been looking anxiously for the Postman's appearance for many days past and when day after day, no letter from you, I have said to myself (and that with a pain at my heart) 'something unpleasant must have occurred to Oxley Parker, or I should certainly have heard from him'. Delighted am I to find, that all my dark forebodings are groundless, and indeed, my dear friend, I think I may safely congratulate you, in having so far got over the difficulties you apprehended, and on being now on the road to much permanent happiness. Thank you for telling me so much as you have done. I suppose it is still a profound secret and shall therefore not spread the intelligence at present. . . .
I always console myself by thinking that I feel sure you remember me, and it pleases me much to hear you say your thoughts have turned towards me often of late, and that you have wished I had been nearer you to offer encouragement and counsel. I always expected that the *heads of the family* would be *quite pleased* at the proposed connection, such an old friend you are of the brother's, and I feel sure they will never be so cruel as to make any serious opposition on the score of *money* (that bane to happiness and yet a necessary

to it also). No doubt the Papa wishes to be particular at first and to understand your affairs and all that, and I trust you will very speedily be able to bring your uncle to the point that all may be settled, but don't alarm yourself with unnecessary fears, that you may not then have sufficient to satisfy the expectation of the sire and brother, for as the former is so rich, if you cannot make a settlement to please him, *you must promise to him to make up the deficiency.* How very much relieved poor Miss Durant must feel to have it no longer a secret, and I pray, her remaining anxiety and your own may be but of short duration and only serve to heighten the enjoyment of the future, or as you once in happy days gone by most ably expressed it.

> 'That your days may be bright,
>   With no sorrows encumbered,
> Save those mere passing shadows—
>   Those clouds which we meet.
> But to make our sky brighter,
>   Our pleasures more sweet.'

And have you yet told your sister? and how does she seem to approve and like it? Would you like me to write and congratulate *her* on your prospects, or no? You do not say if you intend another trip into Devonshire soon—but I suppose you can fix nothing certain, till you get these odious money matters a little settled. (11 November 1846.)

December passed by, and still no progress. Emily wrote on the 15th a chatty letter with news of her little family and a hope

that the subject next your heart is in a more cheering state than when I last heard from you—how glad shall I be when I hear from you that everything is settled! . . . I hear there are to be gay doings on the 29th and 31st—hope you will enjoy no end of Polka—your last winter of dancing probably—by this time next year you'll prefer a cosy evening over the fire to all the Polkas in the world. I hope your party are all well. I had quite a treat on Friday evening—went to hear the Ethiopian Serenaders and was very much pleased—'Lucy Neal'—beautiful, just as Mr. Prior sang it, and 'Mary Blane'—very touching. Have you seen 'Dombey and Son'—the account of the *cold christening* was most amusing, dº Mrs. Pipchin method of managing children—some good hints for me.

The dancing and festivities of Christmas 1846 did not relieve the suspense of Oxley and Louisa. He wrote in January that he was to meet his uncle Charles on the 16th. The reply arrived at Woodham Mortimer on the day before and enclosed was a small purse made by Emily herself and sent as a present with her good wishes:

My little trio are quite well; Miss Emily Louisa will be eight months old on your BD [birthday], so we will drink your health and hers in conjunction and another Louisa will also be present to my mind and our inward hope that health happiness and every blessing may attend her and him she loves for many many years. (14 January 1847.)

In Oxley's diary for 16 January occurs the following brief entry:

Morning at home. Afterwards to Chelmsford to CGP, [his uncle Charles].

He did not write again to Emily until April. Evidently the business of a settlement was decided to everybody's satisfaction, but some opposition came from another quarter, his old friend Richard Durant, who did not want to lose his sister. Emily's comment ran:

I am delighted to hear next month it [sic] fixed for the wedding and hope the brother will thaw before that—he surely could not expect his sister to remain single to please his whims and conduce to his happiness and comfort, and I should have thought *you* of all people (being such an old friend) he would have approved of; however I dare say he will come round after a bit. (13 April.)

She cannot help ending with a sly dig at Oxley's popularity among the unattached girls:

I suppose you mean to have a few of your wedding cards *edged with black* to send to some victims of unrequited affection.

Nobody would suspect on reading the diary that wedding preparations were afoot. Oxley was at Putney the last two week-ends in April and the first two in May, and there is an occasional mention of Saturday shopping, but no more. On Saturday, 15 May, he went to Putney and returned home the same day. The laconic entry for Tuesday, 18 May, runs:

Married at Putney Church.

Oxley Durant Parker gives a rather more detailed account of his father's wedding:

Father married in May, 1847, Louisa, eldest daughter of Richard Durant, of Sharpham; they were married in Putney from the house Mr. Durant lived in there, and drove away from there to King's Cross G.N. Railway Station in a post chaise, and with postillions in red jackets, which they changed en route behind a hedge, turning them outside in, and at King's Cross an old friend of the Durant family, Sir Richard Moon (the Manager of the line) had had a red carpet laid down for them, and refreshments and flowers displayed, before they took the train to Auchterarder, kindly lent by Mrs. Charles' brother, Mr. Rollo Hunter, and during their stay there Father went out shooting grouse or fishing.

Oxley gives in his diary a brief list of the places they visited:

Went to Wolverton, 19th To Lancaster, 20th Bowness, 21st Patterdale, 22nd, Carlisle. 23rd—D°—24th, Glasgow. 25th, Loch Lomond etc. 26th Stirling to Glasgow. 27th, Kyles of Bute, Inveraray. 28th, Oban, [?] 29th, Caledonian Canal. 30th, Inverness. 31st, Balachulish. June 1, Killin. 2, Blair Atholl. 3, Dunkeld, 4, Perth to Auchterarder. 5th, 6th, 7th, 8th, 9th, D°. 10th, Edinburgh. 11th, D° and Roslyn. 12th, Edinburgh to York. 13th York. 14th, Home to dine at Putney. 15th, Putney and Home.

A list that speaks of an energy that is almost alarming.

Apart from a month in Italy when he was an old man (1884) this was the only holiday completely free from business cares that he had in all his life.

61

CHAPTER V

THE TITHE QUESTION AND
THE ORIEL COLLEGE LETTERS
(1827–1843)

DURING THE EARLIER PERIOD covered by these letters and diaries, most of the business of C.C.P. was concerned with the assessing and collection of tithe.

Since the seventh century it had been the custom in England for every landholder to pay one-tenth of his produce to the Church. In early days this was taken in kind and it was usual before the Reformation for the parson or his agent to visit the farms in his parish at tithing-time to pick out the tenth swath of corn or hay out of the harvest which was set out for him. Tithe of corn, hay and wool, called Great Tithe, went to the Rector, Tithe of all other produce, called Small Tithe, to the Vicar. Peas and beans were brought in from the fields, milk was poured every tenth day into a vat in the Church porch or paid in at regular intervals in the form of cheese. Eggs from the parishioners' poultry appeared on the Vicar's table and the tithe of their chickens ran in his coops.

Although there were innumerable disputes, this custom of payment in kind worked out fairly well in the Middle Ages. After the Reformation, however, complications set in. In the first place, not everybody belonged to the Established Church and there was much resentment among nonconformists. Even in Purleigh, the parish with which C.C.P. had so much to do on tithe questions, tithe from the Quakers had to be collected by the Parish Constable. Secondly, the seventeenth and eighteenth centuries saw farming on a much larger scale and a far greater variety of crops. Collection under such circumstances was far more difficult. Hence the practice became more widespread for farmers to pay to the parson money in lieu of tithe in kind. In some places the whole parish made an arrangement to pay a fixed sum per year and the liability for this was apportioned among the parishioners at so much an acre. This was known as a *modus decimandi*, or simply a *modus*.

The practice of paying tithe in money worked fairly well as long as the value of money remained stable. Once this stability was disturbed, however, by war, foreign competition, labour troubles or through any other cause, complaints arose from all sides and it therefore became necessary not only for the owner of a living but even for the larger farmer to have somebody at hand who could act as his agent. Thus we find at the time when the Parker diaries begin, that much of the work of C.C.P. was taken up with the assessing and collection of tithe compensation money. In 1827, for instance, the first complete year for which we have a diary, we find him acting in some cases for the Church and in others for several farmers. A copy of the complete entries on tithe for that year shows how varied were his activities:

January 12. Attended B. Hanbury respecting *Bures* Tithes.

February 10. Wrote Mr. Armstrong respect^g Tithe of Wood North lands—corn, hay etc.

February 17. Attended Mr. Elwin respect^g Tithes of *Bradfield*.

February 26, 27, 28. Journey and attending Mr. Elwin to advise respecting the Tithes of his Parish and attending Mr. Biddell, Mr. Blencowe and Mr. Bruce looking over the Parish—wood etc. Wrote to Mr. Blencowe stating that I thought Mr. Elwin's offer equitable and made mem'dum disapproving adjustment etc.

May 3 Attended Dr. Shuttleworth and rec^d instructions to value Tithes and Glebe of *Writtle* Parish.

May 8 and 9 Attended Mr. W. W. Simpson at *Althorne* Hall and several other farms in the Parish to ascertain what portion lands sold to Mr. Wilson were improperly described in Sale as to Tithe

May 16 and 17 At Writtle looking over Parish as to Value of Tithes

May 18 At Writtle   do

May 19 At Writtle   do

June 2 Attended at Maldon to meet W. W. Simpson to settle award Althorne Tithes etc.

June 11–12 At Roxwell

June 16 At Writtle

June 21 Attended Mr. Lorde to examine several particulars respecting Writtle and Roxwell Tithes.

June 22 Attended at Chelmsford to peruse affidavit Wilson's. Attended at Blue House Farm Purleigh to set out Tithe of Clover and Grass and to point out boundary of Parish to Bowles. Mr. Webster met me here by appointment

June 23 Attended at Chelmsford to make affid^t Wilson's award, Althorne Tithe

June 23 & 26 At Langenhoe surveying Parish for valuation of Tithes —met Parishioners at Mr. Cooper's and agreed as pr Survey Book

June 27 Engaged all day making calculations relative to Survey and entering same

July 14 Attended at Willingale to consult with Mr. Deedes respecting Tithe Comp^n *Langenhoe* when he approved proposals made by me

July 23 Attended Mr. Cockerell to survey *North Weald* Parish to form an opinion as to his interests in the Tithes of the same as Vicar with 1/3^d of Great Tithes

Aug. 5 Writing to Mr. Cockerell to meet parishioners at North Weald

Aug. 7 Wrote to . . . Mr. Otte respecting valuation and Tithe (Plumborough—Rayleigh)

Aug. 16 Attended Rev. H. Cockerell to North Weald to meet Parishioners respect^g Tithes; agreed that Mr. C. should take Comp^n with Mr. Gyles and that each should have 2/8 (per acre) and those Parishioners who do not agree to pay such sum are to give notice to Mr. Kirkby who will take the Tithes in kind and pay the Comp^n for the same to the Rector and Vicar

Aug. 27, 28 At *Margaretting* surveying Parish to value Vicarial Tithes as agent for Parishioners; met Mr. Edward Driver.

Sept. 8 Writing . . . to Mr. Driver relative to Margaretting Tithes.

Sept. 10 Attended Mr. Driver and settled with him the valuation of Vicarial Tithes Margaretting.

Sep. 24 Wrote to Mr. Trevet respect^g Mr. Johnson's Tithes.

Oct. 23 Wrote to Mr. Tufnell respect^g *Wormingford* Tithes and to Mr. Andrews of Epping

Nov. 7 Wrote to Mr. B. Hanbury to inform him I shd be at Wormingford and could attend him if required on the 15th

Nov. 8th Attended at *Purleigh* to receive Tithes

Nov. 15 Rec^d Tithes Wormingford

Nov. 17 Wrote to Mr. Everard and Mr. Bailey respect^g Wormingford Tithes

Dec. 4 Went to Felstead to meet Mr. Gardner previous to Survey of Little Maplestead

Dec. 5 and 6 Surveyed Maplestead Hall and Brick House Farm also the Parish for estimating value of the Tithes

Dec. 17 Attended Mr. Simpson respect^g Althorne Tithes

Dec. 18 Attended at Mr. Forbes' with Mr. Simpson—Althorne Tithes—rec^d instructions to have land measured. Called on Mr. Gardner respect^g Little Maplestead.

Dec. 19 Attended Mr. Bailey respect^g Wormingford Tithes; with much difficulty finally settled Balance (errors excepted)

Dec. 22 Wrote to Colchester Bank respect^g Mr. Bailey's payments on a/c of Wormingford Tithes

These entries, the whole for one year, give a good idea of the kind of work done by a Tithe Surveyor. The list is somewhat lengthy but very comprehensive, even giving an example of the work of a Tithe Surveyor and Assessor. They even show a case of tithe having to be taken in kind from George Nicholson of Blue House Farm, Purleigh, who was behind in his cash payments. In 1827 C.C.P. surveyed at least seven parishes (Writtle, Roxwell, Althorne, Langenhoe, North Weald, Margaretting, and Little Maplestead), in addition to settling differences between incumbents and parishioners, rectifying mistakes made on sale prospectuses, attending parish meetings, sitting in receipt of tithes (Purleigh and Wormingford), going out into the fields and seeing crops set out, and giving information on parish boundaries. In some cases he looked after the interests of individual farmers and in one case, at Margaretting, he was employed as agent for the parishioners.

The 1820s and 1830s were times of serious agricultural depression, and many a farmer struggling for a living with bad harvests and decreasing returns found himself quite unable to pay his full tithe and remain solvent. This led to many requests on the part of the tenants for abatement, and we find that these were commonly acceded to by the patrons, many of whom followed the example of their neighbours with regard to the percentage of abatement. In his correspondence with the Rev. Dr. Hawkins, Provost of Oriel College, Oxford, on Purleigh Tithes in 1831 and 1832, C.C.P. not only advises by what percentage he thinks his client should abate but quotes the percentage abatements that had been made in neighbouring parishes. Even then it was difficult to get the money in and threats were often necessary to take tithe in kind. The result was increased dissatisfaction and numerous disputes which benefited neither party in the long run.

The year 1836 was an important one for those who received and those who paid tithe. In this year an Act was passed which made it possible for any parish vestry to take steps to have a parish surveyed and the amount of arable, pasture, woodland, and common measured. From the measurements an assessment could then be made and the amount every occupier of land should be charged per year could be calculated. This amount was confirmed by a body of Tithe Commissioners and thus every occupier knew what was expected of him, and the income from the parish was fixed for good. When a parish was surveyed the findings of the surveyors were embodied in a map called a Tithe Map with an accompanying index.

During the years after 1836 most parishes took advantage of this Act, and those which followed it, to have their land surveyed and their tithes commuted for cash payments. This meant that there was a rush of work for the land surveyor and valuer.

C.C.P., who had a reputation throughout Essex for being absolutely fair and impartial in all he did, was in great demand for this work. He had, for instance, the valuations of all the parishes under the patronage of the Bishop of London and the Dean and Chapter of St. Paul's, and he was also in charge of their interests in every parish in which they had property. Luckily, by the time all this work came his way he had his son Oxley at home to help him, and his business diaries show the vast amount of work they got through. During the three years, at least, from 1836 to 1839, general work on such matters as repairs and tenancies had to take second place, and that on tithes mounted to enormous proportions.

In 1827, C.C.P. had surveyed seven parishes. Between January and June of 1838 it is doubtful how many were actually surveyed by him and his son, but in that six months C.C.P. attended eighty-seven Tithe Commutation meetings in forty-six parishes.* Some he attended on behalf of his clients, some on behalf of the Vicar, and of some he had complete charge. In addition he wrote innumerable letters on all kinds of matters connected with tithe.

* These parishes were Althorne (9 Jan.), Aveley (17 Apr., 13 June), Barking (12 Jan.), Boreham (24 Apr., 2 June), Brightlingsea (31 May), Chigwell (2 Jan., 13 Feb.), Chingford (27 Jan., 17 Feb., 10 Mar.), Colchester (15 Mar.), Dagenham (27 Mar., 16 May), Dengie (20 Feb., 20 Mar., 14 Apr., 18 June), East Ham (26 Jan., 16 May), East Mersea (3 Mar.), East Tilbury (27 Mar., 16 May), Gestingthorpe (21 Mar., 8 May), Great Waltham (21 Apr., 25 June). Goldhanger (28 May), Hatfield (20 June—Oxley), Horndon (9 Mar.), Lambourne (2 Jan., 17 Jan., 13 Feb.), Langdon Hills (12 May). Langenhoe (3 May, 25 May, 22 June), Latchingdon (30 May), Layer Marney (16 Jan., 3 Mar., 11 April, 9 June), Little Ilford (10 May), Little Leighs (3 Feb., 18 May), Little Mundon (24 Jan., 8 Feb., 10 May), Little Totham (29 May), Little Waltham (26 Jan., 30 Mar., 27 Apr.), Maldon St. Peter's (13 Feb., 12 Apr., 14 June), Matching (13 Mar., 31 May), Mucking (7 Mar.), Peldon (26 June), Rettendon (14 Mar., 20 Apr., 22 June), Stow Maries (4 Jan., 30 Jan., 24 May, 14 June), Sandon (30 Jan., 12 June), Stanford Rivers (4 May), Takeley (4 June, 22 June), Tillingham (12 Apr., 26 Apr.), Tolleshunt D'Arcy (3 Apr.), Vange (8 Jan.), Wakes Colne (24 Jan., 15 Mar.), West Tilbury (17 Mar., June 16), Witham (16 June), Wormingford (24 Jan., 18 May). Today (1960) the list seems fantastic. The farms of Barking, Chigwell, Chingford, Dagenham, East Ham, Little Ilford no longer exist; they are swallowed up in Greater London and covered by houses.

A good idea of what was happening in almost every parish in Essex about that time may be gathered from over fifty letters in the Parker collection dealing with the tithes in Purleigh. These begin at the commencement of 1826 when disaster had struck at many of the farmers through the failure of Cricketts' Bank in Chelmsford. A bundle of some £485 of worthless banknotes in the collection, together with a few letters, show that C.C.P. was not unaffected by it. Dr. Copleston, the Provost of Oriel College, Oxford, who held the living of Purleigh, replying to a letter from C.C.P., refers to it:

Is Cricketts thought likely to pay a large dividend? From some rumours which have reached me I fear the reverse. It would, however, be some satisfaction to me to know which of my own farmers, and to what extent they are involved in this failure.

Just prior to this Dr. Copleston had suggested what he calls a 'moderate rise' in tithe compositions, and had asked C.C.P. to suggest a figure. The bank failure caused him to hesitate.

Considering the pecuniary difficulties of the times, if the farmers are materially affected by them, I may be inclined to postpone that measure. At any rate, I should be glad of a line from you at your leisure, giving me, as you always have done, frankly your own opinion. You are aware that my wish is to be moderate—that is to be rather under than above the average of composition in that country [sic], but I am decidedly adverse to a rate so low as to imply that one is ignorant or indifferent or timid about asserting one's rights. The loss, too, is sustained not in favour of the tenant, but of the landlords.

On 6 March, when the position with regard to Cricketts' Bank had become somewhat clearer, C.C.P. replied. He had not had the opportunity of enquiring which of the farmers were likely to suffer by the bank failure as this business had been interrupted by a second crisis—a run on Sparrow's Bank at Chelmsford. The worst feature of the affair for the farmers, apart from direct losses, was that everything at Chelmsford Market had gone down in price by 20 per cent. He assumes that

Dr. Copleston is not going on with the idea of asking for a raised composition.

I am glad you view the difficulties of the times in their proper light as respects agriculture and are inclined to postpone the alterations contemplated—at least that you do not press serving notices which I think now would create much irritation. I have abstained from any conversation on the subject with your Parishioners and if applied to I shall express my opinion that after what passed last year I have no doubt you will be governed by the time and the crop where payments become due—Your Tithes at present in the aggregate are quite equal to the average of Dengie Hundred and Purleigh is certainly not one of the best parishes as to the quality of the land, nor yielding any green crop on the fallows.

The main thing to notice about these letters is that both parties favoured moderation—a thing which contributed greatly to the good relations which always existed between them and to the general good of the parish.

In 1827 Dr. Copleston was appointed Bishop of Llandaff and in his last letters he expresses his appreciation of the services of his agent:

My connexion with Oriel and consequently with the living of Purleigh will soon cease—but I shall never forget the able and judicious management of my affairs which have been entrusted to your hands—and for my successor's sake, even if you had not desired it, I should certainly have recommended him to secure, if possible, the same valuable assistance. (18 December 1827.)

His successor at Oriel College was the Rev. Dr. Joseph Hawkins who, like his predecessor, was very willing to leave affairs in C.C.P.'s hands and to trust his good judgment:

I had, however, no particular directions to give you respecting Purleigh, about which indeed your judgment w^d be always probably better than my own. (12 November 1828.)

The extent of his responsibilities may be gathered from his reply of 21 November:

The Tithe Meeting was attended this year as well as usual and the receipts amounted to £837-10-0—since then I have received 60£.

I have paid your Land Tax, Poor Rates, Surveyor's d°, Salary of the School Mistress etc 96-3-6, and I have this day ordered 800£ to be paid to your credit as directed. I have several promises of payment, most of which I expect will be performed—but as must be expected in so large a Parish there are a few doubtful—those I shall press for immediate payment and threaten if not complied with. The crop is this year very deficient in this district—and altho' the price is high for most Grain—yet it will be worse for the farmer than a good crop with moderate prices. The Surveyor is proceeding with the admeasurement of the Parish and he has not at present met with any obstruction. . . . Some of the Parishioners are Quakers—the process to obtain their Tithes takes several weeks. As soon as I have received sufficient for a second remittance it shall be paid to your a/c and at the usual time I will send a particular account of receipts and payments.

From 1827 onward conditions rapidly deteriorated, distress among individual cases increased and reductions had to be made, sometimes to the Parish as a whole and, on top of that, further abatements in individual cases. In one letter (9 November 1829), Dr. Hawkins comments on the difficulties of adjustments in one parish causing more requests and complaints in others:

Nothing can be more unfair than the common practice of publishing Mr. So-and-So's reduction of his rent or tithes as a reason why others should do the same when possibly the circumstances of the land or the original rent may be very different in different cases.

In 1830 agricultural distress throughout the country rose to a climax. Riots broke out in various places. Hawkins, while agreeing that this was a time for forbearance (26 March 1830), also agreed that the mere checking of riots was no cure for the cause (14 December 1830).

I have no doubt you are right that to check rioting will not be sufficient unless means are also taken to improve the sad conditions of the labourers. Are there, however, more labourers than are wanted for the work to be performed? If so all that is done is but a palliative and does not reach the real disorder. Nor do I see any real remedy for this case but the creation of new profitable employment, either at home, or if that cannot be sufficiently done, abroad. And this seems the general design of Providence, that the Earth sh^d be gradually peopled. To emigrate and colonise have been the processes always hitherto pursued by over-peopled countries. Some distress however has always led to this. It is a kind of distress which drives the children of our higher classes to the East Indies. I only hope the poor may be taught their own true remedy for their Distress, before they are driven to still greater evils, or before they are driven by the pressure of greater distress to involve themselves and their employers in one common ruin.

C.C.P.'s method of dealing with individual cases varied. George Nicholson of Blue House Farm writes in this strain.

Sir: I attended this Day for Purpose of settling the Tithe due to the Rector of Purleigh But being Disappointed of not being any Money Paid in to the Chelmsford Bank for Me from Dixon owing to Contrary Winds I suppose. But I have no Dout of Being Able to Settle it Next day Not seeing You the Later End of the Market I thought I had better write.

Nicholson's letters arrived with monotonous regularity, always with some excuse for non-payment, but occasionally with the long-delayed cheque. Mr. Nicholson probably remembered that day in 1827 when he had had to set out his grass and clover for tithing in kind.

A second tenant of the same farm, Samuel Baker, complained in 1832 that his tithes were set too high:

I have sent thirty-five Pounds by my Son to pay Messrs Sparrow and Co. on your Account being one year's Tithe. You say it is as low as any Person can wish to have it, but I maintain it is a very high Tithe (viz 5/– per acre for the arable and 3/6 for the grass Marshes) taking into consideration the condition and quality of the land. I understand you have taken off 20 per cent from the other Parishioners and I trust you will do the same to me—when I have received your answer, will pay in the remainder.

The reply shows that in extreme cases it was always possible, though perhaps inconvenient, to go back to the old method.

I am sorry we differ in opinion as to the Value of the Tithe of Blue House Farm—and should you continue to think thirty-five pounds

71   F

too high an annual composition, I must request you will give me notice of your intention to render the same in kind. . . . I have really had so much trouble in collecting the tithes in Purleigh that I must for the future adopt a line of conduct I least expected after the liberality I am authorised by Dr. Hawkins to exercise towards his Parishioners.

It was different again in the case of Thomas B. Green, the lessee of Purleigh Hall, whose tithe was being raised. In October 1829 Green complained to Dr. Hawkins that arrears of tithe to the extent of £18 10s. was being claimed from him whereas he had paid in his own estimation £50 more than he should have done, and that all the facts had already been put before C.C.P., who, when he saw a copy of the letter, wrote to Green:

I regret that I can only reply to yours received this morning by stating that I must inform Dr. Hawkins that your letter to him is from the beginning to the end as far as regards my agency for the Bishop of Llandaff and himself a very erroneous statement.

An interview must have followed this, for a week later this note was received from Green:

Sir: As you stated positively you should arrest me for the £18-10-0 before I could hear from Dr. Hawkins I have desired Mr. Copeland of Chelmsford to settle the Business for me. . . .

In November 1831 Green gave in payment a draft for £50 which was dishonoured, and in November 1831 he was in serious difficulties about the rent of his farm. In August 1832 he was proceeded against for arrears of tithe. In January 1833 Green was in France dodging his creditors, having absconded the previous November:

I begin to have hope that your arrears due from Mr. Green will not be totally lost, as I hear he is still in France and in correspondence with his wife's relations to make some arrangement for him to return to England.

Nothing seems to have transpired, however, for in the following December, in a general account of arrears of tithe, appears the following:

The latter [Green] is still in France defrauding his creditors and deserting his wife and family—if he should return I shall be inclined to arrest him immediately.

In 1830–1, when the agricultural distress was at its height, so many tenants were in arrears that it was difficult to decide how to treat each case. The small sum received that year at the Tithe Audit—£811 16s.—gave him much anxiety:

I wrote on Tuesday threatening our Parishioners and I am fearful I must do the same with a few more.

His attitude to defaulters seems to have depended on the answer to the question, 'Will he be able to pay?' If there seemed no hope he advised legal action. This is illustrated by a series of letters concerning a farmer, J. Speakman, of Purleigh Barns. On 27 January 1830 Speakman wrote:

I received your letter respecting the Tithe which I am sorry is so much in arrear, to pay it now is out of my power and I am not aware that I can give any satisfactory security therefore I must take the liberty of begging your indulgence till another harvest when I mean to leave the farm and pay all their dues.

'I could place little hope in such a promise', says C.C.P. He applied to Speakman's landlord proposing to grant the indulgence if the landlord, Mr. Coape of Maldon, would guarantee payment of the 1830–1 tithe. It appeared, however, that the landlord could not even get his rent and was actually prepared to forgo a whole year's payments if Speakman's relatives would pay a year's rent for him and advance him capital to cultivate his farm properly. This they refused to do, and therefore the landlord too was on the point of taking legal action. C.C.P. advised Dr. Hawkins to do likewise, and added this note:

I think the effect may be beneficial in prompting others to be more punctual in their payments.

To this Dr. Hawkins replied:

I heartily concur with you in the propriety of the liberal offer made to Mr. Speakman with respect to his tithes—and if by any reasonable indulgence granted to him in retrieving his affairs or continuing his farm I should still be glad to do so. But if this is out of the question, as I fear by your statement is the case, I think that this seems a proper case in which to take legal steps to secure some portion at least of what is due to you. It is with reluctance that I authorise you to take legal measures against him, but I know you are far from advising harsh measures and therefore I feel assured that you will not adopt any measures that may seem harsh in this instance until all other reasonable attempts have been made in vain.

The result was a prosecution, and on 7 March C.C.P. wrote:

I have this day been at Chelmsford and have examined Mr. Speakman's schedule by which I find his debts are £518-11-6 and his assets only £13-5-0—his therefore must be considered a lost debt. The landlord under his Warrant of Distress absorbed nearly all the poor man possessed.

To prevent further losses of the same kind C.C.P. therefore proposed sending notices to be served on all those who had given most trouble and from whom he had reason to fear future insolvency.

I do not [he says], recommend this solely to avoid cases similar to Mr. Speakman's but to check with many of your Parishioners a restless disposition as to the Composition received. You need not fear any unpleasant result, for should any Tithes require to be taken in kind I will take that trouble upon myself. The seasons, I am aware, have been very bad but with some of your Parishioners more complaint has been made than the defective crop would justify.

Dr. Hawkins returned the signed notices together with a spare one in case it should be needed, with the remark:

In any case I know I may rely on your discretion and judgment and upon your forbearance towards any Tithepayer to whom forbearance ought to be shown.

Speakman's case, like Green's, ended in disaster. We find

74

from a later letter (21 January 1833) that he went to gaol for debt.

During the period covered by these letters there were three petitions from parishioners asking for reductions in tithes. The first, dated October 1831, and signed by thirty-two tenants, runs:

To the Rev^d D^r. Hawkins, Provost of Oriel College.
The Memorial of We the undersigned Parishioners occupying Land and subject to the payment of Tithes in the said Parish of Purleigh— Most respectfully Sheweth

That your Memorialists beg leave to submit to your consideration that in consequence of a general unexpected and destructive blight with which it has been the pleasure of Almighty Providence to visit our Crops upon the approach of Harvest they are consequently deficient in produce and quality unquestionably less than the moiety of an average Crop and we are without hope of any return whatever for the Capital and Industry upon such a failure of the present Year's Crop.

We solicit permission to furnish a detailed Stament [*sic*] of all the specific Facts of the Case to your Agent Mr. Parker and hope from that Gentleman's Characteristic Conduct, satisfaction may be made reciprocally which is all that we desire, and the application of ruinous Calamity to us your Parishioners may be averted.

Your Memorialists (as becomes them) hold in grateful remembrance your repeated Acts of liberaltiy [*sic*] by remitting a Portion of your demands during three years' continuance of defective crops and it is with great unwillingness we are thus impelled to solicit such abatement from the Tithes of the present Year as will be commensurate with the Circumstances and Situation of our Cases respectively.

C.C.P.'s comments on this memorial take the form of a review of the effects of agricultural distress in the Dengie Hundred:

It is difficult to give advice altho' I am aware that the distress of your Parishioners is generally very great owing to a succession of three wet seasons and now in the fourth year a càlamitous blight of their Wheat and other Corn, the blight very unexpected as in the early part of the year the prospect was flattering. Your Parishioners have but little relief from Stock the greater part of the Parish being

75

heavy arable land and when they do grow a small quantity of Turnips or Cabbages the injury to the succeeding corn crop quite counterbalances the benefit expected to be derived from such cultivation. I have referred to your last year's Tithe and Rent account by which I perceive your present abatement does not amount to 10 per cent in the whole altho' some of the Parishioners have received more than 15 per cent. . . . Any abatement you may think proper to make cannot relieve the whole loss sustained by your Parishioners, but in calamities like the present it is but equitable all should share in part. I will suggest therefore whether a further abatement for one year only of £15 per cent . . . may not be advisable on your part and I trust satisfactorily received by the Parishioners. . . . The combination of bad seasons and the bad spirit of the times make the arranging and receiving of Tithes a most irksome charge but I must as I have heretofore done struggle thro' the difficulties endeavouring to give satisfaction to all parties. . . . When I ask for arrears I am shown a sample of blighted corn which the millers will not buy. I had with me this morning one of Mr. Green's labourers of Purleigh Hall who stated that he did not believe his Master's crop would make sufficient to pay the Labourers until next harvest.

Dr. Hawkins, moved by this letter, consented to an abatement.

I am very sorry to receive your letter containing the Memorial from my Parishioners, both on their account and my own. I perceive that altho' the number of Petitioners is not above half the number of Tithepayers, yet their payments amount to nearly two-thirds of the whole and I take it for granted that no one w^d sign the paper put into your hands who had not really suffered from this blight, which indeed you describe is very general.

 I have no doubt therefore that there is as you say sufficient cause for the complaint and shall be glad to meet it as far as I can. Will you be so good therefore to say that I will make a further abatement of 15 per cent for this year only, and shall be glad to hear that this is satisfactory. You may add . . . with great truth, that I am much concerned to hear of their distress, and *to you* I may say that if on further inquiry you sh^d find that a still greater abatement w^d be just, your discretion will be my guide.

The second, in November 1833, was evidently not general, for it was signed only by fourteen tenants. C.C.P. did not think it justified and promised recourse to payment in kind.

His letter to the Parishioners (3 November 1833) in reply is a gem:

Gent^n: I have with much surprise read the Paper signed by Mr. Saunders and several of the Parishioners of Purleigh and had it not expressed that they considered me a practical Man I should have supposed that it was dictated by some one who had neither knowledge of me or the subject on which he was writing. Let all and every Parishioner take account of the produce of the Lands he occupies and I am well assured that he will not discover so long as the Clergy are entitled to tithes that the Sum required by me as Agent for the Rector of Purleigh as a Composition in lieu of those tithes is more than I ought to recommend being taken—but should any one be of a different opinion I will not require of him the necessary legal notice but agree that his Composition may cease from Michaelmas last but the Parishioners must excuse my recommending Dr. Hawkins to make any abatement this year. I should no longer deserve his confidence if I complied with this request. Wishing to retain his good opinion and that of the Parishioners of Purleigh, I subscribe myself etc.

The third memorial was received on 27 October 1834, and was signed by fifteen tenants. It runs:

To the Rev^d Dr. Hawkins, Oriel College, Oxford, Rector of Purleigh, Essex.

We the Undersigned Occupiers of Land in the Parish of Purleigh beg most respectfully to submit this Memorial to you relative to the Approaching Tythe Audit Humbly soliciting you to give us some abatement this year. In consequence of the Ruinous low prices of Wheat, the Average of which for the last six weeks has only been 43/11 p^r Qr. The Wheat crop is our principal dependance the Spring Crops being almost a total failure in this District owing to an unprecedented dry Season. We most sincerely hope you will give our trying situation your serious consideration and whatever you should be pleased to do for us would be most gratefully received.

The accompanying comment is very different from that of 1833:

Having fixed the Purleigh Tithe Audit for the 6th of next month, Mr. Saunders called upon me yesterday morning with the Memorial herewith sent—and I regret that the prayer of the petition is too true and that if I have your authority to make an abatement of 10 or 15 pʳ cent as I feel it required, the then payment will be more than equivalent to former years—the drought in this district is such that water has been carted for the Cattle on many Farms for months and all our Marshes in the Eastern Coast are as one Common without either feed or Water except near the Brooks. Upon referring to my News Paper this day I perceive the last six weeks Average of Wheat is still less than stated in the Memorial—viz 42s 7d, and the last week 41s 1d. I am fearful we shall experience much difficulty this Winter in finding employment for the Poor the forward Harvest and continued dry weather has caused much winter work to be anticipated.

The request was granted.

Thus the tithe abatement for Purleigh Parish from 1829 to 1834 was, on paper, a constant 15 per cent though, in practice, by making individual abatements according to circumstances, C.C.P. reduced it—at least in 1831 it was little more than 10 per cent—on a tithe assessment of some 5s. per acre on arable and 3s. 6d. on marsh pasture which was generally agreed was a figure below the average. In his letter to the agent for the landlord of Purleigh Hall Farm in the case of Green, he reports other cases of abatement in the Hundred.

I beg to state that Dr. Hawkins two years since authorised an abatement of 15 pʳ cᵗ which, after admeasurement of the parish was apportioned according as quantities appeared correct from estimated measure, some of the Parishioners having more and some less allowed, and he has now desired me to grant an additional 15 pʳ cᵗ exercising my judgment in the apportionment according to the degree of injury to the several occupants. The Rev. Robert Moore of Latchingdon, a similar heavy land parish has abated last year 20 pʳ cᵗ and this year he has ordered his receiver to make a further abatement of 10 pʳ cᵗ making together like Dr. Hawkins 30 pʳ cᵗ: the Rev. Thos Schreiber of Bradwell near the Sea in 1829 abated 50 pʳ cᵗ, last year having good crops in the Parish he made no abatement and this year he has written to me to say that he is abating 25 pʳ cᵗ. (7 November 1831.)

In order to get speedy and efficient assessment of tithes and avoid discontent it was very necessary to have a parish correctly surveyed. This was done in Purleigh in 1828. On 28 May 1829 there was also a perambulation of the parish boundaries and C.C.P. walked with the parish officers from 7 a.m. to 7 p.m. On 19 November of the same year he was present at the annual Tithe Audit which, he says, 'was very fully attended, but I never received so little at any former meeting, the whole not exceeding £650. . . . The Parishioners appeared quite satisfied with your instructions for an abatement which I would not allow in any case to exceed 15 pr ct.'

I made an abatement as I found the quantity by admeasurement agree with what I had before presumed to be correct, and in some instances where the variance was large I took the same as last year for Tithe. I am already satisfied that the admeasurement will be beneficial to yourself and your successors—and I hope I shall not be considered intrusive in recommending a Map book, with each Farm on a separate Page. Such a document will be a valuable Heirloom to the College. But this I cannot press upon you as an expense which will answer your purpose—what is already ordered is sufficient as regards yourself, but surely the College will think it advisable to be at the expense of a Map book. My personal knowledge of the Parish with an inclination to have the survey accurately made will I trust insure the same being accurately finished, if ordered. (27 November 1829.)

This letter was acted on. In reply Dr. Hawkins asked what would be the cost of the survey without the map book, and what was the acreage of the parish. 'It was reckoned I think in 1816 at about 4988 acres, which wd make about 62£ at 3d an acre.' On 1 May 1830 he desired the surveyor, Baker, to make the map book.

The work was put in hand though it was four years before it was completed. In December 1833 C.C.P. wrote:

The Map and book of reference I shall have carefully packed in a case and sent with Mr. Baker's bills as desired. The book of dissected maps which is on a larger scale I shall keep as I am continually required by Parishioners to refer to it to satisfy them as to the quantity in their occupation, particularly when a part of the farm is in Purleigh and the remainder in other Parishes. . . . I consider Mr. Baker to have faithfully performed his contract—he has taken infinite pains to have all the parcels correct and his maps are well executed.

Dr. Hawkins, in a letter of 20 June 1834, sent to C.C.P. a copy of Baker's account for the survey and map—£205 9s. 3d. for a parish of 5479 acres at 9d. an acre, and for the maps including binding of the duplicate forwarded to him £72 14s. 3d. 'The maps are beautifully executed, and I have already shown the Map book to the Fellows of the College.' It appears from the Survey that Dr. Hawkins's report on the estimate of the area of the parish had been over five hundred acres out. Such an error is hard to realise in the twentieth century but it makes us understand why surveys and bound-beating were necessary.

The making of this map was an act of foresight on the part of C.C.P. for in 1836 the Tithe Act was passed making provision for any parish to commute its tithes and make an official survey with map. On 27 July 1837 Dr. Hawkins wrote:

I must contrive to see you . . . that I may consult with you about the Commutation of Tithes. You would scarcely have time for this in a hurried visit at this season of elections. Nor have I yet found time to look into the case of Purleigh, but I have sent papers to Rochester, hoping to examine them there.

In October he wrote again:

When you have occasion to write to me will you tell me whether you know if my Map of Purleigh is such as would be approved by the Tithe Commissioners—I heard the other day that the Bishop of London has refused his assent to several agreements for commutation in Essex. Is this so?

By this time C.C.P. was almost overwhelmed with tithe business. He writes:

I am fearful you have thought me very negligent having so long delayed sending your annual Tithe Account but I have been so constantly engaged attending Tithe Commutation Meetings that I have not had more than one day in the week to attend to other business in the last six months. . . . I am frequently asked when a meeting will be called for the commuting the Tithes of Purleigh— when you have made up your mind upon the subject I shall be glad to hear from you. I consider you may with propriety demand an increase altho' I dared not recommend it when I might hazard involving you in difficulty by notice to render Tithes in kind, which has been threatened. Most of the Parishes in this district are commuted or in process of commutation—your map will be allowed by the Commissioners but it will be necessary to have three copies when the apportionment is confirmed. I am not aware that the Bishop of London has refused many agreements—he has demurred to several, making strict enquiry before he has given his assent.

The Tithe Survey was in due time complete, and the final document drawn up and approved. The figures we have for Purleigh Tithes are:

Before Commutation	1834	£1360 14s.
	1835	£1350 1s.
After Commutation		£1204 17s.

Tithe Commutation throughout England was an expensive business for the parishes, and it put much work into the hands of agents and surveyors. Yet in the long run it was economical, for whereas previously parishes had spent large sums not only on one survey after another for settlement of tithe, poor rate, etc., but also on lawsuits, correspondence, and the costly business of having tithe collected in kind; now it was settled for many years to come, leaving C. C. Parker, his son Oxley, and every other agent free to concentrate on other matters more vital to the well-being of agriculture.

In the Oriel College letters all mention of tithe problems stops in 1838, of tithe itself in 1840, and the series comes to an end in 1843. Possibly the annual Tithe Statements may be found at Oriel College and should be very interesting, but they are not to be found among these letters. There are, however, some comments on those of 1828, 1833, and 1838 which give vivid descriptions of the state of the county and of the diverse nature of managing a parish. Here are mentioned on the deficit side of the accounts such items as tithe in arrear, the insurance of the Rectory at £3 and the new Barn at 18s. That these premiums were increased in December 1830 to £3 6s. and £1 4s. on account of the danger of incendiarism is an interesting commentary on the unsettled condition of the country. Payments figure to a Mr. Sly for glazing at the Parochial School and painting the chancel of the church; to a Mr. Kemp for repairs to the rectory and the erection of a cattle shed. Then out of the revenue the agent paid land tax, poor rate, highway rate, etc., and the salary of the schoolmistress. The amount of general news concerning the state of the rectory and the premises, the confirmation or denial of local gossip and sundry matters makes one realise the enormous amount of written work that was entailed at a time when there were no such aids as typewriters, carbon papers, or duplicators.

*   *   *

Apart from references to agricultural distress and questions relating to tithe, the letters touch on other topics, general and personal. Agriculture leads on to finance, finance to politics. Dr. Coplestone in 1827 ventured to suggest that English agriculture could not do without the Corn Laws.

I am inclined to think that 67/– would be a sufficient protection to the English landholder, or perhaps 66/–. That he is in equity entitled to a legal protection against the foreign competitor to the extent of those burdens to which land in this country is subject there can be no doubt. These burdens are Tithe, Poor Rate, Land Tax, Highway and Church Rate, all of them being imposed for purposes the benefit of which is enjoyed by the other classes of the community quite as much as by the landowner.

Elections come in for their share of comment. In the Parliament of 1831, at the height of the great Reform controversy, one of the two representatives for Essex was William Pole Wellesley, the rakish husband of Catherine Tylney Long, whose profligacy had helped to cause her death and the sale of Wanstead House in the 1820s. This was the Parliament that passed the first Reform Bill. In 1832 there was another election and a new candidate, Robert Westley Hall Dare, was put forward by the Conservatives for the newly created constituency of South Essex. His Liberal opponents were Sir Thomas Barrett Lennard of Belhus and W. P. Wellesley. C.C.P. worked hard in the Conservative interest and Dr. Hawkins wrote to him (11 November 1832):

I thank you sincerely for your free offer of hospitality if I could attend the election but I could not well do so at present. Your cause indeed has my very best wishes. Mr. Wellesley ought not to represent Essex, and though Mr. Dare's name is quite new to me yet I do not doubt from your letter and your son's account of him that he is such a man as Essex ought to send to Parliament. But many reasons make me unwilling ever to do more than give my own vote; and even that I shall probably never do. My *name*, I feel satisfied, had better never appear in any list of supporters of any candidate. It would be of little value any way, *but probably it would rather do more harm upon the whole than good.* And as to money (notwithstanding your account of remittances which I was very glad to receive), between ourselves I have none to spare.

However this may perhaps be an occasion when, if ever, I ought to assist by something better than mere good wishes. And if you wish to tempt me to subscribe perhaps you could take the trouble to send me a list of the subscribers and their subscriptions, and tell me your own opinion of Mr. Dare's character for ability and good character [*sic*], for, as I said, his name is quite new to me and I was obliged to ask your son who he was and what was the common report of him.

A second letter followed on the 20th:

Will you be good enough to subscribe twenty guineas for me to Mr. Dare's cause, and detain it from your next remittance if you have anything of mine in your hands after to-day—if not, I will send it. But even this little paltry sum I can only give on condition that my name does not appear. You can give it as from a Friend, or in your own name or in any way you please so that my name is not known. For I am sure it w^d do harm, in these times especially, if it were ever said that a Parson living out of Essex, and drawing an income from a

Parish there in which he never resided, subscribed from his Tithes towards a County Election, so, you perceive, I send you scarcely more than it w^d have cost me to have given my vote on the two last occasions.

Hall Dare was again returned with Thomas Bramston of Skreens, Roxwell, in the election which followed the short Peel Ministry of 1834–5.

Many other letters bear on what is going on in Purleigh Parish. On 8 November 1832 a note appears in the Diary: 'At Purleigh receiving Tithes.'

An interesting incident occurred on that occasion. The Vicar, R. F. Walker, was also due to attend the dinner which was to take place immediately after the collection of the money. The latter, however, took so long that the Vicar had to leave for another engagement without attending the dinner. He left behind a note of apology to which this is the reply:

Your note was given me as I was going from the Room of business to the dinner Table or I would have answered it immediately expressing my regret that you were not one of our Party. I should be glad to dine earlier could I prevail on the Parishioners to be more punctual in their attendance. As the Meeting is annual and the day always fixed when not only most of your respectable Residents but also many of the non-resident Parishioners attend, I must confess I like to see the Rector or his Clerical Representative present as I am old fashioned enough to be of opinion that there are seasons for all things and that the Pastor of the Parish does good by joining at proper times in the social intercourse of his Parishioners, and particularly at a Tithe Meeting where, most of the Parishioners being present, matters are discussed relative to the good management and ameliora-tion of the labouring Poor and other necessitous Parishioners, whose wants are most likely to be attended to and relieved if recommended by their Pastor. I hope next year you will be able to arrange your engagements so as to favour us with your company.

In December 1832 Dr. Hawkins showed some concern about the inhabitants of Purleigh Hamlet, which lay a good distance from the Parish church.

Will you be so good as to inform me when you next write about what number of Inhabitants there is in Purleigh Hamlet and what is their distance from the nearest Church (for it must be out of the question that they shd go to the Church at Purleigh) and also who is the incumbent of the nearest Church and of what character.

The reply ran:

The Lands in the Hamlet are nearly all attachments to other farms in East Hanningfield, Woodham Ferris [sic] and Danbury and the occupiers reside from ½ a mile to 2 miles from their respective churches. Mr. John North[?] is the Rector of East Hanningfield and Mr. Bridges the Rector of Danbury and Woodham Ferris; in the latter Parish he has a resident Curate. The Rectors are most exemplary characters and the duty is well done and the churches well attended—in each Parish morning and afternoon service.

In March 1833 again Dr. Hawkins wrote:

I thank you for your a/c of the occupiers of Purleigh Hamlet. I had imagined there were many persons living there, and that it might be well for me to engage the pastoral services of one of the neighbouring Clergymen for their benefit. But a curate for one farmhouse probably is not necessary.

Three of the last letters concern another distant part of the parish called Cock Clarks. Dr. Hawkins made a visit to consider what could be done for the inhabitants of this isolated spot. The next visit C.C.P. paid to it he received a surprise:

Since your visit to Purleigh I was driving on a Sunday afternoon by that part of your Parish called Cock Clarks and hearing singing at the Dissenters' Meeting, I got out and went to the door. After the singing was over I heard a very impressive exhortation from one of the attendants stating that they were there assembled for the purpose of promoting the establishment of a school in that portion of the Parish where for lack of instruction many poor persons were deprived of a knowledge of the Word of God, and they hoped from the zeal of their Friends, funds would be found for so good a work. (21 November 1840.)

This eventually led to a speeding up of the plans for a small chapel and school. On 5 January 1841 Dr. Hawkins wrote:

I have not been able to think of anything better for Cockclarks at

85

least for the present than a school with, I hope, occasional, or rather periodical visits from the Minister at the School where he might expound the Scriptures and give some instruction to the old as well as the young. And I shall write to Mr. Walker by this post on the subject. He had suggested the hiring of a room for the present—but the more difficult thing will be to find a proper Master—and the expense will probably fall almost certainly on me. If there is, however, any tolerable prospect of getting a good school with additional instruction I should be very glad to be at the expense of building a good Schoolhouse, if I could find land for the purpose, which you thought the Lady of the Manor might grant, or at least sell on moderate terms.

At the same time a communication came from Mr. Walker, asking for an interview on the matter. Early in 1843 a plot of land was purchased from a certain Mr. Kemp and a school house and chapel erected on it.

A long correspondence such as this cannot but contain many passages of a personal nature. In 1829 C.C.P. lost his first wife after a long period of ill-health. On 29 October 1830 Dr. Hawkins congratulates him on his second marriage:

I could have wished to be the first to congratulate you upon your marriage, as no one is more heartily rejoiced at any circumstance which may tend to increase your happiness.

There are frequent invitations to Dr. and Mrs. Hawkins to stay at Woodham Mortimer Place, and repeated notes of mutual concern about health.

I particularly beg that if you are still unwell [October 1836], you would not trouble yourself about it at all, not even so far as writing to me.

The two men were drawn together by a common interest in C.C.P.'s son Oxley, who was accepted at Oriel College largely through the agency of Dr. Hawkins, who kept a friendly eye on him all through his university career, as was described in Chapter IV.

The correspondence, or at least that which is preserved, came to an end with the death of C.C.P. in 1843. By that time his son Oxley had had enough experience to continue his father's work, which he did for forty-three more years.

It seems worthy of record that all Dr. Hawkins's letters were written in his own hand, conclusive evidence of the important part taken by the Provost in the business of the College.

CHAPTER VI

BUSINESS

THE VARIETY and extent of the work done by C.C.P. and his son John Oxley are revealed in the day-to-day record of their journeys and business transactions. These are entered in forty-one diaries and extend from 10 March 1826 to 15 May 1887, with a break from 3 June 1875 to 1 January 1877 owing to a book being missing. In May 1841 John Oxley, who had joined his father, was keeping a book of his own and this runs parallel with his father's until 10 June 1843, when C.C.P.'s diary stops shortly before his death.

The first diary begins abruptly on 10 March 1826, and this seems to imply that diaries now lost were kept by C.C.P. before that time. They are plain matter-of-fact records of journeys, letters, and negotiations and were used for later reference in case of dispute and as a basis for making clients' bills. The reading of a single month's entries gives a vivid picture of a full and active life. Here is the record for four days in May 1826:

May 2nd Called at Laindon Watch Farm—saw bark measured off—137 yds. Offered Mr. Maling the Topwood and stackwood at £1 per Hd—told Mr. Maling to draw Trees to the back of Barn.
Called at Laindon Hills Hall—marked 18 Trees more in Wood—looked to work of those felled.
Attended Revd Wm. Armstrong at Standford-le-hope to meet Parishioners to receive for yrs Tithe, looked over Glebe Land with view of letting same, recd instructions to have Barn and Premises put into proper repair see Mr. A's Tithe A/c Books.
Attended Mr. Turner respectg Farm—he did not appear inclined to take the Farm at the Rent asked, wished me to see his Uncle Mr. Saml Turner previous to offering Farm to other persons.
3rd Went to London to make Affdt in Handly Benson's Trust Business; detained the whole day—Expenses £3-18-6.

Attended at Bank to examine transfer a/c of Stock to a/c of Mr.
Armstrong's Trustees—wrote to Mr. Hemmington and Mr.
Anderson to expedite settlem^t of Ex'orship a/c. Went to Bermondsey.
4th Attended at Wormingford—to look over Farm in occup^n of Mr.
Constable as to state of cultivation and repairs and alteration and
improvement of Buildings—marked in Fordham Wood 25 trees and
on Hill Farm 5 Oak Trees.
5th Attended Pettitt, looked over Farm—measured 9 Oak Trees to
Edwd Oakley—Mr. Stannard wants 2 or 3 Trees, Mr. Bailey 62 or
63 ft of Oak; looked over Mr. Bailey's Field offered to Mr. G.
Tufnell—stated Field is worth £40 per acre for convenience. Attended Mr. Tufnell at Chelmsford and reported to him what I had
done at Wormingford and Mr. Constable's request about repairs.
Attended Mr. Bramston respect^g £1 due from Mr. Jos. Pledger for
Tithe.

Thus, in four days, travelling on horseback, in his own light
carriage, or by coach he covered at least 150 miles, quite apart
from the business he did. The first morning he probably spent
at Laindon where he was agent for a Mr. Moore, attending to
the felling and sale of wood; then in the afternoon he went to
Stanford-le-Hope (about thirty miles in all) to see to the letting
of a farm. The second day he was in London and paid a visit to
the family estate at Bermondsey. He probably returned to
Woodham Mortimer that night by the Maldon coach, and
early next morning he was off to Wormingford (about thirty
miles) in the north of the county. Whilst here he took in Mount
Bures where he was agent for Colonel Bourchier and returned
via Braintree, calling at Great Waltham and reporting to Mr.
Tufnell at Chelmsford. Here too he probably met Mr. Bramston
and then returned home.

There are blank days in the diary which probably account for
leisure-time and Sundays, and other days, possibly of inclement
weather, when the only reference is to the writing of letters. But
most of the time of C.C.P. and his son was spent in the open air
in active pursuits. The month of May, when the rigours of
winter were over, was always a busy time, and in 1826 conditions must have been very good for journeys, for on the 9th and

10th he was at Bradwell, again busied with stock and farming; on the 11th at Rettendon marking trees, on the 12th at Moulsham selling timber, and at Chelmsford. On the 18th he was again at Great Waltham. Here he

attended Mrs. Tufnell respecting Donkey in Pound. She expressed a desire same may be sold and Salmon[1] is heartily welcome to all it makes beyond expenses.

On the 22nd and 23rd he was in London, on the 25th at Rochford, and after that attending sales and writing letters. On the very last day of the month he was on Tillingham marshes

to meet Jury to inspect 2 Gutters laid from ye Brook to supply Tillingham marshes with water. Mr. Gepp attended with me.

There was no room in such a life for indolence. One day in July 1824, some eight years after C.C.P. had started in business, he received a letter from an acquaintance.

Being aware of your early rising habits will plead an excuse for my making an appointment with you at your House at 5 o'clock to-morrow morning. . . .

He taught the virtue to his son. In the days of John Oxley Parker, Woodham Mortimer Place was astir in good time in the morning. At six o'clock the head stockman walked round the outside of the house ringing a handbell, and the clang of another bell from the wheelwright's shop echoed across the fields to rouse the labourers. The master himself was among the first to be moving. He often went out long before breakfast. On 27 August 1849, he breakfasted at Coggeshall (about twenty miles), and on 2 November he went to Heybridge Hall and returned to Woodham Mortimer to breakfast. On 16 June 1859 and on 25 June 1868 he was out on the ground of the Essex Agricultural Show at 6 a.m., and on 25 June 1861, as Director of the Show Yard, at 5 a.m.

[1] It is thought that Salmon was his bailiff.

This was the kind of business in which there must be no surprises. A man must know everything about real and personal estate and if there were difficulties he needed a good lawyer at hand. C.C.P. could never have thrived so well or made so few mistakes had it not been for the constant help and guidance of his father and elder brother who were solicitors in Chelmsford. Nevertheless, without tact, industry, intellectual honesty, business acumen, and a thorough understanding of how to deal with all sorts and conditions of men he could never have established such a prosperous concern. Nothing came amiss, be it questions of copyhold, trusteeship, tenure, enclosure, surveying, repair of sea-walls, valuations, the construction of buildings, tithes, tenant-finding or tenant-keeping. He served landlords who often expected to reap where they had not sown, parsons who depended on his services for their livelihood, parishioners and tenants who relied on him somehow to save them from ruin in evil days, companies established to make new railways, and landowners who wanted to make profit out of them; and all the time he had to hold in his mind one prime consideration—not just what was expedient, but what was right. It must have been like playing a hundred separate games of chess at the same time with a whole county as his chessboard, and rights and wrongs attached to each piece. Some of the work was of a temporary nature, that is, for single valuations, sales or leases; some, such as tithe accounts, made heavy seasonal demands round about November. The stewardships of other estates went on for years and years and added to this he farmed 2000 acres.

It was in 1836 that C.C.P. had a pleasant compliment paid to him. In the previous year the Land Surveyors' Club had been formed with a membership limited to thirty-nine for all England. Within a year of the formation of the Club he was elected a member, showing that he was well known outside his own county, and on his death in 1843 his son J.O.P. was at once elected a member.

The efficiency with which C.C.P. and his son did their work is evidenced by the long period over which they kept their clients. On 9 September 1829, C.C.P. attended at Mount Bures Hall to commence the survey of the estate of the late George Caswall. Colonel Bourchier, who became possessed of part of this estate, employed C.C.P. to manage it. After his death in 1843 his son Oxley continued the work which did not come to an end until 1865 when the Colonel's son, Captain Bourchier, sold the estate. Sir Charles Drummond Smith's estate at Suttons, near Passingford Bridge, was in their hands from 1831 to 1884; Sir George Pechell employed J.O.P. from 1860 to 1887, although Sir George twice gave notice (16 August 1878 and 23 September 1879) that he would manage his own estates. From 1836 to 1865 he administered Frame Farm, Tolleshunt D'Arcy, for the Taylor family, who were the most exacting of clients. In 1826 C.C.P. had charge of the Heybridge Hall estate for O. Hering. His son continued to look after it until his death in 1887. Also, in the first of the diaries appears the following entry:

1826. Nov. 9. Attended Purleigh Tithe Audit.

And in the last:

1886. Nov. 18. Purleigh Tithe Audit. Dr. Hatch and the Provost entertained the principal payers at a dinner at the Rectory; smaller payers lunch at the Bell. All passed off well. Some of the payers expressed their disappointment at not having any abatements.

The connection between Oriel College, Oxford, and the Parker family has lasted many a lifetime.

These are only a few of the lengthy associations which father and son maintained. When C.C.P. died, Oxley, who had been assisting him for some years, sent letters to all, asking them to continue to employ him. Only one declined. His father had only recently been employed on extensive repairs to Layer Marney Towers (1842), and in the same year Oxley had collected evidence there about the disputed position of a fence.

Mr. Quentin Dick, however, does not seem to have required his services any longer, and there is some indication that he was influenced by his bailiff, for J.O.P.'s answer runs:

As regards the past management of your estate, it affords me much gratification to learn from your letter that the trust reposed in my late Father has in your opinion been so fulfilled as to render any further particular superintendence unnecessary.

As regards the future I have no doubt but Mr. Blyth will be extremely glad to be rid of any interference and trust that he will do his best to protect your property.

At the same time that I thus close this account between my late Father and yourself I cannot help observing that I do so with some regret from the circumstance that had you been pleased to transfer this administration to me, I should have had the satisfaction of retaining every single appointment of the kind held by my late Father.

The wide connections C.C.P. had with farmers and landed gentry often caused him to be called on to find purchasers or tenants, sometimes under interesting circumstances. On 25 April 1834, Maldon Wyck Farm and a house in Maldon, both the property of Mr. J. S. Hance, were sold to meet the claims of his creditors. One of these was Miss Elizabeth Shaw who lived with her brother Edward Shaw at Polwin Cottage, Helston. Since February 1833 C.C.P. had been working on behalf of Miss Shaw, pressing her claims on Hance and endeavouring to hasten the sale. On 18 February 1834 he was at Maldon Wyck Farm to assess its value which he gives in his diary as 'n^m House n^{c}EO', the only entry in code in the whole series. The principal creditor was a certain Dr. Warneford, who had a prior claim on the estate amounting to £9900. Before the sale he demanded that a high reserve be put on the property, hoping thus that all his demands would be met. When the prospective bidders heard of this, many of them walked out of the auction room. The result was that the reserve was dropped, the farm was sold for £8500 and the house for £920, nearly £500 short of Dr. Warneford's claim. C.C.P. reported the result to Edward Shaw.

I am vexed I cannot give you a better account. . . . I am fearful both your sister and William Hance will lose their claims as well as other creditors. . . .

On 10 May Shaw replied. The loss had been a severe blow to his sister, now 'much behindhand in the world', not having received interest for three and a half years.

However, instead of sitting down and regretting the circumstances I have put my shoulder to the wheel to help her as far as possible and owing to the kindness of friends of whom I can boast a great many I do not fear getting out of the difficulty.

The solution was to sell the farm which he and his sister possessed and which was situated at the head of the Fen at Woodham Ferrers. He therefore asked C.C.P. to find what the farm was worth and to offer the first refusal to James Pertwee, the tenant. C.C.P. replied on 3 June:

If offered for sale by auction I doubt whether it would make £2200, but I think Pertwee may be induced to give more. . . . I will try what I can get offered by private contract, subject to your approbation.

Pertwee made an offer of £1995. In the meantime C.C.P. was negotiating with the Rev. H. DuCane who wished to purchase enough land to give him a vote in the Southern division of the county. He offered him the farm at £2200. This he reported to Edward Shaw with the comment:

I know it was necessary to ask more than the farm was worth to obtain a bid for near its value.

On 19 September C.C.P. was able to send good news:

I am now in my brother's office arranging an agreement with Jas. Pertwee having sold the Fen Farm at Two Thousand Two Hundred Pounds and the timber to be taken at valuation. Mr. Pertwee could not make up his mind until the day previous to that fixed for Mr. DuCane to view, and on that evening most reluctantly complied.

His client in Cornwall was both relieved and thankful.

We are much gratified by the contents of your letter, and perfectly satisfied in every respect by all you have done in the business and I

94

assure you that we consider it a fortunate circumstance that we had a friend to apply to in our necessity. . . . I must repeat my former observation that you must let us know every expence you have incurred. . . .

It was almost a year before the legal difficulties concerning the title to the farm and its identity were settled, but on 8 May 1835 £2100 was paid over to Miss Shaw, clear of all charges. In view of her unfortunate losses C.C.P. produced no account for professional services. Her letter of thanks was his only remuneration (20 October 1835):

. . . and now, my dear Sir, what can I say for the very friendly way in which you have taken so kind and active a part respecting my unfortunate affairs, believe me I know not how to express my gratitude, but I hope I shall always retain a proper sense of it, although I cannot look forward to being able to remunerate you in any way for the trouble you have taken, my Income having as you know been so sadly reduced, and in consequence of such an accumulation of Interest, and the Law expences falling on me to discharge, involved me in debt which it will take several years to extricate me from; but still my heart acknowledges a merciful God in having left me so many blessings, and raised me up so many kind Friends, yourself not amongst the least of them.

In December 1840 C.C.P. conducted a very delicate negotiation which was concluded in four days and involved a transfer of £36,400. This concerned the Coptfold Estate near Margaretting, which had been bought in September 1828, after valuation by C.C.P., by Mr. E. G. Stone. It comprised the Hall and five or six outlying farms let to various tenants. In February 1840 a certain Mr. Attwood had proposed buying this estate, but negotiations had broken down. Mr. Stone, who had been out of England for some time, returned in 1840 and decided that when the lease ran out in a few months he would go and live there. His preparations to take up residence were interrupted in December by a letter from C.C.P.:

Mr. Attwood's agent has been with me this evening and I have fully explained to him that £33,500 for the Coptfold Hall Estate and

£1500 for the moiety of Webbs Farm is no more than the Property has actually cost you or rather will cost you before you can convey the same to a Purchaser and as to the Timber felled that its value has been expended on the Property. I have also stated that you will retain the Furniture to convert to your own use and be paid for Fixtures Garden Crops Implements etc—and that it is with great reluctance you allow me to offer the Estate upon these conditions— he in reply states that Mr. Attwood will not take any thing at a valuation but always desires to know the total sum demanded and either purchases or relinquishes as his whim dictates. I will therefore thank you to state what sum must be added for Fixtures Garden Crops Implements etc—and whether the Greenhouse and Hothouse Plants are to be included in such valuation or retained by you with the Furniture. It should also be stated when you are to be expected to quit possession. The Agent is to see me again on Wednesday on his way to the Maldon Club. I shall not return home until midday Wednesday. It is perfectly understood that all that passes on the subject is to be strictly confidential.

When Mr. Stone received this letter he was astonished. He imagined C.C.P. knew quite well that he had intended to occupy Coptfold Hall. C.C.P., on the other hand, seeing a chance of a good sale, imagined that his client would be willing to dispose of it even at that late juncture.

Mr. Attwood [wrote Stone] must now pay the penalty of his own indecision and, if I am, in order to meet his present views, to incur again the great expence and inconvenience attendant upon moving, I must ask some further inducement.

He thought that £35,000 would make up for all his trouble, authorising C.C.P. to sell at that figure, and enquiring about his charges. The reply must have been most satisfactory:

As to your note of this day's date I will follow your example and be candid in my reply. While in business I do not expect to work either in body or mind without a satisfactory recompense and I trust my charges have never been considered extravagant, in a case like the present a negotiation having been before on the carpet, a percentage for sale according to custom cannot be thought of—but should a treaty be entered into and a sale made upon satisfactory terms, any sum you may think me entitled to I shall be satisfied with—you have had sufficient opportunities of learning what ought to be done in such cases that I shall feel quite easy in leaving myself in your hands and trust you will ever find me

Yours very faithfully
C. Comyns Parker.

Mr. Stone, however, was still very undecided. He wanted better conditions of sale and a still higher figure:

. . . I have been altogether taken by surprise by Mr. Attwood's change of mind in again asking to become the Purchaser of my Coptfold Estate, and fear I have already been too precipitate in renewing my offer upon the terms I have. However, it might not now be thought honorable in me to retrograde, and therefore (disliking the annoyance of Valuers as much as Mr. Attwood can do) give you a plain statement of the sums the Fixtures have cost me. . . .

I leave you now to act on my behalf as you shall deem right, only again cautioning you, that if any form of Agreement be drawn up, as between Mr. Attwood's Agent in [sic] yourself, it shall be so expressed that I am not led into any after disputes or difficulties—in short, that Mr. Attwood takes the Estate, as before mentioned, subject to all charges as to land tax etc, to which it may be liable, upon paying the clear sum of £35.000 and the further sum of £1400 for Furniture, Garden Crops, Plants, Implements and Manure upon the Premises, I myself retaining the Furniture, Drawing Room Grate and Mantelpiece, which, though of no extraordinary value to any one else, I have private reasons for desiring to keep.

Excuse this repetition, but I am so fearful of being misunderstood. . . .

The entry in C.C.P.'s diary for Thursday, 10 December runs as follows:

Attended Mr. Stone at Coptfold Hall afterwards attending Mr. Baker and went with him to Mr. Attwood's to endeavour to arrange a treaty for Coptfold Estate, afterwards attending Mr. Stone at Perkins and Gepp's with Mr. Baker.

Between them they persuaded Stone to accept a somewhat lower figure than the £36,400, and then C.C.P. took his leave. Afterwards he received a note from the purchaser's agent:

After you left Mr. Stone vacillated and at last left in great uncertainty, stating that he should hold himself until 12 o'clock to-morrow open to change his opinion without any derogation in point of honourable conduct towards Mr. Attwood. Under the circumstances if you can therefore be at the Office by 11 o'clock you may enable us to effect the object.

The two met, and Mr. Stone was finally persuaded to sell at the reduced figure of £35,200. In the evening he signed the agreement.

He had been served very well, and the estate had been bought by a man who had not even taken the trouble, at least on this occasion, to have it valued. Moreover, he seems to have been freed, as he stipulated, from further trouble, although in the following month C.C.P. had to attend to examine an affidavit stating that the price at which the estate had been sold was £2200 over its real value. For on 5 May 1841 the following entry appears in the Diary:

Attended at Westminster Hall to [be] examined by the Judge after sitting respecting sale of Coptfold Hall.

To find a good tenant at a reasonable rent was always a triumph. To keep a good tenant in bad times, sometimes facing the opposition of the landlord, was a continual struggle. To get rid of a bad tenant before the end of a lease was very difficult. The many problems which an agent faced in dealing with the conflicting interests of landlords and tenants will be dealt with later, but the story of Gate House Farm, Birch, gives as good an illustration as any of the troubles attendant on tenant-finding.

Gate House Farm, Birch, belonged to Mr. C. G. Round of Birch Hall, whose family had been clients of the Parkers for half a century. In 1865 it fell vacant. On 9 March J.O.P. visited C. G. Round to consult as to its future tenancy. He decided to offer the farm to Samuel Polley of Copford on the same terms, £284 a year, as it had been held by the previous tenant, Barnabas Pettit, but it was declined. C. G. Round thereon sent a letter to J.O.P., with another suggestion:

Advise, pray, what may be done now. What say you to young Mr. May? Is he a sober-minded young man and a good churchman? A communicant? The Mays are a highly respectable family, Conservatives, and the young man is engaged to be married. A fast young man would terrify us quiet people.

Within a fortnight Mr. Round had been satisfied as to the question of religion. May was both a churchman and a communicant and the farm was offered to him at the former figure.

'Young Mr. May' was fortunate to have a good business man for a father. First he objected about the penalties for non-observance of the terms of the lease as being 'so frightful you would think the Landlord was a tyrant'. Then he queried the acreage on the schedule and said that the rent was too high.

Indeed, if Mr. Round get the same rent under the severe restrictions imposed by the Lease, it is quite certain that the new tenant will be in a much worse position than the old tenant where he could do anything he pleased. . . . I should like my son to have it so that he could pay the rent cheerfully . . . and think Mr. Round would not wish for more. . . . (4 April.)

When the parties met at Chelmsford it was plain to J.O.P. that May was not going to be an easy tenant to catch. Backed by his father he not only raised the same points but he also complained of the insufficiency of the buildings and the restriction as to working the gravel-pit on the farm. J.O.P. reported this to Mr. Round.

I have given him to understand that I will not entertain at the same time reduction of rent and expenditure on additional buildings to meet his requirements, but as I have no doubt that he will make a good Tenant and will put the whole thing into quite a different state to its previous mode of farming, I am ready to advise that if he takes the farm some further shedding accommodation should be provided —a stable and chaise house built so as to make him comfortable in the place and as there really need not be dissight [sic] or annoyance from the gravel pit if it is properly worked I do not fancy it worth while to stand out on this point. I think Mr. May will now want to hear from me and I therefore shall be glad to hear whether I may grant these concessions if he is willing to take the Farm at the stipulated rent of £284. (12 April 1865.)

To May he suggested letting the farm at £280, reserving the gravel-pit for the farm alone, but this was turned down. 'The £4 you name would not meet the question.' On the 18th, five weeks after Mr. Round's initial suggestion, they came to an agreement:

Met Mr. May and his son and agreed to advise Mr. Round to accept him as Tenant at £275 per ann., additional buildings to be erected, but Gravel Pit not to be worked except for use of the Farm.

The story of 'Young Mr. May' shows that J.O.P. realised how important it was for a landlord to secure the right man for tenant. The farm was soon in his occupation and in August the repairs were put in hand.

In the meantime a crisis had arisen on another part of the Round estate. When in August J.O.P. went to Birch to view the progress of repairs at the Gate Farm, he noticed that things did not seem to be going well on Heath and Luke's Farms which were occupied by a widow, Mrs. Orpen. Two years previously, when this woman's husband was alive, the tenancy of the farms had been granted to him at a rental of £280. To help him to start, Mr. Round had also lent him £600. Since there had also been a rearrangement of land on certain of the Birch farms, a new homestead had to be put up at some expense to accommodate the Orpen family. Before the homestead was complete Orpen had committed suicide. The building of the house was, however, proceeded with, and Mrs. Orpen was allowed to carry on as tenant.

When J.O.P. saw the state of affairs on the farms he immediately reported this to the landlord. He also wrote to two of Mr. Round's tenants who he knew would be able to give him help on the matter. The first was his friend Philip Smith of Jay Wick Farm, Clacton, a man for whom he had a great respect, and to whom he gave the only unsolicited testimonial in the whole series of diaries (16 November 1874). The second was Mr. John Bromley, another of Mr. Round's tenants. Between these men, the landlord and the agent, there seemed to be the greatest goodwill and a perfect understanding. Together they set about to help the widow. J.O.P.'s note to Smith runs:

I hear from Mr. Round that you are likely to be at Birch to-morrow or Thursday. I am sorry that I am so engaged as not to be able to meet you. I was there a few days ago about matters connected with the Farm lately in Mr. Pettit's occupation, but in my drive I could not help noting that things do not look as I could wish on Mrs. Orpen's farm. Unless the management is really under the control of a man of experience and knowledge of business there is really very little hope of her doing any good in the farm.

It may be as well that you should not mention that you have heard from me—but I cannot help asking you to use your eyes and judge for yourself, and if you think as I do it may be advisable to confer with Mr. Bromley as to whether it would not be better for the poor woman to realize what there is on the farm and save the chances of further loss. You know as well as I do that Mr. Round would be likely to look with great leniency upon such demands as he may have on the estate.

I write this without any sanction or knowledge on Mr. Round's part, and in confidence to you, but I think it is worthy of the consideration of yourself and Mr. Bromley as friends of the poor woman and her Family.

Mr. Round was aware of the increasing seriousness of Mrs. Orpen's affairs, for she was already behindhand with her rent:

I must observe to you *in confidence* that poor Mrs. Orpen's farm is a more serious affair. Since I wrote to you I have had a walk through part of it: the condition of some of the fields and the fences is melancholy. It is said that the losses of the *last* season are very heavy: and I must in honour and compassion regard the rent to Lady Day as gone. It may be necessary to apply the same rule to the losses of this present season. What is to be done? The younger son, I humbly conceive, is quite unequal to the management, and when advice is given him he does not take it. This is a very uncomfortable subject. I touch upon it to you in confidence: and I hope to do so to Philip Smith in order that he and Mr. Bromley, Mrs. Orpen's friend, may consider what they recommend. (17 August 1865.)

On 30 August Mr. Round received Philip Smith and John Bromley to talk over the widow's affairs. 'Mrs. Orpen . . . still clings to the farms; we think it will be best for her to give them up', wrote Smith. Bromley stated the matter more clearly:

. . . we find it impossible for her to get thro' the coming year without a further loss of over £200, and advise at once to give up the farm. Mr. S. waited on Mr. Round the same day when he expressed himself very liberally disposed towards Mrs. O., indeed I think excessively so. On Friday I communicated to her the result of Mr. Smith's interview, when to my great surprise she seemed quite to repudiate the idea of giving up the occupation but if possible (as she says) to struggle on.

Have written to her by this post again strongly advising her to give it up and throw herself unreservedly on Mr. Round's kindness which if she declines to act upon I intend to have nothing more to do in matter, the state of the Farm itself being calculated to bring me into disrepute in the neighbourhood and further incur the displeasure of Mr. Round.

J.O.P. replied to both letters regretting the decision of Mrs. Orpen to stay on. He knew it was the wrong course, and that if the farm went from bad to worse she could not again expect such liberal treatment from her landlord. He determined to visit her.

I think that instead of going to Colchester by railway on Wednesday afternoon I shall drive by way of Birch and see Mrs. Orpen on the subject.

On that same Monday afternoon he set off with Mrs. Parker to visit his relatives at Canons in Hertfordshire, enjoyed a day's shooting there on Tuesday ('29½ brace and 1 rabbit—knocked up at the end of the day from the heat'), transacted business in London the following morning, was home at Woodham Mortimer to lunch, and set off for Birch in the afternoon,

in consequence of a letter from Mrs. Orpen that she had changed her mind as to giving up the farm. Advised her to see Mr. P. Smith and be guided by his opinion.

PLATE III *Christopher Comyns Parker*

PLATE IV *John Oxley Parker in later life*

From Birch J.O.P. drove to Colchester and thus concluded the business of a very arduous day.

This interview probably turned the scale and persuaded Mrs. Orpen to pay more attention to the urgings of Smith, Bromley, and her brother-in-law, Newbury. Mr. Round was specially anxious that any rumour that she was being turned out should be quashed, and was alarmed when he heard that young Mr. May was already hoping to get the farm. In a letter of 14 September J.O.P. tried to put his mind at rest:

I thought . . . that Mr. May had better not appear in the matter in the first instance. He wrote to me stating that a rumour had reached him that Mrs. Orpen might give up the farm, and asking me to speak on his behalf. I replied that it was projected, but that he had better not say anything about it at present. When the time came he should not be forgotten. I was anxious that nothing should occur to enable anyone to say that Mrs. Orpen had been put out to make way for Mr. May.

Thus the combined pressure of four people induced Mrs. Orpen to leave her farm. Immediately J.O.P. wrote to her landlord (12 September 1865):

I feel certain that Mr. May will be glad to have so much of the farm as you may think fit to re-let, and that he will probably take the things as valued to you.

Mr. Round was just as eager.

I feel that I may be wrong in not accepting your advice at once and I have the most entire confidence in Philip Smith's integrity and ability, and his friendly feeling towards Mrs. Orpen—*but he is my friend*. Is it impossible or improper to open the whole of the present state of affairs to Mr. May, and learn from him what he is willing to do?

I shall be glad to let the whole of the land to him, stipulating that the one field between our house and the Church should remain in pasture.

He instructed J.O.P., however, to do as he thought best. The question of Mrs. Orpen was therefore most amicably settled and the farm was offered to young Mr. May. He immediately began to quibble about terms (22 September 1865):

My father and myself have been and looked at Mrs. Orpen's Farm this morning and find it very hot soil. The corn being all threshed we could learn the produce of the past year and find it very deficient being only 5 Combs per acre everything, which at the present price must be ruinous. Taking the stock by valuation also makes a difference as there are many articles that I should not want. There are a great number of acres sown with young clover which fails in plant also no Mangles and several acres of Turnips missed and I shall have to pay the same as if they were, only ¼ of Turnips planted which will increase the valuation to no purpose. Upon enquiry I find that £1000 has been sunk upon the farm during the past 4 years, and I should be sorry to be in such a case I am very desirous of enlarging my occupation and therefore beg to offer you £250 a year for the present occupation.

On the same afternoon as this letter was written J.O.P. set off for Conway. On the Saturday morning he caught the early train to Penmaenmawr and breakfasted there, having first walked round Conway and the castle and through the tubular bridge:

36 years since I was at Conway!... The tubular bridge greatly destroys the effect of the old castle and the railway yard and the fine new houses outside the gates takes away the impression of the grim old isolated fortress.

He spent the day with his relatives the Gepp family. Next day he was at the service at the new Llanfairfechan Church, visited a new farm and gardens, and spent the afternoon walking in the village. He does not say how he found time or inclination to reply to May's letter and take a copy of his reply before posting. This time the landlord was in the stronger position. J.O.P. suggested that May was declining the offer:

I am sorry that your inspection of the farms lately held by Mrs. Orpen leads you to the opinion that you ought to decline my offer. Taking into consideration the average of really useful land comprised in the occupation I cannot feel justified in offering the Farms at a lower rent. I know that a portion of the Farms is hot land but you are well aware how such soils can be well worked for sheep farming— with new and commodious premises and so much receivable from the second Farm house, cottages etc, I must hold the farm at liberty until my return. As regards valuation of turnips if there is misplant you certainly lose the benefit of the growing crop but you will recollect that by Essex valuation you only pay for ploughing and manure. Nothing is taken out of the land.

Somehow on this day he also found time to write to C. G. Round stating May's reasons for asking for a reduction of £30 on the £280 asked:

Now considering all that has been done in the creation of commodious premises etc., I do not feel inclined to yield any portion of the Rent and have therefore written that I must hold the Farm at liberty till my return. In the meantime I think it will be advisable that your Bailiff should take the control and should do such work as is necessary to prepare for the coming seed time and all which would be repaid by an incomer. I rather hope that Mr. May will reconsider his decision, but if he should not I do not apprehend difficulty in letting the Farm. I of course mentioned the intention to retain the 22 acres adjoining the drive and wish that the field next the Premises near the Church should remain in grass. My movements for the next few days are somewhat uncertain but letters will be forwarded to me from Woodham.

J.O.P. did not err in judgment in calling Mr. May's bluff. Within a very few days a number of good offers had been received by Mr. Round and on 3 October J.O.P. was able to write:

This is exactly what I expected, and the applications which you have received are also what I expected.

I have no doubt that he now wishes to reopen the question but after these applications from good substantial men it is for you to determine whether you will let these Farms off-hand to Mr. May or to a resident tenant. The latter course would probably entail some larger expenditure about the House, but, as regards the former, having in the first instance allowed me to offer the Farms to Mr. May, I daresay if he should now offer to come to terms you would be unwilling to refuse him. I think that he almost deserves it. The graceful thing to have done would have been to take the Farms and valuation without a word, but some people fancy that anything of the nature of a bargain can hardly be done rightly if there is not some *haggling* about it.

C. G. Round was delighted with developments. On 5 October he replied:

My dear Mr. Parker,
  Welcome home! Many thanks for your letter, in which you have exactly hit off my thoughts about Mr. May. He almost deserves to have his answer 'No': but the offer having been made, you and I will not be 'huffy' if he comes to terms.

The Mays, father and son, now found it advisable to agree very quickly. On Friday of the same week, market day in Chelmsford, J.O.P. met them and agreed for the hire of Heath and Luke's Farms as held by Mrs. Orpen at £280—'and that they shd take the Valuation as made by Messrs. Cook to Mr. Round'.

Mrs. Orpen moved out, satisfied; Mr. May moved in. Within six months there were other matters in which he disagreed with his landlord, but these were settled by J.O.P. by a judicious mingling of forbearance and firmness. The main consideration was that a first-class tenant had been obtained.

*   *   *

Whenever a tenant was found it was the agent's business to advise in the drawing-up of the terms of the lease. In most cases the agreement between landlord and tenant followed the lines of previous ones, perhaps with alterations in the amounts of rents or in penalties for breaking various clauses. Some of these were often a matter for lengthy negotiation.

In letting or leasing land, both landlord and tenant took considerable risks and it was the function of a good agreement to minimise these for both sides as much as possible. After all, a farm worth many thousands of pounds represented a value that had been built up through many generations of hard labour and careful attention, and this value could be greatly reduced in a few years by negligence. Even before the hiring was thought of, the landlord and his agent had to consider whether the prospective tenant had enough capital, for the lack of it would quickly destroy a farm's value. Thus references to the possession or lack of capital by prospective tenants abound in the diaries.

To Mr. James Allen stating that I had received satisfactory references as to his perseverance, manner of farming etc, but that I was afraid he had scarcely sufficient capital for Berwick Farm. (Sir C. C. Smith, September 1848.)

Also reported application from Mr. Cracknell who afterwards appeared before the Trustees and provided it could be shown that he had sufficient capital . . . the Trustees accepted him as Tenant. (Dean Clark's Trust, August 1851.)

Went with Mr. Jolliffe Tufnell to Israel's Farm. Saw Mr. Stock— gave him to understand that he could not be allowed to remain after Mic'as unless his Friends should enable him to pay Rent and farm the land better for the future. (J. J. Tufnell, February 1861.)

Something also had to be known about the character of the applicant. Was he an energetic farmer? Did he know his job and use his initiative in the doing of it? If he did, the farm would have increased in value by the time his lease ran out and he stood a good chance of renewing it on advantageous terms. If not, the lease was offered to another and his reputation after having lost a farm made other landlords chary at granting him a lease.

At the end of a lease, the material interests of the landlord were to some extent safeguarded by the 'custom of the country'. Before conclusion of a tenancy it was usual to value the dilapidations, i.e. the diminution in value as a result of a tenant's occupation, and usage of property which belonged to the landlord. These dilapidations were paid for by the tenant, and he had to leave on the farm the hay, straw, and manure which could be made use of on the farm by the next tenant.

The general rule about keeping hay and straw to be used on the farm was a very important one. There was a great temptation to the tenant in need of money to sell these, as may be seen from the many references in the diaries:

Also went to Barking, found that Mr. Plows had threshed out his wheat and sent away the straw and was doing the same with the barley—told him that he was doing extremely wrong and that I must acquaint Messrs Parnther and Fisher with what had been done. (Mrs. Thoyts, 11 September 1849.)

When a farm changed hands the straw and hay had to be left behind 'according to the custom of the country' for the benefit of the incoming tenant:

Pointed out that Mr. Allen had hired Berwick Farm on the same terms as are expressed in the agreement to Mr. Aldham and had come into the farm on those terms—that the straw must therefore be left for the incoming tenant, he paying for threshing and carrying out. (Sir C. C. Smith, 10 August 1855.)

Among the collection of documents are many of these agreements, two of which are quoted in an appendix (below).

The fixing of an annual rent was often a very difficult matter. Conditions in farming changed quickly, and what was thought a reasonable rent in one year could be deemed very high or very low in another. Nobody knew this better than J.O.P., who tried continually to obtain abatements of rent on Bovill's Marsh Farm which his father had leased from the Frere family at a time when rents had been high. Some prospective tenants even demanded the assurance from the landlord that they would be protected in bad times. On 7 September 1850, the tenant of Stamford's and Hill Farms, Latchingdon, refused to take out a new lease unless he could be guaranteed from loss. J.O.P. asserted that this was only possible by making a rent which varied with the fluctuations in the price of corn. In some cases such rents were agreed on. In April 1852 he made a proposal to renew C. G. Round's leases to the tenants of Layer Hall and Layer Rows Farms 'based on a graduated scale of the price of corn', commencing with the highest rent when corn was at 60s. and decreasing by £25 with each diminution of 5s., 'the averages to be by prices of Colchester market'. In the same month he endeavoured to obtain a tenant's approval of a rent which consisted of one-third fixed (£100) and the remaining two-thirds on a sliding scale varying with the price of corn. In March 1845 he offered Philip Smith '£350 minimum rent, £370 if wheat is at or over 52/–, £390 if at or over 56/–, £410 if at or over 60/–'. In April 1851 the Rev. John Bramston agreed to his letting Torrels Hall to Richard Boyton for twelve years 'at a rent of £200 and 75 quarters of wheat by the average price of Chelmsford Market'. Thus Boyton's rent could be expected to vary between £200 plus (75 × 60s.) = £425, and £200 plus (75 × 45s.) = £368 15s. The fact that such negotiations were carried on is an indication of the importance of corn-growing in the economy of the Essex farmer at that time.

Unexpected stipulations are occasionally to be found with regard to the letting of farms. In July 1848, J.O.P. had a meeting with one of C. G. Round's tenants who did not want to take a long lease on a farm.

I stated that I could not abate my previous proposals, but if he was afraid of the rabbits etc., I was willing to introduce a clause allowing him to give a 12 months' notice to quit and to receive payments by valuation for improvements.

Rabbits were a pest serious enough to influence the terms of a lease. Here a conflicting interest showed up as between landlord and tenant. Rabbit-shooting was good sport, and, when shooting was let out, could be a good source of income. J.O.P. in his diary gives several instances of large numbers of rabbits shot in one day.

Shooting in Hazeleigh Hall Wood. . . . 42 P[heasants], 12 H[ares], 295 rabbits—349. (29 November 1883.)

On the other hand, they were often the source of great damage to crops, especially on fields which were near to woodland. In July 1831 C.C.P. recorded in his diary:

Darby and Brights looked to damage done by rabbits, estimated Mr.

Smith's damage at £46, Mr. Darby's at £10, Boultwood's at £30 without allowing profit on crops.

One tenant took the extermination of rabbits into his own hands. His action was followed by a stern reproof from C.C.P. and a reference to the Landlord:

Attended Mr. Dennis at Mr. Gepp's respect^g Agreem^t for his Farm —denied ever giving authority to kill Rabbits; recommended him to see Mr. Attwood and disabuse his mind on the subject. (15 January 1841.)

Many prospective tenants refused to consider hiring unless rabbits were controlled. Some insisted on being allowed to shoot them on the land they held.

Afterwards to look to damage by rabbits in fields adjoining Kiln Wood. Found five acres in Brick Kiln Leys damaged at least 1 qr. an acre, and 3 acres on Higgles Ley 4 bushels an acre. (T. W. Bramston, 27 August 1861.)
Mr. Faux and Mr. Eve as to agreement for Heybridge Hall Farms. Agreed to certain alterations in covenants and after long discussion allowed him [Mr. Faux] to destroy rabbits. (Trustees late Sir John Milbanke, 8 July 1872.)
Eventually agreed to accept £110 rent and to give £20 for damage by rabbits. (Trustees late C. G. Round, 15 May 1875.)
Also saw Mr. Brand who said he could not take Traceys Farm unless the rabbits were kept down. (Sir C. C. Smith, 30 August 1878.)

In 1848 Archdeacon Wilberforce insisted that the tenant of his farm on Potten Island should attend church, and most landlords had a distinct preference for Anglicans over Non-conformists as tenants.

In 1853 a tenant of J. R. Tufnell's at Wormingford Hall applied to be allowed to use a steam threshing machine, and the landlord insisted on an extra insurance being taken out on the premises. On 1 May 1869, 'at Dean Clark's Audit, Mr. H. Crabb complained of being called upon to pay extra insurance of Steam Engine next Barn'. On the very same evening the barn caught fire from a spark thrown out of the chimney of the engine 'but extinguished by the exertion of the labourers on the spot'.

Both C.C.P. and his son recorded carefully in their diaries the places they attended and the main items of business transacted. Farms had to be visited regularly, for once a tenant was found and installed it was the work of an agent to see that his client's property was not suffering either direct damage or damage by neglect. The periodic visit was also good for the tenants, giving them the chance to voice their complaints. Note was taken of all these. The state of the farm concerned was entered up, often in great detail, and the record acted as an aid to memory and a source of reference in case of dispute:

Attended at Standford-le-hope met Mr. John Turner to measure Elm and Oak Timber saw Mrs and Mr Turner, both appeared determined not to hire at 500£ a year proposed having dilapidations valued which for the present was not acceded to; finding the Lease does not allow Timber for repairs informed Mr. Turner that I should not allow same if he persisted in patching the repairs—found great fault with him for the manner in which many of the Timber Trees had been pruned and many Spires also felled and found fault with the backward state of the Fallows and hoeing of the Lands in Peas and Beans. (C.C.P., 18 April 1826.)

Or again, forty years later:

To Birch to meet Mr. Grimes and Mr. May. Went over works recently done and found same satisfactorily carried out—gave orders for new hen houses—repairs to lean-to, to Barn, weatherboarding etc and tarring and flooring chaise house and spouting to shed, and repairs to House late Mrs. Orpen, and placing new sheep shed at Heath Farm. Also walked with Mr. May to site of Luke's Farm to determine as to portion to be laid to grass and left same for further consideration. Afterwards at Round Bush Farm planning new sheds and giving directions to Hutson to proceed with same. (C. G. Round, 7 March 1866.)

Accounts of proposed and completed agreement were usually written up in some detail. On 25 February 1835, C.C.P. took the trouble to record a complicated arrangement he had made with Captain Fanshawe for the reletting of Bridge Wick and Dengie Hall Farms:

Attended Captn Fanshawe to report to him resp^g arrangement for my reletting Bridge Wick and Tile Barns. Stated that I did not expect to obtain more than 20s an acre for all the land within the Wall—the Tenant agreeing to do the Repairs and Improvements at Tile Barns and the Wyck and to enclose the Saltings being allowed £100 annually out of the rent reserved, but to expend the money in advance if he thought proper. Capt. Fanshawe agreed that such an offer should be made to the late Mr. Page's exec^{rs} (late tenant of Bridge Wick).

J.O.P. was no less precise in his recording. In the first diary he kept (1841–3) there are many detailed accounts:

February 2nd, 1843. At Wallasey Island to look on Shearwood's Farm—Lord Wynford's. Mr. Allen [the tenant] not there on account of the weather. Went over land—found same in improved state of cultivation. The Wall in good order—1 man and 2 boys replacing chalk and stone—ab^t week's work—requires one load Piles one ld. of Stone and one ld. of Chalk dropped along the Wall where wanted and laid in with judgment to make same in most substantial condition—new Gates wanted—Buildings, Sluices etc bad—Tiling and Thatch requiring repair. House wants 2 coats of tarring and brick open Gutter to be laid in cement round the House to throw off water—same now soaks through the underpinning.

Many instances such as these may be found in every volume of the diaries.

Repairs were an important factor in the negotiations between landlord and tenant. The general custom was for the tenant to receive the premises in good repair and to keep them so, receiving rough materials such as timber and bricks free. The timber was usually taken from the hedgerows or the woodland, if there was any belonging to the farm, and was cut down and sawn up by the farmer after being marked by J.O.P.; and some farms had their own brick-kilns. The conditions were, however, varied in many ways, and both landlord and tenant had to be very wary of being led into greater expenses than they had reckoned on. On 27 July 1827 the tenant of John Moore's farm at Stanford-le-Hope, a Mr. Turner, offered £450 a year to renew his lease but would make no contribution towards repairs. These terms were not accepted, but a lease was eventually agreed on. On 30 May 1829 C.C.P. attended on Moore at Stanford, looked over the farms,

and explained the dilapidated state of the same, informed Mr. M. that the repairs would not be less than £1000—exclusive of Timber —received instructions to proceed with the repairs.

Some tenants were not so lucky—or far-seeing—as Turner. On 31 March 1849 J.O.P. recorded:

Went to Plumborough and afterwards to meet Mr. A. B. Croxon at East Wick [owned by Sir J. T. Tyrell]. Went over the Farm— inspected land lately broken up—examined repairs required to be done and eventually proposed to recommend Sir John Tyrell to grant lease for 14 or 21 years at £380—Mr. Croxon agreeing to expend not less than £200 in repairs during the first 4 years being allowed only rough timber for the same. Bricks for walls etc. to be made on the Farm at the Tenant's expense.

Thus the total rent for the farm was £430 for the first four years, exclusive of material and labour taken up in repairs. Many factors were involved in the drawing-up of this lease. The first was that the tenant had broken up pasture land and converted it into arable, which usually carried a penalty, the second that the repairs were urgent and likely to be costly. The tenant in this case must have had capital to tide him over the first four years, but after that he stood to reap considerable benefit for, after the last payment of £50 in March 1854, his premises were in first-class condition and he was freed from all future payments for repairs. In June 1854 we find him authorised by the landlord to retain £100 out of the rent 'on account of the repairs in progress'. Thus the actual rent he paid in that year was £280 as against £430 in 1850.

For more than sixty years father and son continued to arrange leases not only in Essex but in many other counties. Experience taught them what to adopt and what to avoid, how much weight to give to length of lease, repairs allowances, rights to shoot and course, to lop timber and to work sand-pits and gravel-pits. They had to know which were the best types of agreements for light and heavy land farms and how much a tenant should have to do with the keeping clean of gutters (i.e. dykes), and maintaining of sea-walls; they knew how the onset of bad times was likely to affect a tenant, where the pressure was likely to be and whether or not abatement of rent ought to be given, and in what form. They laid great stress on the drawing-up of sound agreements and went to great trouble to explain both to landlords and tenants why these were important. In July 1846 J.O.P. gave wise general observations to two tenants of Sir Charles Smith:

. . . It is highly necessary under present circumstances to advance as far as it is possible the onward progress of agricultural improvement and inasmuch as such improvement cannot be carried out except at a considerable outlay of capital it is highly desirable that some form of agreement should exist between the owner and occupier of the soil as should give to the latter in some measure a security for his expenditure. Whereas in your case there is good faith existing between the Landlord and Tenant the occupier may fairly expect that no one else will be allowed to reap the benefits of his outlay, and under the guarantee of such an impression he may be induced to farm *well*, but with a written agreement which shall ensure compensation for certain specific and permanent improvements, I think there can be no doubt that he would be induced to farm *better*, and at the same time that it has this good effect I am also inclined to believe that the power of referring on either part to certain definite terms of agreement may prevent in future those misunderstandings which sometimes arise in cases where the only mode of settlement (should any difference of opinion occur) is left to the undefined and often ill-understood rules which are applied by what is termed 'the general custom of the country'.

On another occasion, in 1864, J.O.P. gave very sound advice to G. M. W. Peacocke, M.P., whose property, Reeves Farm, Mersea, had suffered badly through a misplacement of the obligation to repair. Previously the farm had been leased at £480 per annum, the tenant doing all repairs to buildings, sea-walls, and sluices, finding all materials and also paying land-tax. These obligations had the effect of materially increasing the actual rent, but they offered the temptation to the tenant either to neglect them or carry them out badly. The result on Reeves Farm is described:

The arable land of the Farm appears to have been very fairly cultivated, but no levelling or improving of the grazing marshes has been done, no hard roads formed round the Premises, nor any such works as would better the condition of the occupation. . . . The Farm has that useful combination of good arable upland with the extensive grazing Marshes [which] ought to place it amongst the best class of Farms of the Neighbourhood—but to enable it to hold this position the House and Premises must be improved, a better supply of water provided, the grazing Marshes divided into convenient enclosures, the gutters lowered to provide better drainage, and hard roads formed round the yards and premises, and for proper communication with the Marshes.

The sad condition of this farm had, he said, been caused by the negligence of a tenant who was under obligation to do his own repairs. It could be made good, not by calling on the tenant to do more, but by valuing the dilapidations and asking the tenant to pay a reasonable amount so that the landlord could have repairs done.

His general observations on repairs show the wisdom of taking the middle course of co-operation between landlord and tenant.

I consider it very detrimental to a Farm to be let, as this has been, on a long Lease with every obligation to repair, find all materials etc, imposed upon the Tenant. The result is almost invariably the same— as little as possible is done. Old buildings are patched up from time to time to make them last through the term. No improvements are made and the Property reverts to the owner in bad condition. Where on the other hand all rough materials are provided at the cost of the landlord, and the Tenant is only charged with the expences of labour, repairs and renewals of buildings are done in a substantial manner and the character of the Premises is often at the end of a course of years materially improved.

Though the day-to-day work of C.C.P. and his son may have been concerned with more ordinary matters, there were occasions when both made notable sales, valuations, or purchases. On 10 December 1842 C.C.P. received an application from Sir Claude de Crespigny for the purchase of Danbury Park from J. Round. Nothing came of this but on 22 April 1845 the following entry appears in J.O.P.'s diary:

Wrote to Mr. Round and Mr. Hoggart informing them of the Bishop of Rochester's visit to look at House and Grounds and stating that when pressed by him to name a price I had said £25,000, Timber included.

Ten days later, one of the largest sales of all was completed.

Went to London by 3 o'clock train. Called on Mr. Hoggart and learnt that the Bishop of Rochester had agreed for the purchase of Danbury at £24,700.

Thus Danbury became the residence of the Bishop and was known as Danbury Palace.

In 1857 J.O.P. was instrumental in making a purchase which involved an even larger sum of money. On 6 November he was instructed to look over the Fitzwalter Estate which was advertised for sale. On 1 December he bought it for £30,000. 'I trust that I have done a good day's work', he wrote to his client, the Rev. G. Gretton Townshend. Twenty-two years later he surveyed the same estate. He accompanied his detailed statement with a short note:

The Property consists of *814 acres* in what may fairly be called a ring fence. The present Rental is £1445 per annum (exclusive of the Woods in hand) but with the addition which will be put to the Rent of 'Palmers Farm' under a new Lease, the gross rental will be as near as may be, *£1500*. If from this amount shall be deducted, say £250 for Tithe paid by you, and for repairs, and something be added for the value of the shooting, at 30 years' purchase the Property is worth over £38,000 exclusive of the value of the Timber. But I cannot consider that the value of this Property is to be limited to the ordinary rule of calculation. A compact Estate of this kind is not to be met with every day. At £50 per acre the value would be £40,700. It might realize more, but under any circumstances I cannot put it less than £40,000.

Sometimes the work they did led them into unusual situations. On 7 March 1833, C.C.P. received a letter from William Gosling, one of his clients:

I . . . should much wish your going to Hassiobury on Monday the 10th Inst:, I propose if possible to be there on the Sunday before to meet you, but should I not be able I will write to my Servant there to have everything ready for you. She will give you the key of my Cellar sealed up which you will have the goodness to take and return to her upon your quitting my House making use of what Wine and other liquors you may want. Upon recollection it is the key of my Desk in which is the key of my Cellar, have the goodness to return the key to her sealed up.

C.C.P. replied with a very detailed report on the state of the farm.

In all transactions involving sale or purchase hard bargaining was the convention and proceeded on an acknowledged plan. Every vendor, lessor, or agent demanded more than he knew the property was worth; every prospective buyer, lessee, or agent offered less. Then, with such things as length of lease, repairs, shooting and coursing rights, timber, revenue from subletting and many other considerations as makeweights the two parties gradually gave way a few pounds at a time until, if both sides pursued the bargaining, a point of common consent, if not of complete agreement, was reached. This process is well illustrated by the selling of Steeple Grange for J. J. Tufnell to St. Bartholomew's Hospital in 1856. The first figures were £16,000 and £14,000 and finally met at £15,000. If there was no possibility of demand and offer ever coinciding the negotiation was broken off. Sometimes, as we have seen in the case of 'young Mr. May', one party almost overreached himself, so that an agreement was concluded only through the forbearance of the other.

A most amusing example of hard bargaining to very little purpose concerns a tree felled by mistake on Curtis Mill Green. A letter of Sir Charles Smith's tells what had happened:

When I was marking the trees on Curtis Mill Green I marked among the others, one standing in a little plot of garden ground, which has been apparently cribbed from the green and which stands opposite Strange's cottage, to whom it formerly belonged. I marked it, thinking it belonged to me in the same way as the other trees near it and in fact my impression when I did it was 'There is a tree standing very awkwardly in the middle of a poor man's garden, how much better it would be away'. Since it was taken down I have received a letter respecting it from Mr. Postans who claims it as belonging to Mr. Brown to whom it appears Strange sold the garden; on enquiry I find that the piece of ground has been enclosed a long time, before the trees were sold to me, so I suppose I cannot claim it, though I think it is still open to a doubt, whether Brown has an unquestionable right to it. As I did not wish to have any dispute about it, I wrote at once to Mr. Postans to say, that no part of the tree had been removed and that he could do what he chose with it. I enclose his reply. I should have imagined that having the tree felled, stripped and the top wood tied at my own expense, would have been sufficient compensation for the invasion of his property, if invasion it is; of course in many situations such would not be the case, but there can be no reality in the tree having any ornamental value where it stood, in fact half the garden was spoilt by it. Do you think he has a right to compensation and if so how much?

The enclosure from R. W. Postans was humorously abrupt:

I shall be sorry if I am obliged to take proceedings against you for the trespass committed on Mr. Brown's property by your orders, but if you have no proposal to make I must ask you to furnish me with the name of your solicitors.

At first, J.O.P. saw the funny side of the situation:

As to the question of the disputed tree, I could not help laughing at the whole story. I quite remember where it stood and am not at all surprized at your marking it. It would have been such a very simple way of preventing the cutting down to have made a claim to the tree as soon as it was marked, that I should very much like to know whether Mr Brown was aware of the intention. You may have been allowed to proceed just for the sake of having ground for compensation for the invasion.

One would have thought that between gentlemen of substance such a small matter as a tree felled by mistake could have been easily settled, but Brown either thought it had been felled intentionally or was venting some animosity or other.

Mr. Brown will of course take the tree bark but as he had no intention of having it felled and in fact would not have had it cut down on any account I think he is fairly entitled to receive some compensation for the trespass and injury to his property by the removal of what I understand was a very handsome and ornamental tree.

J.O.P. countered by offering compensation of £1 for the damage. By this time the tree was becoming very valuable, especially to the complainants:

When I tell you that Mr. Brown bought the piece of land with the idea of building himself a house on it and that the tree being a very handsome one was the chief inducement to him to fix on the spot for building you will better understand how mortifying it was to him to find the tree felled and that its removal is in his view a real detriment to the property. . . . I will advise him to accept £5 and I think that is the very least that should have been offered for the injury inflicted.

Thus all preparations were made for the bargaining process, in which argument and counter-argument were advanced with as much seriousness as if the damage involved had been thousands of pounds. J.O.P. suggested that the decision be left to a third person, but immediately followed this by an offer of £2 and costs, and, of course, the tree.

The reply of Postans was uncompromising:

My client . . . has directed me to say that he will without prejudice agree to accept £3-3-0 provided my charges which I estimate at about 2 guineas are paid and the amount realised by the sale of the bark and top of the tree is handed to him.

This would have meant a total bill of £5 5*s.*, five shillings more than the first demand. Here was obviously no chance of a gentlemen's agreement. J.O.P. detailed his moves to Sir Charles, adding:

I have spoken to Mr. Gepp about it, and he says that he should be afraid to take it into court and the only thing is to pay. I don't like it but I suppose we must give in.

'Is this', he wrote to Postans, 'your client's final proposition?'

I think it is not an unreasonable one [replied Postans]. If Sir Charles could replace the tree it would be quite a different thing but the injury is one he cannot repair and one which an expression of regret alone will not compensate for.

The reply infuriated J.O.P. He railed at 'the miserable nature' of the transaction and even threw doubt on the straightforwardness of the solicitor:

I know that a solicitor cannot rule his client but I do not believe that you or any respectable solicitor would wish to support a claim where it turns out to be *morally* wrong. I am informed that Mr. Brown told a person in the neighbourhood that he should have taken the tree down himself only he should have waited till the winter before doing so. If I can prove this to be the case will it make any difference in your view of the matter?

This last argument was promptly countered:

My client . . . says that in a conversation which he had with Mr. Palmer about the tree he told him that if he had intended to cut down the tree he should not have done it at that time of year but in the winter but he denies having said that he intended to cut down the tree. . . . He directed me to say that rather than have any further contention upon the subject he will accede to your proposal to pay £2. . . . You can therefore send me your cheque for £4-2-0.

J.O.P. was by no means satisfied. He set about trying to prove that Brown had intended to have the tree down, and collected notes from John Palmer and from Strange, the occupier of the cottage. The trouble, however, was that nothing could be done without going to a great deal of expense, and at a risk of losing an action. He wrote to Sir Charles:

Is it worth while to stand out any longer? In equity you certainly ought not to be mulcted in this way but I am afraid law would be against you. When I pay the money I shall not fail to tell him my mind about the whole transaction.

So he did a day or two later:

. . . I send you a cheque of £4-2-0 in accordance with your last letter. I never wrote a cheque with greater reluctance in my life because, as I said before, I consider it a most miserable exaction. . . . I believe that your client has the law on his side and I am unwilling to carry it further, but as to the pleas of damage, unwillingness to have the tree down etc, they are positive moonshine, and I can prove them to be so. . . . I have ascertained who Mr. Brown is, and I am not surprized at a man of his class thinking to make a market of such an occurrence, but I am much surprized that he was not differently advised as to the mode of proceeding.

There, after a dispute lasting six weeks, the matter rested.

*   *   *

It was the duty of land agents to handle a great deal of money. When administering an estate their practice was to take in all rents and other income, pay all bills, and to produce an account for annual audit. Money was usually paid in by cheque and a note sent to the recipient when it was remitted. In all cases receipts were collected and accompanied the annual statement to the audit.

On one occasion J.O.P. had difficulty in getting his receipts. The Rev. J. H. Stephenson of Corringham received a cheque from him in September 1844 for £64 14s. 7d. in payment of tithe on the Cliffs Estate, and a receipt was requested.

I am aware [wrote the Rev. J. H. Stephenson] that it is not unusual for those who take money to be required to give a stamped receipt, but checks are not generally considered money and therefore such of my Tithe Payers as tender them are satisfied with the endorsement of my name on the back of the check.

With this remark—a foretaste of a recent reform in banking practice—he registered his protest. J.O.P., however, still insisted on 'a receipt on stamped paper which under the circumstances I am obliged to require'.

The Rector enclosed a receipt with the observation:

You will allow me to observe that as you put me to the expense of a stamp I must request that in future you will either send me cash or an order payable in London. A check payable at Romford is to me as inconvenient as one payable at York.

On business transactions of all kinds a commission was charged, and this was rarely queried. In 1829, however, after a survey of Writtle Parish for tithe, Dr. Shuttleworth of New College expressed his disappointment on receiving a bill for £140, which he stated was 'beyond the proportion he had been paying other gentlemen for similar assistance under the like circumstances'. C.C.P. detailed his charges: 2½ per cent for valuing lands to let and 5 per cent on tithes. He stressed that he had made an actual survey, visiting every field, and that upon consulting his day-book he found that the survey would have cost more had he imposed a daily charge for time spent.

This is the first time [he wrote] I have had my charges questioned, and I hope the explanation is satisfactory.

It was not satisfactory, and Dr. Shuttleworth asked him to reconsider his charge, reducing it to 2½ per cent. This he refused to do, and offered to submit his accounts to any other respectable surveyor, saying:

. . . the Society must excuse my committing self-destruction. If the Tythe Rental of a large Parish like Writtle could be acquired with accuracy with less difficulty than in numerical proportion to the smaller parishes, charges might reasonably vary, but as the demand is large so is the labour and the ability to pay it.

The dispute went on for months. C.C.P. pointed to other people's charges which were higher than his. Dr. Shuttleworth quoted the opinion of C.C.P.'s brother Charles Parker that they should have been lower. This brought forth an acid comment on the legal profession:

I am not surprised at the observation you state my brother to have made—he is like all other legal men who although they do not forget to charge for their own exertions do not appear aware of the time, trouble and responsibility that attaches to the duties of those who value landed property, also that it takes them generally far from home at considerable expence instead of being transacted in the office where the greater part of the business of legal Men is performed by their Clerks and from precedents.

It was July 1830, seven months after the first protest, when the account was finally settled.

In a letter of 1831 C.C.P. gives a full statement of his scale of charges. He had been employed to find a new tenant for one of William Sotheby's farms in Latchingdon, and his bill was queried by Sotheby's solicitor, George Rickards.

My charges which are similar to others in the same line of business are and have been for many years, for valuing Lands of Houses 2½ per cent on the Rental and if employed to procure a Tenant an additional 2½ per cent—for valuing Tithes, for marking and measuring and selling Timber and for the superintendences of repairs and arranging and settling the accounts 5 per cent—other business where my opinion is required to govern the proceedings of the Persons employing me—references, valuations of Stock and Crops etc, 5 guineas a day.

He goes on to say that in this valuation he has more than saved his client's money by extricating him from further heavy losses.

Rickards replied saying that Mr. Sotheby 'still feels very sore on the subject of your Bill', and asking him 'to satisfy the mind of a client', to take £55 or 50 guineas.

C.C.P.'s politeness did not conceal his disappointment.

It would ill become me pertinaciously to resist the feelings of any one who had favoured me with their confidence by employing me to transact business for them . . . but regret that Mr. Sotheby should have expressed any dissatisfaction which I am sure can only arise from his want of knowledge of the trouble the various interests and arrangements took.

After again going through the particulars of the work he had done, he left the matter of payment in the hands of his client. Both C.C.P. and his son gave very generous treatment to all the poorer people who consulted them. As we have read, J.O.P. excused Miss Shaw all payment and left the question of charges on the sale of Coptfold Hall to E. G. Stone, who, after all, was a rich man. In 1854 he sold Enfield Mill, for Sir Charles Smith, to the East London Water Works for £15,250. His charges were 1 per cent on the first £1000 and ½ per cent on the remainder, a total of £81 5s., which was more than reasonable, possibly because Sir Charles had been his friend and client all his life. In 1856 he valued Thaxted Park Farm (£7330), charging £69, a much higher rate. In 1847 he valued timber on the Danbury Estate at 2½ per cent and in 1868 he was paid 10 guineas for valuing the small Millworth Farm at Great Wakering. The standards he worked by were originally set by his father, and as he was a member of the Land Surveyors' Club, presumably he could not deviate far from the usual rates of commission.

Notes of appreciation were numerous; marks of dissatisfaction were rare. In 1835 the integrity of C.C.P. was questioned because after he had valued a farm in Thundersley the tenant imagined that since he was supposed to be friendly with the landlord he had overvalued the dilapidations. He replied to the accusation:

. . . whether the matter is large or small, it equally claims my unbiassed attention if I engage in it. . . . I know as little of Mr. Nash as it is well possible to know of any one whom you have only seen a few times and certainly not since I have been applied to on this business.

On one occasion when a party to a dispute sent a letter to J.O.P. before the dispute was settled and before he had had time to consider and report on the value of the estate in question, he broke open the letter, but on the first glance at the contents, closed it again without reading it. (6 April 1856.)

An equally groundless charge was levied at him on another occasion by his friend Sir Charles Smith, who accused him, on the evidence of his bailiff Baker, of canvassing his tenants at the time of a General Election. This was not hard to answer:

It is a serious charge to make against me without any other evidence. In reply to it I can only say that I have had no communication with any of your tenants on the subject of the Election and I trust that I should be incapable of taking any means to influence their votes.

It says much for the forbearance and common sense of both men that their long friendship was not destroyed by this unconsidered accusation.

To most complaints there was one good answer: 'You admit your dissatisfaction with my services?'

That shall be if you please the close of my charge of your farm, and I can only express the hope that the management in whose hands it may be placed will give you more satisfaction in the future. (J.O.P. to C. E. Sotheby, 13 June 1877.)

His client was too wise a man to lose a good agent and the contact between them was only broken with J.O.P.'s death in 1887.

* * *

During the life of Christopher Comyns Parker there had been little room for enterprise outside his own particular sphere, for he was hard at work building up and maintaining a business. In his day Essex was far removed from the places where industry was attracting capital. His life was drawing to a close before the railways invaded the county.

With his son it was different. The prime of his life was spent in the Railway Age and he was quick to see the possibilities in the making of new lines. Much of his land business was connected with the railways either on behalf of company or landowner, and he was one of the prime movers of Sir Morton Peto's abortive effort in 1856 to make a line from Tilbury to Colchester. Had he lived in an industrial county his abilities might well have made him one of the railroad pioneers. All his life he was keenly interested in machinery and visited every show and demonstration that was held within his reach. Year after year he accompanied the Land Surveyors' Club on their annual excursions to some of the finest farms the in country. In 1879 he joined in a project to market a mechanical device called the Darby Pedestrian Steam Digger. A patent was taken out and it was regarded as so promising that the young company refused an offer of £3000 for American rights. On 17 July 1879 it was tried out at Boreham but failed in many respects:

Did not keep strength to its work, or turn over the spits of earth as moved. *Lucky that no trial was made before the public!*

In February 1880 the company was wound up but improvements must still have been made on the digger, for in May 1881 J.O.P. tried one on his own farm and noted that with very little further improvement it would be an effective implement.

In 1847 he had married Louisa, daughter of Richard Durant of Sharpham, Devon. Mr. Durant offered to invest £30,000 for him in Hodgsons' Brewery at Kingston-on-Thames which was owned by his cousins, but J.O.P. felt that as a Justice of the Peace he ought not to have any interest in a brewing concern. Other avenues were explored. In the diaries from 1848 onwards there are references to insurance. In November of that year he presented a claim for £301 17s. to the Board of the Essex Economic Fire Office. From then onward he was a member of the Board. In October 1850 he was on the Board of the East of England Life Assurance Office which, in July 1857, was amalgamated with the Reliance Assurance Office. In 1868 he was elected a director of the Essex and Suffolk Equitable Insurance Co. and was appointed vice-chairman in 1883 and chairman in 1887.

In 1859 came a chance of joining the banking firm of Messrs

Sparrow Tufnell and Co, Bankers, at Braintree, Chelmsford, Maldon and other places in the Eastern Counties. He joined the firm in 1859, and Mr. Durant found £10,000 capital . . . and it proved a good investment.

In January 1865 he opened a branch of the Bank in Southend. On his journeys in Essex whenever he was near Ongar or Southend he would call at the branches and check the till. From about 1870 onwards he paid regular visits to the Maldon Branch on a Tuesday and to the Chelmsford Branch on a Friday which was Market Day. On one occasion, 3 September 1874, his diary reads:

Maldon Bk early—told up till—£50 short. To Chelmsford—found deficiency to be in silver.

On 30 July 1877 he attended the annual meeting of the Bank:

Renewed discussion as to admission of Partners' sons. W. N. Tufnell at Aldershot. Sparrow still opposed any arrangement and stating WNT to be the same.

By the following year this dispute must have been settled, for under 6 August 1878 we have a note concerning J.O.P.'s eldest son:

Chris went to work at Chelmsfd Bank.

He started his banking career the day after the sixth August Bank Holiday.

On several occasions C.C.P. and his son Oxley had had to decline requests that they should take new clients. 'I cannot spare a day either in January or February from other engagements', wrote C.C.P. in 1839. Towards the end of his life he was just as busy. His son, however, became more involved in the banking business as he grew older. It was nearer home, easier to manage, and it did not mean travelling far and wide in all weathers. The employment of Christopher in banking meant that this, rather than land surveying, would be the direction of the future. Perhaps J.O.P. recognised signs of coming agricultural depression, for in 1873 there were already many vacant farms, stewardships were growing irksome, and old friends among the Essex farmers were passing away one by one. Towards the end of his life, therefore, the number of his clients diminished and he avoided taking too many new ones. On 28 October 1873 he turned down an agency which forty years earlier he would have gladly accepted:

Afterwards to Terling. Had long conversation with Lord Rayleigh as to management of Estate and farms now vacant, and with reference to Brook Farm Woodham Ferris [sic] of which the Tenant had just now failed. Stated that I could not undertake any general management but that I would visit the Brook Farm and advise what should be done.

In those days when typewriters and carbon paper were unknown, the writing of letters was an arduous business. C.C.P. wrote in his own hand a copy of all his letters. In early life J.O.P. did the same, but later on the copies are frequently in the handwriting of his eldest daughter Maria, and he was very proud of her business abilities. Towards the end of his life we find him using a special copying ink, and the letter was placed in a book consisting of flimsy paper which was damped and then placed in a press. The copy was liable to smudging, and if the paper was not adequately damped the copy was so faint as to be undecipherable.

As the end of the century approached, the family business of land agency gradually gave place to another. Between them the Parkers, father and son, had played a unique part in creating nineteenth- and twentieth-century Essex.

APPENDIX I
LEASES

1. *Sherwoods Farm, 1836*

EXTRACT from Lease of Sherwood Marshes in Wallasea Island in the Parish of Canewdon dated November 9th, 1836 from Lord Wynford to Stephen Allen—by admeasurement 1810, 380ᵃ 1ʳ 17ᵖ but now found to contain 371ᵃ 3ʳ 31ᵖ.

Term 14 years from Michˢ 1836—Rent £350 the first year, £400 the remainder of the Term—received quarterly clear of all parochial or other Assessment Land Tax Quit rents Tithes Rent charges Sewers rates or other charges.

Twenty pounds increase Rent for breaking up old pasture Lands. To keep Premises in repair (the same being first put in repair by Lord Wynford) being allowed rough Timber within ten Miles (Sea Walls and Sea gutters excepted). To cleanse and new make full one hundred rods of Marsh ditches annually of the full width and depth.

To cultivate Lands as stated—one sixth summer fallow annually with at least six clean tilths at proper distance from each other and leave one sixth summer fallowed in the last year being paid and allowed for the same. Not to have two white straw crops in succession from any part of the Lands.

Not to have more than thirty acres of brown Mustard in any Year. Not to carry off the said Farm any Hay Straw or Fodder except Wheat or Rye Straw and Clover Hay for which the Tenant is to bring on a full sized tumbrell load of rotten dung chalk or lime for every load taken off. All other produce to be consumed upon the farm and the manure etc spread where most necessary except the manure of the last year which is to be left for the Landlord he paying for the same. Hay of the last year to be left Tenant to be paid for the same by Landlord. And shall not break up any of the newly laid down pasture lands without laying down the same or a greater quantity of Arable land with good grass seeds in the previous year with the first crop of Corn after a clean summer fallow. And to continue the same until a like quantity is laid down in a previous year to breaking up the same, so as always to keep the same quantity in grass as there is at the commencement of the Lease.

2. *Plumborough, Hockley, August 1840*

Plumbro' Mount Farm in the Parish of Hockley in the County of Essex containing by admeasurement exclusive of the Woodlands about three hundred and seventeen Acres, late in the occupation of

Joachim Otte esq^{re} deceased and now of the Trustees and Tenant for Life of the said Estate.

I agree to become Tenant of the above Farm on a Lease to be granted for fourteen Years from Michaelmas next subject to the following Covenants and Conditions—Rent to be three hundred and seventeen pounds a year or one pound an Acre provided the admeasurement stated is correct, clear of all taxes, rates or parochial assessments whatsoever—Tithes or Rent Charges to be apportioned in lieu thereof (Land Tax Quit of Fee Farm Rents excepted)—the Lease to contain the usual Covenants as to Timber, Rent, Repairs, Hay Straw and Manure, Tillage of Fallows, Underletting or assigning etc. Penalty of £20 an Acre increase Rent for every Acre of the Pasture Field called front Field containing about 13 acres, the Hoppets containing about 9 Acres that shall be broken up or converted into Tillage and the like penalty for any land that shall be broken up if the same shall have been laid down by the Tenant with Grass and so continue in grass for five successive Years. The Tillage Lands to have as near as the size of the field will allow 1/6th clean fallowed annually with at least five clean tilths, one other sixth part Clover or other artificial Grass seeds, and no part to have two white straw crops succeed each other under penalty of £10 an acre increased rent for each breach of covenant, Beans, Pease and Tares for Seed if well hoed and kept clean not to be deemed a crop. Rye, Turnips or Rape seed, Mangel worzel Tares or other Green crop if fed upon the Premises may be allowed upon the Fallows. Rye Turnips or Rape seed if seeded to be deemed and taken as a white straw crop. Landlords to put the Premises in good tenantable repair, and the Tenant to keep them in such repair being allowed enough Timber, Bricks, Tiles and Lime upon the Premises or within 10 Miles of the same. Tenant carry on the said Farm annually Chalk Lime or Manure, the produce of other Lands at a cost price of not less than £40 a Year or feed with oil-cake to an amount that shall be considered equal to the same. Tenant to thresh and carry out the Corn now grown upon the Farm, being allowed the Straw and Chaff for the same, and upon quitting to have the arrangement with the Landlords, the distance of carrying such corn not to exceed ten miles, the foregoing stipulations subject to the approval of the Trustees.

C. Barnard

As Tenant for Life I approve of the terms herein proposed on behalf of the Trustees, myself and the said C. T. Barnard.

Walter Otte

APPENDIX II

NOTES FROM THE DIARIES
ON THE MANAGEMENT OF ESTATES
AND COVENANTS

(With variations on the Rent Theme)

27th January, 1832. Attended at Mr. Gepp's to sign circulars to Tenants of Skreens Est. desiring them not to cut the Banks of the Fences nearer than 3 ft. from the Stake or where the Stake ought to be and not to lop any Pollards unless where fences are made nor to prune any Timber Trees or Spears likely to bear Timber without permission of Mr. Bramston or his Agent.

17th September, 1839. Went to Withemans Farm and looked over the same with Mr. Hunt as to cultivation and repairs found all in very creditable condition informed Mr. Hunt that he must not expect Mr. Otte to do any repairs but that he would find Materials as pr the Lease.

January 23rd, 1841. Went to John Pavitt to look at Pasture allowed same to be broken up and cultivated as arable Land on paying 20ˢ an Acre increased rent. (Lady Smith.)

14th June, 1843. Met Mr. Allen and walked with him round Farm and inspected Buildings—told him to have slight repairs in tiling weatherboarding etc immediately done and that as soon as completed I wᵈ give orders for new gates or other work most required to the amount of £50—did not find him willing to join in a thorough repair and improvement of the Premises. (Lord Wynford.)

June 27th, 1844. Agreed with Mr. Wayling to hire Black House Farm for 14 years at £160 per annum on the same terms as by former lease, and that the alterations proposed in estimates prepared by Mr. Kemp shᵈ be done, the Landlord paying £120, the Tenant £80.

October 4th, 1844. Agreed with Mr. John Dennis for the hire of Guys Farm on the same terms as to Mr. Barrett, provided the Landlords agree to put everything in repair and permit the tar for repairs as well as rough timber. (Trustees of late Chas. Bullock.)

February 15th, 1850. Had long conversation with Mr. Thos. Dowsett respecting Fallows to be left at South House stating that according to the custom of the country I considered he ought to leave in fallow a fifth of the arable land (J. J. Tufnell.)

27th June, 1850. Went to Gt. Clacton to inspect the state of the Sea Wall of the Wash Farm. Met the Tenant Mr. Salmon and Messrs P. and J. Smith and Mr. Dean. Found the Wall in most dangerous condition, the wharfing much decayed and broken away and several serious cavities in the face of the Wall. Advised Mr. Salmon for his own sake as well as his neighbours' to withhold the Rent due and expend same in repair of the Wall. Also desired Mr. P. Smith without implicating his Landlord to join with Mr. Salmon in doing certain temporary work such as stopping the cavities with bushes, piles etc, and gave him to understand that he sh^d be repaid the expense of same. (John Round.)

24th February, 1854. Met Mr. Saml Blyth and went through lease of Duke's Farm, when he objected to the clause requiring him 'to paint and tar' thought the same should be allowed by the Landlord—and also to the obligation on him to leave in good Tenantable repair. (Rev. Arthur Pearson.)

25th January, 1855. Morning home and to Bradwell. Met Mr. Page by appointment respecting renewal of Bridge Wick Lease. Mr. Page produced plans of improvements to House, yards, stables etc, and erection of 2 cottages, and stated that if Lease was renewed and these improvements carried out that himself and Brothers would be willing to pay good interest on the outlay. (Admiral Fanshawe.)

29th June, 1855. Met Mr. Allerton respecting rent of Great Potton. Found that he had had a meeting of which I was not aware with Mr. Wilberforce and Mr. Comyns and that he had written thro' Mr. Wood proposing to pay £600 per annum and to bring on £50 a year in chalk but that he shd not be required to do the latter during during the last 7 years of his Lease. Rec^d the Rent at the rate of £600 in money (allowing £50 cash and £50 chalk on the year). (Archdeacon Wilberforce.)

13th January, 1859. Suttons Audit. Gave the Tenants to understand that Sir Charles w^d take repairs upon himself, and that I should meet them and arrange what additional Rent sh^d be paid by each Tenant in lieu of the labour of Repairs. (Sir Charles Smith.)

19th April, 1861. Met Mr. Josling and offered him Barnish Hall £350 first 7 years and £450 last 7 of 14 years. He offered £300 first 7 and £350 for the remainder of the term. (T. W. Bramston.)

15th November, 1961. Saw Mr. Clark and explained to him that Sir. G. Pechell was extremely unwilling to incur the cost of new gear to

Mill, and that he w^d rather let it to him at a low rate than incur the outlay himself—though he should pay interest upon it. (Sir George B. Pechell.)

27th June, 1864. Mr. Page to be allowed £25 towards painting House and erecting a Porch and Front door. (Smith's Charity.)

May 27th, 1867. Met Mr. Edward and Thos Knights . . . and after very long discussion agreed for lease of Stanfords and Hill Farms for 14 years at £300 per annum, Mr. Sotheby to spend £300 in repairs and improvements to Premises. Mr. Knights to be allowed to spend £86 dilapidation money in improvements to House and bringing water from Hill Farm to the House at Stanfords. If all shd not be spent the bal. to be paid in towards general repairs. (C. H. Sotheby.)

May 7th, 1870. With Mr. Inglis advising as to Gull's future rent. Stated that £200 a year for Bastards' Farm and White Hart Land w^d be a moderate Rent, but that he might have it £200 for 7 years and 7 years at £220. (Trustees of late C. G. Round.)

October 21st, 1870. Met Mr. Offin and agreed with him for hire of Eastbury Marshes at £380 per annum, Mr. Thoyts to allow £20 towards fencing off sewer, and timber for repairing gates, fences etc. (M. G. Thoyts.)

26th April, 1872. Met Mr. Robert Page, and agreed to contribute £1000 and pantiles, oak and timber towards the reconstruction of Premises at Eastlands, Munkins and Dunbirds, Messrs Page paying the amount of dilapidations as assessed by Mr. Stammers, and also bearing the moiety of all further charges, and finding all bricks free of cost, and all carting and roadmaking etc. (Farms in hand, Bradwell.)

November 5th, 1874. With Mr. Tufnell at Church Hall. Considering plans of proposed reconstruction of Premises and arranged with Mr. Pettitt that the same should be carried out in the Spring Mr. Pettitt undertaking to superintend and execute all the proposed works, Mr. Tufnell contributing £650 towards the expense. (J.J. Tufnell.)

27th July, 1874. Had interview with Mr. Hurrell as to future tenancy of Jenkyns Farm—unwilling to hire except at reduction of Rent. Eventually agreed for 7 years at the same rent £325 per annum, but Landlord to do certain present repairs as I shall think necessary. (Sir G. B. Pechell.)

133

February 11th, 1877. Attending Mr. Evans and arranging terms of lease of Pewitt Island and Bradwell Creek to Bradwell Oyster Company. Terms—21 years determinable by the Promoters at 12 months notice. Rent £3 per annum for first 5 years, £10 for next 8 years and £15 for remainder of term. Promoters to be allowed to remove any building erected for Trade purposes, but any wall or defence to be left, and Promoters to pay all costs incurred up to this time in consequence of the application of the Promoters and pay for the Lease. (Admiral Fanshawe's Trustees.)

April 18th, 1878. Met Mr. Page with reference to new Lease of Marsh House. He asked that he might be allowed the new Lands as he liked till the last 4 years, and for some alterations in farming covenants, but made no objection to my proposal of £800 first 7 years, £850 next 7 and £900 remainder. (Dean and Chapter of St. Paul's.)

9th October, 1870. At Kingsmoor. Tried to induce Mr. Todhunter to take lease of Maunds Farm. His only offer is to take the farm from year to year and will quit at Mic'as 1880 unless repairs are done by Landlord and £50 allowed out of this year's Rent towards expenses and draining, and rent from Mic'as 1880 for the two farms £100 per annum. (Winchester College.)

CHAPTER VII

AGRICULTURE

CHRISTOPHER COMYNS PARKER started farming in 1796 and
he could not have taken it up at a better time. The war with
Napoleon had given a great impetus to agriculture, for imports
were at their lowest ebb, prices of foodstuffs were high; wheat,
which in 1792 had been 43s. a quarter rose to 113s. in 1800 and
119s. in 1801, and though lowered to 52s. in 1806, it rose rapidly
in the latter years of the war, reaching 126s. 6d. in 1812. Corn-
growing was the most profitable side of farming. Land which
had been long in cultivation was improved, land never cultivated before was taken in, and much pasture-land was put
under the plough. The war years thus gave the enterprising
farmer time to find his feet.

It was during this time that C.C.P. began to develop his
business as land agent, for, with the rise in the value of agricultural products the demand for land was stimulated and
increasing stress was laid on the most profitable methods of
land utilisation. This was an ideal period for a competent
farmer to branch out into land agency, surveying, and estate
management.

In so doing he was to some extent following in the steps of his
father, the first John Oxley Parker. Today the family possess a
silver salver and a silver soup-tureen, presented by Wadham
College in 1813 and inscribed:

TO JOHN OXLEY PARKER ESQ.

Presented as a token of esteem and regard
by the Warden and Fellows of Wadham College, Oxford.

MDCCCXIII

They were given in recognition of his services in looking after their estates in Essex.

Then in 1815 came the end of the long war and the dislocation of a sudden return to a peace-time economy. Foreign corn was again available on the British market and demand for the home-grown product fell in spite of the Corn Laws of 1815. These entirely forbade the importation of corn if the price in Great Britain was less than 80s. a quarter. Though they did something to aid the British farmer, they contributed very little to ensure the stability of corn prices owing to the time-lag between the rise above the 80s. level and the actual arrival of the foreign corn. It was just as necessary at such a time, as in the previous days of prosperity, that a landlord should have recourse to a good agent, for outlay following expert advice and assistance was money well spent. Thus, by 1826, when the Parker diaries begin, C.C.P. had a long list of clients all over Essex.

The effect of the depression on the labouring classes was devastating. Wages were low. In some parts of England they were implemented by payments in kind or from doles out of the parish poor-rates. Bad as it was, the lot of the Essex labourer did not approach that of the textile operative nor, though discontent was rife, was it as vocal as that of the labourers south of the Thames who rioted in 1830 and were savagely punished with hangings and transportation. Yet all the while it smouldered, and the most innocent measures on the part of landlords, such as surveys of farms, brought fear of disturbances. In November 1830 C.C.P.'s daughter Elizabeth wrote from school a letter expressing her shock at the disturbed state of the country and the distress of the working-classes. Her father replied:

I assure you, my dear child, I intended answering your political Epistle with which I was much pleased, as it affords me another proof of your thinking and benevolent mind.

He goes on to comment on the situation:

When you wrote I was in London as I had a ticket given me to attend the procession with the Merchant Taylors' Company, and I

had started before I was aware of the King's visit being put off. . . .
I decidedly approve the conduct of the late Ministers in putting off
the procession as I feel convinced there would have been a Riot had
the King gone to the Guildhall—immense masses of evilly disposed
persons were called together from various parts of the Kingdom for
the express purpose of mischief, and a very strong excitement was
raised against the New Police, a most useful and well-conducted
body. This no doubt stimulated pickpockets and every other
description of thieves and vagrants who are most annoyed by the
good order preserved in the streets and environs of London. . . .

The evil, in my opinion, is created by a combination of various
causes and effects, but most particularly by the change from high to
low wages without a corresponding change in the prices of the
various articles of food and necessaries required by the working
classes. The value of these can only be reduced by a reduction of
taxes affecting them, which cannot be dispensed with but by
economy and retrenchment in the State, or by a tax on property. I
am well assured we have ample resources if properly applied, and
among responsible classes in society a loyal and well-disposed
people; but the working classes must be employed profitably before
the disturbances will cease in Kent and other districts, which I trust
the good sense of this Country will soon comply with. . . .

Here we have the very first hint of C.C.P.'s politics—those of
a Tory—in that he believed that the beginning of reform must
necessarily come from lightening the burdens of the farmer by
reducing taxes so that the capital thus released could go towards
providing sufficient employment, which in its turn would raise
the wages and allay the discontent of the masses. He thus
desired improvement within the constitutional fabric, without
tampering in any way with the constitution, but relying on good
relations between the farmer and farm labourer, between
employer and employed, to return to a better footing on a
personal and a paternal basis. Hence, he repeatedly stated to
his clients that, always bearing in mind the financial and social
obligations contracted by the ruling class, economic burdens
should be shared. This was not merely a belief inspired by the
desire to see the workers comfortable, but by a reasoning which
led him to a conclusion that a landlord's own interest was best

served by keeping the tenant on his feet in bad times. Hence, at the time of the riots, C.C.P. advised the Rev. T. Schreiber of Bradwell to abate his tithes by as much as 50 per cent and enjoined continual abatements year by year on Oriel College. Dr. Hawkins agreed whole-heartedly with him.

The same attitude towards the labouring classes was shown by Colonel Bourchier of Mount Hall, Bures:

You will be kind enough at all times in acting for me to believe that my wish is to do all that is liberal and right towards my tenants and I am persuaded my interest is best consulted in doing so. (4 November 1830.)

Colonel Bourchier, however, was not convinced that the solution would come as the result merely of abatement of rent, which might conceivably have no effect on the well-being of some farmers, but might be frittered away on other things than the stocking and upkeep of their farms. He far preferred to make allowances for repair.

It has struck me that in many cases where the landlord is desirous of bettering the labourer's condition, his object is not necessarily attained by lowering his rent unless he ascertains at the same time the sum retained to the tenant will be expended in employing more hands or paying those already employed, better; and that the simplest means of arriving at the desired end would be for the landlord himself to expend the sum he intended to reduce from his tenant's rent in employing more hands, which would not only secure the money being expended as he intended, but would of course improve his own property. (28 December 1830.)

He was no less concerned about the poor labourers:

Being totally ignorant of the number of poor in the parish of Bures I cannot decide whether I am doing enough in giving but £10. Of this point I will get information. . . . I think perhaps an additional £5 in reduction of the price of coals would be certainly desirable in this inclement weather.

Though Essex suffered badly from the agricultural depression, there is very little indication of violence in these letters and diaries. Only in one case, at Belchamp Walter, do we find it threatened, (21 January 1831), and there is one report of fires in Laindon and at Basildon Hall. On 15 December 1830, John Moore wrote to C.C.P.:

The labourers in our county appear now quiet in all parishes, having made arrangements for employment at fair wages.

The passing of the 'thirties brought little relief from the depression. In 1835, Colonel Bourchier was still abating his rents and making more than his usual donations to the relief of the parish poor. In the same year John P. Eliot, tenant of Patch Park, Stapleford Tawney, writing to C.C.P. requesting an abatement of rent, said:

I have hitherto been supported by the hope that so remarkable a depression must be followed by a corresponding reaction. In that hope I have, however, been disappointed.

The existence of such a depression is too generally admitted to need any corroborative testimony; . . . When I took Patch Park what was selling at 60/– is now 40/–; oats, beans and barley have fallen in the same ratio although they are at present maintaining a higher nominal value in consequence of the last defective crops. . . . That grazing has very considerably suffered is equally certain, but instead of multiplying words to prove what probably no one will deny, I again appeal to your own and to general experience to confirm.

In his reply C.C.P. admitted the existence of this prolonged depression. It lasted as long as he lived, prevented his business making the progress it ought to have done, and may have contributed towards his ill-health during the last years of his life.

In April 1836 he gave evidence before a Select Committee of the House of Commons called to enquire into the depressed state of agriculture. He mentioned in evidence that he was farming 2000 acres and had the management of 20,000 acres farmed by others.

The condition of farmers [he said] in my neighbourhood has been very bad. I cannot exactly state the amount of reduction of rent, but beginning with 10% and 15%, and many 20% and 30%, and some 50% and even more than that within the last 3 or 4 years.

. . . I know farms that men of capital were occupying that were 25/– and 30/– an acre and they offered 20/– and they have since been let for 12/– or 14/– and 15/– an acre; and I believe that had they been reduced to 20/–at that time those tenants would now have been in possession of them and they [the farms] would never have been impoverished in their cultivation. . . . It has been by insisting on the high rents that the farms have been worked out of condition and then no person would take them except at a very low rent.

He was always a keen supporter of the Corn Laws. He considered that ten shillings a quarter was a fair duty and was enough to protect the Essex farmer, but he admitted that in his part of Essex during the four years ending in 1833 rent had been paid out of capital.

He never changed his mind. In 1836 he wrote to Colonel Bourchier:

If the Parliament will but let us alone and not tamper with the Corn Laws, I consider that the landlord and tenant may easily adjust what Rent can be afforded.

And in 1838:

The present high price of corn is a bonus to the Eastern district where the harvest was early, but the crop is deficient. I hope the farmers will increase the wages of their Labourers in proportion to the price of flour, and prevent clamour against the Corn Laws which are now working well, and show that, when foreign supply is required, the operation is as near Free Trade as possible.

The 1830s saw a Whig Government begin to change the aspect of the British Constitution. First the House of Commons was reformed, then the municipal corporations and the poor law. In the late thirties and early forties the Anti-Corn Law League was active, but Christopher Comyns Parker did not live to see what followed its agitation. His son John Oxley had only lately taken charge of the family estates and business when Peel announced his conviction that Repeal and only Repeal would save the country.

The farming interest believed that he was making the whole economy of Great Britain over to the manufacturers. T. T. Clarke, for whom J.O.P. administered Down Hall, Bradwell, wrote (17 March 1845):

The truth is that if we do not keep Sir Robert up to the mark— complain, howl, tear our hair, gnash our teeth, he will increase rather than lighten our burdens; it acts likewise as a good set-off to the Manufacturing whiners.

Nine months later, when Repeal was a certainty, he continued in the same strain:

What do you think of the aspect of affairs? As I individually fancy it is only a question of time (and that a short one) for a protective duty to remain to us agriculturalists. I would fain hope that the *evils* as well as the blessings are too much magnified by their respective adherents. Notwithstanding muck manuals, scarifiers, tiles, Mechi's and Liebig's, I despair of being able to compete with the foreigner, and if such is the case, down goes Rent, down goes the Landocracy and up the Cottonocracy, and the present social position of this country extraordinarily altered.

J.O.P. fully agreed with these sentiments, and did all he could during that fateful year to forward the Protectionist cause:

February 6th. At Chelmsford. Numerous meeting of Protection Society to memorialize Her Majesty to dissolve Parliament on the question of the Corn Laws.

It was all in vain. Repeal came later in the year, and Peel's Tory government fell before Young Disraeli's vigorous onslaught. Happily, this 'selling out to the Cottonocracy' did not immediately bring such dire results as the agricultural interest had prophesied. There was no sudden catastrophe.

There was a constant increase of the island population, which had still to be fed mainly on home produce. The gold discoveries of the 'fifties raised prices. In the 'sixties, while wars raged in Europe and in America, England was at peace. Great progress was still being made in livestock breeding. Improved draining and manuring; the gradual introduction of machine ploughing, reaping and threshing into one county and village after another, the work of the Royal

Agricultural Society, the capital invested and the pride taken by the great landlords in the improvement of their estates—all these things brought more fields under the plough in Palmerston's England. (Trevelyan, *English Social History*, p. 536.)

J.O.P. was keenly aware of all these developments, and, in the relatively prosperous times of 1847–77 he reaped the full harvest of his father's industry and his own enterprise.

April 28, 1845. Went in afternoon to Staplehurst by Dover Railway to see Drain Tile making machine (Hutchin's) at Benenden Kiln. *May 9th, 1845.* Went to Cottam and Hallen and ordered tile-making machine on principle invented by Hutchin of Benenden. *October 15, 1847.* Rode to Kingsbridge (from Sharpham, Devon) to inspect double plough made by Messrs Webber. Ordered one.

Trevelyan's statement on the post-repeal changes in English farming had almost an exact parallel on the one-man scale in the letters and diaries of John Oxley Parker, with the one difference that the social historian was speaking *after* the events, the enterprising and far-seeing farmer *before*. A fragment of his letter to Mrs. Frere from whom he rented Bovill's Marsh Farm, Mayland, is prophetic.

Now, as to Protection, I am not one who clings to a high price of wheat as the only hope of the Farmer. I may say that I have given up all idea of it since the very first passing of the Repeal of the Duty. I fully believe that other things will in time accommodate themselves to the price of corn, and that, under a new state of circumstances, the energetic and skilful farmer may prosper again as he has done.

Throughout the middle years of the nineteenth century J.O.P. was in the forefront of those who worked for a solution of the agricultural problem by promoting the idea of mixed farming among a community which had been used to rely for the past hundred years on the growing of wheat alone. The Royal Agricultural Society and the Anti-Corn Law League had both been founded in 1838, and both in different ways worked towards the broadening of the basis of British agriculture. J.O.P., a Protectionist, favoured the approach of the former. The meetings of the Royal Agricultural Society at Chelmsford

in April 1856 gave him and other forward-looking agriculturalists their chance. An entry in his diary for 18 December 1857
runs:

Early to Chelmsford. Meeting of Committee of R.A. Society for
disposal of surplus fund. £200 for Sebastopol gun, remainder for
agricultural objects.

The Sebastopol gun was purchased, and on 17 July 1858 it
was duly placed on its pedestal in front of the Shire Hall,
Chelmsford. The balance of the money was put to a purpose
which in the following half-century helped to alter the face of
agricultural Essex. On 22 January 1858 J.O.P. was present at
the first meeting of the Essex Agricultural Association, 'the
surplus fund of the Royal Agricultural Society Meeting being
used to establish it. From that time on he was a zealous committee member. He attended the meetings of 12 March ('Sitting
from 11 to 5') which arranged the prize list for the first Show,
and of 26 March which elected the Secretary. From 10 June
onward he threw himself enthusiastically into the arrangements
for the first show at Chelmsford. On the 12th and 14th he
officiated as a Steward, arranging the show field, and his diary
for the 15th runs:

In show field at 5 o'clock. Engaged as Steward of Horses, arranging
show etc. Very hot day. Show went off well.

The Essex Agricultural Society was thus in part his creation,
and there were few annual shows in which he did not take a
leading part. The entries in his diary show the emphasis he
placed on things other than the growing of corn:

June 12, 1860. Essex Agric¹ Show, Walden. Good show of Stock etc.

June 24, 1861. Evening to Romford to prepare for Agric¹ Show on the
following day. Found that the local Secretary had forgotten to
secure me a bed. After some difficulty obtained bed through the
kindness of Mr. Pertwee.

June 26. In the show field at 5 o'clock as Director of the Show Yard.
Good show, particularly of Shorthorns and Cart Stallions.

June 11th, 1867 (Braintree). Early on Show Ground. Good show, fine day. All went off well. Shire heifer, 2nd Prize.

June 11, 1872. Halstead. Agricultural Show. Capital exhibition of stock, horses etc, and all well arranged, but torrents of rain all day. Drove about all the morning in a char-a-banc, but so wet by 1 o'clock that I was afraid to stay out longer.

June 10, 1880. In show field by 7 o'clock. Splendid day and good attendance. Won prizes for cow and 2 heifers. Show of carthorses specially good, and Channel Islands stock. . . .

June 11, 1880. Fine day. Good attendance again. Sir Claude de Crespigny riding in jumping class. *Both days pitched over his horse's head, he on one side the hurdle, his horse on the other.* . . .

June 15, 1881 (Southend). Splendid weather, and fine show of horses, animals etc. Not so numerous as on some occasions but excellent in quality. Obtained prizes for cow and 2 heifers. Large attendance. . . .

He was Hon. Director of the Show almost all his life and had the honour of being elected President in 1887 when the Show was held at Chelmsford.

In 1858 J.O.P. began to accompany the Land Surveyors' Club on their summer outings having been elected a member of that select body on the death of his father. At first they were for one day only, to places like the Royal Domain (1858), Blenheim (1859), the Dukeries (1860); then, after 1861, when two days were spent in Derbyshire and a visit was paid to Chatsworth, many of the excursions were for longer periods, and on occasions the Club ventured as far as Scotland (1877). Not only were new methods of farming inspected, but visits were made to sewage farms (Barking) and to see areas of reafforestation, housing, and land improvement.

July 5, 1874. Marlborough. To early service and afterwards walking out to the Common and College.

After breakfast drove out in brake to Savernake through the drives in the Forest, and to several farms to inspect new covered and open homesteads recently erected. . . . Premises admirably arranged and most substantially built, the whole being done under the 'Land Improvements Acts'.

From such excursions as these, from visits he paid to the Royal Agricultural Society's Show and from data he stored up from observations while on holiday, especially in Devonshire where his wife's family lived, he evolved a conception of farming and estate management in keeping with the new age when corn-growing was in competition with overseas sources and other outlets had to be found.

On the whole the period 1847–74 was one of prosperity though there were some reverses in Essex, as his diary shows. There were a considerable number of rent abatements early in 1850, probably owing to the cumulative effect of a very bad harvest in 1848, when the land was drenched with rain, an indifferent harvest in 1849, and disease among the sheep and lambs in the same years. Another bad harvest in 1852, when the weather was so wet and stormy that the reaping machine pulled up the barley by the roots, brought about more distress and a second series of abatements. In August 1865, thirteen years later, the Rinderpest or Steppe Murrain found its way to England from the continent and there were thousands of casualties among the cattle. J.O.P. lost no time in looking for remedies.

August 8 (1865). Afternoon. Had long interview with Professor Gainger and Dr. Brewer on the subject of the Cattle Plague. Very little apparent confidence or agreement amongst veterinaries as to its treatment. Isolation, diet etc, urged more than medicine.

August 11. Third cow seized with Cattle Plague. Attending meeting at Chelmsford. Gave details of the cases under my eyes and the treatment I had adopted on Professor Gainger's advice.

August 14. . . . Symptoms in the various stages of the disorder— dullness and staggering, loss of milk, running at the eyes . . . etc. Opened the carcase of one before buried—no water; lungs congested, other parts apparently healthy except the inflammation of the 1st stomach.

The plague spread so rapidly and so fast that an effort was made to found a Cattle Plague Insurance Society, and J.O.P.

made another journey to London for information. Before this society could be set on foot, however, the disease had begun to decline and, in November, the money which had been subscribed was returned. Nevertheless, the epidemic was so serious that prospective tenants in some parts of Essex were afraid to sign leases, and in March 1866 a 'Humiliation Service' was held at Woodham Mortimer Church.

The thirty years' relative prosperity ended in 1874. By that time the United States had recovered from civil war, and in Canada's Middle West a corn-growing area was opening up. The acreage under corn in England began to fall rapidly. J.O.P.'s belief in the future of mixed farming was fully vindicated during the succeeding twenty years, but by that time considerable damage had been done to British agriculture by a community that undervalued it and a large town working-class which of necessity sought the cheapest foodstuffs.

It is now generally agreed by those who look back on this period, that, given the government assistance, which it deserved, to meet new challenges, British agriculture could have been maintained in a healthy, if not a highly prosperous, state. J.O.P.'s letter to his son in July 1876, describing the Colchester Show, goes to prove that the quality of farm produce was still as high as any in the world, and that, in spite of adversity, progress was being made in livestock production which was to yield handsome returns in the mid-twentieth century. His account of the accompanying festivities evokes a pleasing picture of mid-Victorian social life.

. . . I rode to the Show ground and had a look round at all the preparations for the morrow. I found John Barker and his companions had arrived and the animals comfortably in their places, and everything connected with the arrangements was in thorough forwardness and quite satisfactory. We have never had a nicer place for the show, and all was well laid out. When I got to Lexden House I found that the girls had arrived in the char-a-banc about ½ past 5, and had had a pleasant drive, and quicker than they expected. Lawn Tennis was going on till pretty well ½ past seven, and besides the party in the house 2 officers came to dinner. I was obliged to make my arrangements for early morning, and said I should breakfast on the ground, but in spite of all I said, there was breakfast ready for me at ½ past 6 and I was on the ground very soon after 7. The night had been very hot and there was a thick fog when I started out, but it soon cleared off, and we had the brightest and hottest day of the season. I rode about all day with my umbrella over my head. It was the best exhibition of the kind we have ever had in Essex. The Horns and shorthorn cattle were first rate, but the Alderneys were such a collection as has never been assembled before at any show in England. They numbered 97, and some of the most charming animals you can imagine. Mr. Macintosh's 100 gns. Challenge Cup which could only be won by the same person having the best animal (Shorthorn) in the yard 3 years in succession was carried off by the Rev. Mr. Kennard, the Rector of Markhall, where John Lyon used to live. He is said to have been offered £5000 for his heifer 'Queen Mary', the winner. In a small way I was successful, winning the first prizes with the few animals which I sent. John and his companions were very proud to walk up Maldon Street with the animals decorated with their rosettes.

The Ball on Wednesday night was not a success in point of numbers. People were tired with the day, and Mrs. George Round had had an evening promenade concert in her grounds (which I think was a great mistake) but neither Mr. Round nor Mr. Twiss would go, so I escorted Mrs. Round, Maria and Eva. There were only 75 present but everything was nicely arranged—good music, good supper, and all enjoyed it immensely. We did not get home till after 3.

Thursday morning I took more leisurely, and did not breakfast till ¼ to nine. The day was hot enough in all conscience, but not so scorching as the day before. I ought to tell you that on the first day Edward Round let the rest of the party go off saying he should look in in the afternoon, but he spent the whole day lying on the Lawn in the shade reading and playing with his puppy, and said he was quite sure he had had much the best of it. . . .

I thought it would be well to get home early on Friday, so I sent Thomas walking off to Marks Tey Station and rode there on Topsy to catch the 9–40 train. This got me to Maldon at 10–40, and I had nearly 2 hours at home before driving off to Chelmsford. . . .

This seems quite good going for a man aged sixty-three!

CHAPTER VIII

'POOR DIRTY ACRES'

JOHN OXLEY PARKER's notable letter to his son was written in the last good year British agriculture was to experience in the nineteenth century. Competition from overseas was driving down the price of wheat, and after 1877 it never averaged more than fifty shillings a quarter.

Long before the end of the 70s the shadow of depression had been gathering over English farming. As early as 1876 J.O.P. wrote to C. H. Sotheby concerning one of his tenants who was contemplating giving up a farm:

I am very apprehensive that difficult times are in prospect. I have a farm on hand for which I cannot get a tenant. There is one about 4 miles from this lying vacant, and nothing done upon it. I should be very unwilling to let Knights [the tenant] go, on the chance of finding a successor. . . .

Then came the disastrous season of 1879 when the old saying that the English summer falls on one or two days only was almost literally true. In that year J.O.P., uneasy about late sowing and meagre crops, began to scrawl his account of the weather across the top of his page. It is a lamentable record. Whereas here and there we have 'Fine, dry', or 'Fine breezy day', the greater number of the pages in the diary are marked 'Rain', 'Rain, rain!', 'Flood', or 'Wet—*wet*—WET!' The truth of the statement in agricultural history that the rains of 1879 brought disaster to the English farmer is brought home in all its grim detail in the diary as it is nowhere else. On New Year's Day he records that the snow was so heavy it broke down the branches of trees. On the night of the 2nd there was a rapid thaw. Next day his mare was lamed by melting snow caking

148

under her hooves and he was compelled to go home early from a Cattle Disease Committee meeting by heavy floods.

It was a bad beginning to a bad year. In February the land was still very wet, in March the wheat at Southminster was more backward than he had ever seen it. There were more floods in April, and from the beginning to 10 May there was a bitter east wind with frost every night.

Tom Royce has stripped bark for 50 years—never knew it so cold. (5 May 1879.)

The ice in May was 'as thick as a penny'.

So the dismal entries go on. Work on the land was still impossible at the end of May. The Essex Agricultural Show at Haverhill on 24 June was swamped out—'the whole ground a sea of mud'. The Royal Agricultural Show at Kilburn had no better fortune:

Raining all day—ground only passable on planks laid along the lines of shedding and corduroy roads made with old railway sleepers for the passage of carriages.

In August the land was as wet as in winter; there were floods in all parts of the country, and the steam plough was bogged down at Hazeleigh and immobilised for a fortnight. Cricket came to a standstill, the lambs were being fed on cabbages and dry food, but were dying daily:

Do not expect to save more than 250 out of more than 400.

His bailiff Deadman was at his wits' end as to what to do. In September there was white frost on the ground mornings and cold east winds in the evenings. The land was caked so hard from the August floods that October ploughing was made almost impossible. This dismal year ended with six weeks' almost unbroken fog and frost, with temperatures going down as low as 32° below zero and with the wheat still not sown on the heavy land. The last entry for the year, on 31 December, recites some of the damage done:

No such trying time for farmers for the last 50 years. Many farms in the hands of the owners; others paying no rent, and in this district Great and Little Gibcracks, Blue House Farm, Tile Hill, Southminster Caidge and the Heybridge Hall and Gapwell Farms unoccupied.

The farms in the Dengie Hundred suffered worst of all from this terrible season because of the heavy soil which was turned to paste by the floods and thus made unworkable, and then dried to an almost unbreakable mass by the sun which followed. The report of R. H. Pringle to the Royal Commission on Agriculture in 1894 gives a vivid description of the kind of soils the Dengie farmers had to contend with:

Between the Great Eastern and the sea, much of the soil is stiff, tenacious, bluish grey or brown clay. . . . To plough it three horses are required. In the best of seasons it is expensive to work and at all times it is 'season land'. It cannot be touched in wet weather, and if allowed to become sunburnt the clods will yield to no implement of husbandry.

The following graphic description of the subsoil in the Dengie Hundred I extract from a letter received from Althorne. 'Our soil is stiff, tough, numb, dumb and impervious, so that during heavy rains the vegetable mould and manures are washed off the surface on to the great mud beds of the Crouch and Blackwater rivers.'

On clay-bottomed soil the character of the season is *everything*. To attempt tillage in wet weather is not only a sure way of destroying all chances of a crop, but a certain step towards causing the clay to 'run together' and largely increasing the cost of subsequent cultivation.

In respect of the stiff clay soil one point must be noted with reference to the indirect loss consequent upon the run of bad seasons. Not only were farmers unable to do justice to their land for want of means, but the summer fallowing season failed to exert that beneficial influence which under favourable circumstances it generally produces. The strong soils, instead of being ameliorated by the repeated operations of tillage, instead of being cleaned, sweetened and pulverized, got into a hopeless state of weeds and confusion.

None knew better than the man who was dealing with a number of farms the damage and deterioration that could be caused by leaving them unoccupied, and J.O.P. had always been prepared to go to almost any length to prevent this. He tried to keep good tenants even if it meant much sacrifice in other ways. In 1850, when the Rev. George Heathcote reported that one of his tenants was unable to pay his rent, he wrote:

It is an awkward dilemma to know what to do, and I should like to go and look round the farm before giving a decided opinion, but my impression is that if he is only going on tolerably well and showing a disposition to do justice to the land, that *you must keep him on his legs* and let him pay from time to time on a/c of rent as he is able. . . . It would not do to get rid of him as you would have difficulty in getting a tenant at all.

In the same year, when J. Shapter's farm at Latchingdon was without a tenant, J.O.P. made arrangements to carry it on himself, and thus avoid dilapidation.

In the meantime I have sent implements and horses from a neighbouring farm to carry on the necessary cultivation, and trust that I shall be able to work it in this way without putting you to the expense of purchasing a regular complement of stock. . . .

In 1877 the tenant of the same farm was unable to keep up his payments and J.O.P. writes to the landlord:

It has really come to this, that many tenants are allowed to go on without present payment of rent in the hope that it may come hereafter, rather than run the risk of having the farm vacant, without the chance of getting another tenant.

You have no idea of what heavy land arable farmers have had to contend with during the recent wet seasons. I have acted for you as I would do for myself under similar circumstances. You have an honest tenant, working the farm fairly and rightly, but unable in these adverse seasons to continue to do so and to find the rent at the usual time of payment. He could do so by selling off, lessening stock, but an impoverished tenant would be no use to you on such a farm. I have considered that forbearance and delay were the better course and have trusted to the future to bring up the arrears. . . .

Delays in payment and abatement of rent were general from 1878 onwards. In that year and the next, the two largest landowners in Purleigh abated their rents 20 per cent; others

THE OXLEY PARKER PAPERS

by 10 per cent. A third landlord granted a new lease from 1879 to 1882 at a reduction of 30 per cent and a fourth was left with two tenantless farms. Lands which in the good days of the middle fifties had been fetching 15s. to £1 an acre were being let in 1879 at 9s. and what was not taken up was often offered at 5s. to whoever would come and work it. Landlords were going to any length for the mere sake of keeping tenants. One of J.O.P.'s own tenants came to him in the autumn of 1879, owing two and a half years' rent, and was cleared up to Michaelmas 1879 on payment of the rent for one year only.

Labourers could not be kept in full employment and migration to the towns took on alarming proportions.

I will not worry you [wrote J.O.P. to Dr. Hawkins] with any further recapitulation of our Purleigh troubles, but there is one fact which in such a list might hardly be left unnoticed—that besides some old cottages which have been taken down here, there are now between 40 and 50 cottages unoccupied in the Parish. No doubt this is partly owing to the inclination of the rural population at the present day to migrate to more active scenes of labour, but I consider that it has also arisen from the inability of the farmers to keep the labouring population in full and continuous employment.

From 1879 to the time of his death seven years later, Essex farming did not recover from the shock. There were better seasons than 1879 and, here and there, joyful entries of fine warm weather, but other factors prolonged the distress. Abatements were forced on landlords year by year. The bad harvest of 1884 brought another spate of appeals. Characteristic entries in the diaries run:

September 28th, 1884. [Wrote] to Mr. Todhunter in reply to letter giving notice to quit Manor Farm [Parndon] if rent is not reduced to 10 shillings an acre. (Winchester College.)
October 18th. Afterwards at Mr. Inglis' office to meet Mr. May (C. G. Round, Birch). Long discussion as to reduction of rent. Mr. May said that he could not give more than 10 shillings an acre.
Saw Mr. Royce and agreed that his rent should be £150 instead of the nominal amount at which it had been—£200.

On 20 December, and again on 3 January 1885, meetings were called by the Mayor of Colchester, but on both occasions J.O.P. was obliged to go home early owing to the shortness of the days. At that time he was nearly seventy-three years of age.

In April 1885 he was at Latchingdon hearing appeals against Income Tax Schedule B assessments and wrote in his diary:

. . . relieved nearly all cases. Losses on farms from £50 to £500 and more.

On 2 January 1886 one farmer offered £500 if he could be released from the remaining term of his lease because of his already heavy losses. The rents of Shoats and Canney Farms in Steeple, which had been £760 in 1873, went down to £460 in 1886 and between 1886 and 1891 were only £1 per annum. (Report to Royal Commission.)

J. Todhunter, tenant of Manor Farm, Parndon, put the position very clearly in a letter of October 1886:

The prospects of agriculture grow more hopeless day by day, and I can really see nothing for it except the poor clay lands abandoned. Whether, on the better and more easily worked lands whose crops are less costly and more certain, farmers may, by great economy, still be able to go on, I cannot tell. What is demonstrated beyond a doubt is that spending money on poor land is simply throwing it away. I fear this will be a bad winter for the labourers and we shall find them drifting into the towns and into the workhouses.

In another letter the same farmer lays the blame squarely on the shoulders of Gladstone who, by introducing Free Trade had, in his opinion, wrecked a vital industry and precipitated a social change which one day the country would regret.

What times we live in! I do think the iniquity of that old man will yet be visited upon his head. You cannot get away from principles. What he has applied to Ireland has come home to him in London, and now he dares not face the issue. Will the English people bear it much longer? As to farming, I really look upon it as done. The land must go out of cultivation.

J.O.P. was not so pessimistic, even in the worst of times, but when his landlords complained, his tenants remonstrated against what once had been reasonable rents, his labourers left their cottages, and farms one by one went out of cultivation, he must many times have had his doubts. Yet he struggled on, keeping farms going where he could, advising, bargaining, doing everything possible to save his own clients from the calamity that was fast becoming general.

Reading this gloomy story at the present time (1962) it is of interest to recall that somewhat similar conditions arose in parts of Essex in the 1920s, soon after the end of the First World War. Much of the heavy land between Maldon and St. Peter's Chapel at the mouth of the Blackwater did not pay to cultivate, and went into 'cold storage'—impoverished grassland. It was rescued from this condition by Government help, by tractors that replaced horses, and finally the necessity to grow food during the Second World War.

CHAPTER IX

VARIATIONS ON A THEME

COMMANDER SIR GEORGE RICHARD BROOKE-PECHELL was a veteran of the Napoleonic Wars who had lived a life of public and court service. From 1835 till his death in June 1860 he was Whig Member of Parliament for Brighton. On 18 July 1854 J.O.P. was present at the sale in which he bought Ulting Hall for £18,000. Among his lands in Essex were farms in Peldon, Paglesham, Rivenhall, Ashen, Hazeleigh, Purleigh, and other parishes. He was succeeded by his son, also Sir George Brooke-Pechell, who, in July 1860, was wanting the services of a competent agent. He was introduced to J.O.P. by another client, M. G. Thoyts, and this began an association which lasted until 1887. Nothing shows more clearly the difficulties of landlord, agent, and tenant in those grim days than the letters which passed between Sir George and John Oxley Parker.

During the 60s the two men became great friends. When the agent went to visit part of the estate the landlord often went with him, and they made a day's pleasure out of the journey. In September 1864 they went together to West Hall, Paglesham, in a new tandem belonging to Sir George, and in taking the tandem to Stisted with his own horses J.O.P. upset it on an uneven patch at the corner of Woodham Mortimer Glebe, breaking both the shafts. They went on to Stisted by light cart, then back to Ulting Hall. Within four days the tandem was repaired and Sir George went gaily off on a drive to Southampton by way of Gravesend. On another occasion Sir George engaged his friend to look over his estates in Ireland, and the two, with a small party, enjoyed a pleasant holiday-cum-business trip.

In Hazeleigh and Purleigh there are three farms, Mosklyns, Hazeleigh Hall, and Jenkyns, and it is of these that the main events of the story treat. During the 1860s all went fairly well, but at the beginning of the 70s signs of the coming distress began to show themselves. Mosklyns was let to a tenant named Brackenbury who in 1873 declared that he was unable to carry on. In a long interview J.O.P. persuaded him to do so. Even in August, when a bad harvest decreased any prospects of success, J.O.P. was still hoping to keep the farm on.

I believe him to be honest. I know he is hardworking, even to the injury of his health. Other farms will be flung on the market, and heavy ones in such a season will not be in favour. . . . The poor fellow was in tears when talking to me, but do not suppose that what I have written is the mere work of compassion.

It was all to no purpose. Sir George, after expressing some concern that Brackenbury might do a 'moonlight flitting' with his stock, leaving the landlord to whistle the tune of 'The Girl I Left Behind Me', agreed to let the lease go, and efforts were to be made to find a new tenant.

All through the winter of 1873–4 Brackenbury lived in the farmhouse and J.O.P. sowed some of the land. Then, under the date 22 July 1874, appears a note in the diary:

Home and to Mosklyns Farm. Met Mr. Norden and afterwards drawing agreement for hire of farm.

On the 25th he notified Sir George that Thomas Norden had agreed to take the farm, 126 acres, for fourteen years, the first four at £100, the remaining ten at £125.

I am sure [J.O.P. wrote] you will be glad no longer to call *yourself* a farmer, and it is a real satisfaction to get it off my hands.

The triumph was short-lived. The undertaking was signed, but two months later he was writing to Sir George:

Oh, this unlucky Mosklyns Farm! Shall I never be free from bother about it? I thought we were safe in arranging with Mr. Taber's friend [Norden] and that it would be off our hands again, but having heard nothing of him for some weeks I began to get nervous and wrote saying that it was time to arrange about the valuation etc. and asking who was to act on his behalf. In reply I have a long letter that he is disappointed of help that had been promised him, that he cannot take his share out of the family business, hence he will not be ready with the payments of valuation etc. . . . Mr. Norden has signed an agreement but it will be no use to try to keep him to an engagement which he cannot carry out. All I can say is that I will do the best I can under the circumstances.

Almost the same thing happened again and again. In May 1875 Mr. George Taber of Rivenhall recommended a second young man but nothing came of it, then George Taber himself considered taking it at a reduced rent. He was a man of substance, and, as Sir George said, 'a good solvent tenant is a scarce article'. Again nothing happened. The autumn passed and, in December, Sir George received a gloomy letter from his agent:

I have felt a good many times that I ought to write to you, but I really had nothing pleasant to communicate, and I have to be the bearer of evil tidings. I thought that Mosklyns was off our hands, but luckily I did not write to tell you so. I waited till the thing should be really settled. A man had agreed to take it and all seemed to be arranged. He had seen the farm once or twice—I think more during fine weather. The wet autumn came and when he made his move to Purleigh, with implements and horses and household goods, the farm was drenched by recent rain. It was in such a state of mud that he was fairly frightened. He came to say that his things were on the road but on going to the fields he cried out to the man at the farm, 'I'm not going to stop here; I shall be ruined if I do!' and he stood in the road till the carts and wagons came up, turned them round and went straight off back to his own country on the borders of Cambridgeshire. . . . I am not sure that there was not legal hold upon him, but I did not think it worth while to add litigation to other troubles. . . .

Sir George's reply showed that he not only had tolerance but also the saving sense of humour to smile, if rather grimly, at his own misfortunes. In stating that the man was probably the loser in not knowing the mine of agricultural wealth in the heavy land if treated well and with ample resources, he was quite correct, but the man came from the borders of Cambridgeshire where such conditions did not exist. However,

the matter must have had a ludicrous side to it; the good man standing in the road, watching the arrival of his teams and turning them round and absquatulating forthwith, would make a capital cartoon for 'Punch', especially if all the expletives and adjectives (few of them probably in Johnson's dictionary) descriptive of the land and possibly of ourselves too, were added by way of explanation!

The story of Sir George Pechell reminds us of some dismal musical theme with all its variations. First the subject was introduced by Brackenbury and Mosklyns. Before it had been properly resolved, a second strain was added, this time at Hazeleigh Hall. In June 1875 Sir George had met two of his tenants who had told him that Taylor at Hazeleigh Hall was, as they put it, 'very badly off'. Sir George suspected that he was impoverishing the farm by selling the straw 'preparatory to a flit in some shape or other'. When the matter was gone into it turned out that Taylor, unable to meet his dues, should really be given notice to quit, but with Mosklyns already on his hands, J.O.P. preferred, by judicious leniency, to put off the crisis for a further year.

By the end of 1876 Sir George was feeling the effects of a greatly reduced income.

This Mosklyns account is something dreadful. . . . Please write to Taber and get him to take it if it is possible to accomplish it. If we fail we must simply abandon it and throw it out of cultivation—anything is better than such a ruinous return as it is now making. It will evidently affect my income so much that I must put down my carriage, and my horses will go to be sold next week. (1 January 1876.)

Mosklyns had now been vacant three years, Hazleigh Hall was on the market, and another variation of the distress theme came from West Hall, Paglesham. The tenant, here referred to as 'Old Stebbing', seems to have been in the habit of sending regular appeals every half year to have the day of payment deferred, and this had generally been allowed. In June 1876 the old man died, and his son did not wish to carry on the farm. Again the question arose of finding a tenant who had enough capital. Meanwhile no success whatever had attended the efforts to find tenants for the other farms and Sir George was protesting that it was downright ruin for him to keep them.

The tide of agricultural distress was rising. Even on the lighter soils farmers were beginning to feel the strain. In August 1876 Sir George wrote from his home in Alton near Basingstoke that within eight miles of him there were eighty farms left on the landlords' hands. His anxiety was increased by the poor return from his farms in Ireland where one tenant had gone bankrupt and a second was leaving. He suggested that Hazeleigh Hall should be put into the hands of a London agent (23 February 1877), then, four days later, that J.O.P. should try to let Hazeleigh Hall and Mosklyns as one farm, lamenting the stagnation in affairs by quoting the French proverb, *Il n'y a rien de plus mort que ce qui ne bouge pas*.

In his letter of 27 April 1877, J.O.P. announced yet another impending disaster, the approaching vacancy of Jenkyns Farm.

Thanks for your letter [answered Sir George]. It ought I think to have been written on black-edged paper considering the nature of the contents.

Again he suggested that if the negotiations in hand with one prospective tenant failed, the business should be put into the hands of a London agent.

They have lots of applicants from other parts of England and can be very persuasive when it suits their purpose. It is very clear that it has a bad name locally whether it deserves it or not, and a stranger would be more likely to take the bait than a native. (28 April 1877.)

In May another prospective tenant appeared and for three months it seemed that this man, Captain Delf, would hire both Hazeleigh Hall and Jenkyns. On the 14th, in a letter to Sir George, J.O.P. wrote:

You said that my last letter ought to have been written on black-edged paper. I hope that as time goes on the sad border may be narrowed, and that by and by I shall be able to adopt the old-fashioned gilt-edged for my letters.

Again, however, after much exploring and bargaining, Captain Delf declined the two farms.

It is a comfort [wrote J.O.P.] to find that you can take these disagreeable matters so philosophically. (19 June .)

The whole story is told in his diary:

1877, May 22nd. Had a long interview with Mr. Delf re H. Hall. Offered lease for 21 years at £325 p.a. including shooting, £200 towards repairs and rough timber. Hay, growing grass and manure to be taken by valuation, landlord to harvest the barley and oats now growing. Thought that he had acquiesced mainly on these terms, when he produced his own mem^d requiring that lease should terminate at end of 8 years on 4 years' notice and rent not to exceed 10/6 per acre including shooting. Stated that I could not take less than had been originally proposed.

June 9th. Had long interview with Mr. Delf. Offered Hazeleigh Hall, Jenkyns and woods and shooting at rent of £550 and to lay out £300 in repairs. He offered £450. Stated that I cd not accept it but that if he chose to appoint Mr. Fenn to act for him to meet me on the part of Sir George Pechell, we might possibly come to terms.

June 16th. Mr. Delf. Long interview at Mr. Fenn's office. Eventually offered to let Hazeleigh Hall, Jenkyns and woods at £500 and spend £300 in repairs. Refused by Mr. Delf.
June 17th. Wrote to Mr. Fenn in reply to letter that Mr. Delf would accept terms if £500 was laid out. Replied that I could not do it.

Better fortune followed. On 26 July Jenkyns Farm was let for £315 to a man named Golden Fairhead, and in August £100 a year was offered for Mosklyns. By November both these farms were off the landlord's hands leaving only Hazeleigh Hall remaining in that district, although the farms at Peldon and in other parts of the county were still giving a great deal of trouble. It seemed that nobody with enough capital would come forward and make an offer for the Hall. In March 1878 a young man named Payne from Virley became interested, but it was soon found that he had not enough resources to take up the tenancy. In April Sir George was in Scotland and from there he sent a most interesting letter.

A few nibbles at the bait [Hazeleigh Hall] are always interesting to the angler, and I had been thinking lately with some anxiety about the float staying so long at the perpendicular without signs of a bite.
  I have been lately in the North of England and Scotland. . . . When in Scotland I heard that there are a great many young farmers wanting farms in England—they have a notion that they know a thing or two which we don't, and that if they could get cheaper labour and cheaper rents, which are to be had in the South, they could see their way to an eventual fortune. I propose therefore advertizing in The Scotsman if this Payne(ful) nibble does not end in a bite.

The Report to the Royal Commission on Agriculture states that the Scottish invasion of Essex started about 1880 when a Wigtonshire farmer was there on a visit and decided that he would like to take up a farm there. This letter and the advertisement which followed it seems to prove that both the idea of Scotsmen settling in Essex and the advertisement of Essex farms in Scottish papers preceded this event by two years. Between May and August a number of Scottish farmers made enquiries about Hazeleigh Hall. In all his replies J.O.P. gave particulars of the farm, including acreage and rent (£250 a year), but, to use Sir George's figure of speech, no fish rose to the bait. In one of his letters he drew out the simile:

The Hazeleigh Fly is a curious article, green wings, ginger hackle for dirty legs, whipped all over with a dun hackle from the neck of a bird called 'Debit Sheet'—hook Limerick, very sharp but well concealed by the ginger hackle representing the dirty legs. This I think would be a fisherman's description of the Hazeleigh fly, not a tempting article, but fish will rise sometimes, if greedy, at very curious attempts at flymaking, particularly on a cloudy day and when used by an expert in agricultural fly fishing.

When none of the Scotsmen rose to the bait, Sir George took

another line. It happened that in a previous letter, J.O.P., in commenting on an offer made by Taber, wrote:

. . . He has written offering £200 per annum for 21 years' from Mic'as 1879—that is, no rent for the first year and nothing for the present and to pay nothing for the manure on the farm etc. . . . I certainly cannot believe that you would accept such tenants as these. It is virtually offering about £150 a year for nearly 300 acres. I have told him that if it is to be let at such a rent as that I would offer to take it myself. (6 May 1878.)

Now Sir George took him at his word. Though J.O.P. was not very desirous of taking Hazeleigh Hall, he was in possession of it by December 1878.

It is very probable [wrote Sir George] that you may not make both ends meet at Hazeleigh Hall at first, but altho' I do not see the silver lining at present in the agricultural cloud, yet things can hardly go on for long in their present depressed state, and if this is a day of loss just now, the day of profit must come at last. (25 February 1879.)

Unfortunately neither letters nor diaries give any indication how the rent asked of J.O.P. compared with the £225 asked of the Scottish applicants.

Meanwhile conditions on Sir George's other farms were deteriorating as the depression set in. The letters refer to one after another of his tenants being in arrears. As payments lagged behind dues Sir George talked more and more about direct and vigorous action—a line which J.O.P., knowing how tenants as well as landlords were suffering, was unwilling to take except as a very last resort:

. . . is dreadfully in arrears [wrote Sir George]. Really you must threaten him with something uncomfortable; his holding being simply a field and nothing more, we have no security whatever. . . . (25 February 1879.)

The failure of his rents to come in, and the disagreement between landlord and agent as to the right measures to take with tenants, led to a situation in which, during 1879, Sir George interfered more and more in concerns which were really part of his agent's province. We find him engaged in direct negotiations with tenants, sending information to J.O.P. only when interviews were over or when deals were done. The disagreement came to a head over a complicated negotiation concerning his farms at Peldon in which he took into his own hands the settlement of a difference with a tenant. Confusion and disagreement arose because J.O.P. was dealing with the tenant at the same time. It was plain that, sooner or later, Sir George would take the management of affairs into his own hands. He had already declared his intention of doing this in August 1878, and of closing the agency at Michaelmas of that year. Nevertheless it continued into 1879 with misunderstandings growing, largely owing to Sir George's precipitate actions, until, on 23 September, he gave notice that from Michaelmas he would terminate the agency. In a letter of the following week, he wrote:

Regarding yourself, personally I have every confidence in you, but I do not think your judgment has always been for the best, and I think direct action with the tenants will often cause less friction than transactions thro' a third party. (30 September 1879.)

On 20 October J.O.P. sent off to Sir George a number of agreements. The two met on the 24th and discussed the situation on all the estates and they parted on the understanding that Sir George would collect the rents himself the following Michaelmas. It took some months to produce the accounts for the period ending at Michaelmas, and in the correspondence which ensued, J.O.P. gave an account of the financial obligations of all the tenants. The rents that year were exceedingly small, and Sir George wrote:

. . . I daresay we shall find some day a pair of pantoscopic spectacles that will put matters right. (10 November 1879.)
I have been hoping to hear from you with the a/c from Michaelmas '78 to Lady Day '79. The last remittance I had from you was £172-5-2 . . . being the balance on the a/c ending Mich^s, 1878. In fact, after so long a fast I am getting rather hungry. (3 December 1879.)

In reply he received a timely reminder:

You have suffered through the same causes that brought disaster to your tenants. (8 December 1879.)

The mention of depression to a suffering landlord, such as Sir George was, made him angry. Who then had caused this agricultural depression? he asked. Todhunter had blamed the 'wicked old man' Gladstone. Sir George had another explanation:

Really, these are hard times, nor can I say that as a nation we do not deserve them. Well, liberals foretold that if a Conservative government came in, we should have to take the cup of adversity, and if you contrast the state of the country now with what it was when the present gov't came in, there is no 'take' about the prophecy being true, and most of it is owing to the policy of the government. The worst of the matter is that the squires, farmers, parsons and the drink trade will all go in for anybody that calls himself a conservative even tho' he be really the biggest radical to be found in a day's march, and that will I fear keep the present government in without the smallest reference to their well or evil doing. You will have to shell out more of your Hazeleigh profits to pay for their extravagance and folly before long. You have only yourself to blame, for certainly you left no stone in the country unturned to get them in, and no doubt you would do so again. (12 December 1879.)

We have since learnt that political machinations are not the only things that may bring either prosperity or depression, and in this case it is true that the onlooker sees the game better than he who is actually playing it.

All that now remained to J.O.P. of the former relationship was the tenancy of Hazeleigh Hall. Occasionally Sir George wrote to him with news of his tenants, mostly defaulters, and on small matters connected with his own tenancy. One of these was concerning shooting rights over Jenkyns Farm for which J.O.P. had applied and which he had not been granted. He was very disappointed, and in March 1885 he gave notice to quit as his lease was due to expire.

I am unwilling to burden my sons with the responsibility of continuing the farm. The disastrous seasons which have occurred since I took the lease have caused the occupation to be a very serious loss, and I can only undertake to continue it on very different terms.

He asked for a reduction of the rent to £150 and the liberty to quit the farm any Michaelmas after giving six months' notice:

You are aware that I took the farm for the sake of the shooting for my sons, and they are now desirous of holding it for no other reason, and are really ready to urge me to give it up at Mic'as next. It was a great disappointment to them that my application to have the entire shooting of Jenkyns was not granted, and I certainly felt hurt myself that so little consideration was given to my letters written long before the termination of Mr. Fairhead's tenancy, and at a time when arrangements could have been made without any difficulty.

In reply he received a note from Sir George accepting his terms.

The tenancy lasted a year longer, and on 28 September 1886 the whole of the stock of Hazeleigh Hall was sold off by auction and realised £539 1s. In February 1887 he sent off to Sir George the final payment of rent.

I hope [he wrote] the farms will be so managed that with a revival in agricultural affairs they will bring in better results in the future.

That desired revival was to be postponed for many many years.

CHAPTER X

LANDLORDS

DURING THE SEVENTY or more years they were in business, Christopher Comyns Parker and his son were concerned with many of the largest estates in the County of Essex, especially in the south and east. Among these were those of the Mildmays, the Tufnells, the Round family, T. W. Bramston, and Sir Charles Smith. Besides these, they had many smaller properties to manage, in some cases, like those of J. C. Boodé (Rettendon), Mrs. Taylor (Tolleshunt D'Arcy), W. Otte (Plumborough, Hockley), Miss Haselfoot (Boreham), J. Shapter (Althorne), Archdeacon Wilberforce (Potton Island), and Lord Wynford (Wallasea Island), consisting of a single farm or little more. These were widely scattered throughout the Hundreds in the south and east, as were the properties of the various corporations such as the Charterhouse (Southminster, Bicknacre), New College, Oxford (East Hall, Bradwell), Chelmsford Grammar School (Tilbury), The Dean Clarke Charity (Tillingham), University College (Margaret Roothing), Oriel College (Purleigh), Winchester College, Oxford (Roydon and Parndon) and the widely scattered estates belonging to the Dean and Chapter of St. Paul's Cathedral.

Relationships varied in degree of intimacy. The Gepps (Mayland), the Griffenhoofes (Galleywood) and the Parkers (Bradwell, St. Lawrence, Dengie) were relatives. Sir Charles Smith (Stapleford Abbots, North Weald, etc.) was a friend of lifelong standing. On 15 September 1848 J.O.P. wrote in his diary:

At Suttons. President at Dinner at The Talbot given to the tenants on Sir C. C. Smith coming of age. 31 dined—passed off well. Got home very late. Went to town in the morning to engage vocalists who did not come.

On 15 February 1855 he went to Sir Charles's wedding.

. . . After the wedding called in Grosvenor Place, and then to breakfast at Miss Cave's. Large party. Shopping with Louisa and to Princess Theatre to see Charles Kean as Louis XI.

In 1887 he had looked after Sir Charles's interests for nearly half a century, fixing his rents, seeing his tenants, appearing for him at manor courts, looking to the state of his many farms, and only on one occasion was there the slightest hint of misunderstanding or disagreement. (See page 125.)

Twenty-seven years after the marriage almost to the day he again wrote in his diary:

February 14th, 1882. Drummond Smith's coming of age. Drove with Sir Charles to see preparations in Town Hall Epping for Ball in the evening. Decorations and preparations for supper all satisfactory. Afterwards to Ongar to see how arrangements for dining room were progressing. Evening Ball, 200 guests, dancing kept up with spirit till nearly 4. Agreed on all hands to be a great success.

This friendship and mutual trust was largely the result of Sir Charles's own sensible attitude towards the affairs of his tenants, an attitude which is apparent in all his letters on problems of rent. In the middle of the depression of the 80s he could write of a tenant:

I saw Knights to-day, who laid his lamentations before me and the heavy expenditure he had incurred for his son, and asked what he was to do.

I suggested that instead of paying any rent this year he should, when the proper time came, pay me 5 per cent on money due and make use of the rent so retained for the purpose of stocking and improving his farm, till such time as it was convenient to pay it; he appeared quite satisfied with this arrangement and so am I (under the circumstances), if the money so kept back is really and properly employed in keeping the farm in good heart and cultivation.

I would much rather forego my rent and see the land well done by, than get it simply through starving and deteriorating the occupation. (20 October 1881.)

Sir Charles lived at Suttons, Romford, and was therefore in close touch with the affairs of his estates. Another landlord of the same kind was C. G. Round of Birch, who was not only the landlord but also the friend of his tenants. He was very concerned, for instance, that his tenant, May, should do nothing which would spoil the good looks of his village. With regard to the enclosure of a piece of land he says:

I wish that you, by some persuasive power of yours, could induce Mr. May not to attempt to take in the little piece of waste which lies on your right hand on the low ground as you go from the Rectory to the Church. It will not be of sixpence value to him when he has done it, and it must be a bad job, for the two runs of water that meet there are both lower than the level of the road, and they must remain, whatever other fence, or fence and ditch, may be made. I have expressed my wishes as pointedly as I could to him, but he seems to think that the little piece of waste is of consequence, and that he will gain something by the enclosure. The waste and the adjoining freehold did not belong to the same person until lately. Come to the assistance of our friends at the Rectory, for their walk to Church is made pleasant and pretty to them by the unenclosed little piece. (24 November 1866.)

The enclosure had originally been suggested to May by J.O.P. with the idea of making a verge of grassland from rectory to church, but he now asked him to refrain from carrying it out in deference to Mr. Round's wishes. May, the tenant, willingly did so. J.O.P. acknowledged his own part in the proposed enclosure and stated that it would not be proceeded with, though he had intended it as a preliminary to planting a long line of trees the whole way along the range of pastures. (25 November 1866.)

Some absentee landlords were just as concerned with their estates and the welfare of the people on them. Every year Colonel (later General) Bourchier gave £10 to the poor of

Bures where his land lay, and in bad seasons he increased his gift by a further £5. On 29 November 1830 he stated:

In a time of such serious excitement amongst the labouring class who, I lament to think, have too much real cause for discontent, it is the business of every landlord and proprietor to inform himself of the condition of the poor resident on his property whether it be extensive or not. Though mine is of trifling extent I should feel happy to reflect that as far as it goes the labourers upon it were in a condition which left them no real cause for complaint. I am satisfied you will have the goodness to ascertain for me whether they have employment and are sufficiently remunerated for their labour, or whether there are any paid out of the rates. My wish as well as my interest is that the condition of the labourer should be render^d as good as he has a just right to expect it should be, and I shall be ready to adopt any suggestion you may oblige me with for accomplishing such an object. (29 November 1830.)

After General Bourchier's death a change came. His son, Captain Charles Bourchier, sought to make himself independent with a certain income of £820 a year and no worry about rent or tenants. (8 June 1863.) In August 1863 the Bures estate was sold for £23,340. In January 1864, in the full expectation that the usual £10 would be forthcoming, the money was spent on the poor, and J.O.P. received a letter from Henry Morrell, tenant of Mount Hall:

With regard to the £10 for the poor, it has been already distributed to the people and they wished me to thank Captain Bourchier on their behalf for not forgetting them the last year, but I suppose now it is no use sending the message! I hope upon quiet consideration he will change his mind and leave a name behind him of a good and kind landlord. (18 January 1864.)

The captain did not change his mind, and in August 1864 another letter was received:

I certainly did not expect Captain Bourchier to behave in so scurvy a manner as he has done. I enclose . . . a note to him which if you think well will you please forward it. . . . I certainly think he ought to have some one tell him his mind. . . . I hope Captain Bourchier will make the most of his £10 at the seaside.

Among the letters relating to single farms, by far the most complete set is the one concerning Frame Farm, Tolleshunt D'Arcy. These are noteworthy because they show us another kind of landlord—the absentee who has adopted an expensive style of living, relies on his agent to produce the means to keep it up, irrespective of the struggles of tenants, and begins to complain as soon as payments lag behind.

Mr. Edward Taylor, of Liverpool House, Dover, was the brother of Lieutenant-General Sir Herbert Taylor, G.C.B., a friend of George IV, who held high office at court. One of his properties which he had in the right of his wife was Frame Farm, Tolleshunt D'Arcy, let to a certain Mrs. Cardinal—whose family had been on the farm about 150 years—at £300 per year. In spite of a continual abatement of rent of 10 per cent, the tenant was regularly two, three, or four months late with her payments, and Taylor was in 1836 recommended by a friend to put the farm into the hands of Christopher Comyns Parker. By August 1836 it turned out that Mrs. Cardinal could no longer find the money to carry on the farm and it was let by C.C.P. to a farmer named Francis at £270 a year on a fourteen-year lease. This was later altered to a twenty-one-year lease.

At a very early stage in the negotiations it became apparent that the Taylors were badly in need of ready money. First Mrs. Taylor, when the proposal was made to her to fix the rent at £270, tried to have a proviso inserted in the lease that this should be raised to £300 'if corn should materially improve in price and the value of land be higher than at present'. C.C.P. replied that he could certainly not make such a proposition to Mr. Francis,

as he has been induced by family connexions living near to give more than I should have felt inclined to ask for the farm had it been upon the market.

Francis soon showed that he was the right type of man to make a farm which had been badly neglected and almost stripped of its essential woodland into a going concern.

He is farming with very great spirit. I have rarely seen a farm so much improved in so short a time. I was very fortunate in procuring so good a tenant, and with ample capital to restore our overcropped and ill-conditioned property to a creditable state of cultivation. (12 December 1837.)

The rent for the farm was due on 24 June and 21 December. Even if only a few days late, the landlord sent reminders:

July 10th, 1838. I have such heavy outgoings on account of 5 sons that I am sure you will excuse me for being particular.

January 2nd, 1839. I have always so many payments to make at this time of the year besides the allowances to my sons and servants' wages that it would be a convenience if . . .

July 3rd, 1839. I shall be obliged to you to let my tenant Mr. Francis know that it wd be a great convenience to me if he would remit me his half year's rent on the days appointed. . . .

So it went on. In a letter of 1 July 1841 he complained at having £40 14s. 3d. deducted from his rent for expenses towards the Tithe Map of Tolleshunt D'Arcy. This was admittedly a large sum but in that decade of Tithe Commutation it fell with equal severity on all landlords. His complaint was followed by an account for 15 guineas for four years' services when C.C.P. had attended tithe meetings and conducted business in connection with the commutation.

In March 1842 Edward Taylor had an unpleasant surprise in the shape of a demand for £2500 legacy duty to be paid immediately on the property (including Frame Farm) left to his wife by her uncle. In June he had the satisfaction of seeing it substantially reduced, but begged C.C.P. to try to secure a mortgage on the farm for him.

Francis still continued to be the tenant. In 1843 both Edward Taylor and C.C.P. died, and Mrs. Taylor went to Italy for three years. At that time a minor agricultural depression set in, and Francis's rent began to fall behindhand. In January 1850, Mrs. Taylor wrote from Paris:

The rent of this farm forms so large a part of my income and I have such heavy calls upon me from my numerous family that I miss this payment very much. . . . Mr. Francis sh^d consider for how many years he has had the Frame Farm under such advantageous circumstances, as the rent used to be much higher and the landlord took all the advantage of the timber. . . .

The same thing happened in the June half-year, and in September Mrs. Taylor wrote again asking for the rent. J.O.P. replied with suggestions that Francis's rent would be abated in consideration of the hard times. (2 January 1851.)

Your tenant has applied to me several times for an abatement of rent. I have endeavoured from time to time to ward off the question and have managed to keep him in pretty good temper though he complains loudly of the times, the indifference of the crops and the lowness of the price. In the present year the underwood in the Grove was in the course of clearing, and I have recently been to look at it with the view of having it cut and finding a purchaser. At present I have offered it at £5 per acre (there are 5 acres of it), but without success. It has struck me that it would be a good opportunity of showing some consideration to your tenant if you were to give him the underwood in abatement of rent. He is an excellent tenant, pays a full rent for the farm, manages it remarkably well, and keeps the premises in good order. He is therefore deserving of encouragement. . . .

Mrs. Taylor, in assenting to the suggestion, made a noteworthy comment:

. . . I hope ere another Xmas that the times will improve by something being done for the farmers—or by a war, which does not seem improbable.

In August 1851 Francis wrote:

The pressure of the times must call for an alteration of rents in future, hoping Mrs. Taylor will be prepared to do so next settling day. . . .

In the end a temporary reduction of rent was agreed on to allow Francis to put up a new brewhouse and shed. From that time Mrs. Taylor received her rent promptly and in full save for payments for repairs and improvements. For many years she had spent most of her time abroad and wintered regularly in Nice.

I have tried winters in England and always passed them in my bedroom, whereas in this sunny bright dry climate (with its lovely blue sky and sea) I can walk out or drive in an open carriage any day, and sit with windows open and no fire, and the room full of summer flowers.

In 1861 her son William Taylor wrote asking what the farm was worth if, in the event of his mother's death, he contemplated buying it. He was given a figure of £7500 exclusive of timber and was advised to give the tenant Francis a new lease.

Without any security in the farm, and at your mother's advanced age, he is unwilling to invest further capital. If a lease be given he will farm with spirit and will improve the property.

Mrs. Taylor died in Nice on 21 January 1864. Francis remained in occupation, paying an annual rent of £275. The farm was sold in 1865 while Francis was still there, and J.O.P.'s agency was brought to an end.

One can only conclude, comparing this set of letters with many others in the Parker collection, that the Taylor family were exceedingly lucky in their agent, who found them a tenant such as Francis, able to put money in the farm and, compared with others during those hard days, comparatively prompt, producing the full rent every half-year.

CHAPTER XI

THE LANDLORD AS TENANT

CHRISTOPHER COMYNS PARKER took a lease of Bovills
Marsh Farm in the parish of Mayland shortly before his death,
for £420 per annum, with the idea of carrying out an experi-
ment in the growing of corn on land formerly marsh pastures.
This had been done with some success in various places, and in
the few years before 1843, the year of his death, when the
farmers were recovering to some extent from the disasters of the
early thirties, the idea appealed to him. When he died, his son
was left as tenant, paying £400 a year rent. During the recession
of 1849–50, however, he found that the farm was not promising
as well as he and his father had hoped. On 10 December 1849
he therefore wrote to the landlord asking not for an abatement
of rent but that an experienced surveyor should go over the
farm and give an unbiased opinion as to its value:

I flatter myself that you will give me credit for not being inclined to
trouble you with a recital of grievances and complaints unless there
was, at all events in my opinion, fair ground for the application
which I now venture to make to you. . . .

The rent which you have received of me for the Bovills Marshes
for the last two years has been entirely out of capital and not from
the produce of the farm, and I therefore now beg that you will take
into consideration the altered circumstances of the time. . . .

My father took the farm for the present lease under somewhat
peculiar circumstances, and from the unwillingness to give up the
occupation of this farm while the adjoining farm was still held under
an old lease, he was induced, with the liberty of ploughing up a
certain portion of the grass, to give an enormous rent for it. The
advantage of ploughing up these marshes has never been realised to
the extent that he then anticipated, and in good times the farm has
barely paid its way, but my losses are now so severe that I cannot help

174

appealing to you, and I trust that the manner in which I have done so, will suffice to show you that I do not wish you to depend upon my statement alone. . . .

The farm was owned at that time by two sisters, Mrs. Mary Frere and Miss E. Forster. Mrs. Frere conducted the correspondence. Her reply was not reassuring:

With regard to your application, my friends consider it (as I do) at all events very *premature*.

Mr. Hotchkiss informs me that he has just been receiving rents from various partys; and that not one tenant has said more than, 'Well, sir, *if things do not improve in the course of another year or so*, we shall have to hope for some abatement etc etc.

It was but lately that corn bore a most extravagant price, meat was also high (and tenants do not come forward on such occasions *to volunteer increased rents*).

Moreover both Miss Forster and myself have to remember the hundreds of pounds which for a course of years your father persuaded my husband, for himself and Major F. to abate, which our friends have considered a great mistake and which, *if he had consulted an experienced surveyor*, would not have been sanctioned.

Of this neglect you, as your father's son, have reaped the benefit.

And when you mention having paid the 2 past yrs. rent out of capital, I must beg to quote the words of an excellent man and tenant of Downing Coll., who said to me,

'We must expect to take the *rough with the smooth*, and if in a bad year or two I have had to draw money from the bank to pay my rent, I must remember that for *many a year* I have been making good savings out of my profits from which, when a bad year comes, I must expect to draw, and not to flinch directly the shoe pinches etc etc.'

Moreover, I cannot agree to all the complaints of the times. As to corn, the *increased quantity* grown by improved management makes up the difference. (We grow 9 Coomb wheat per acre instead of 6.) Corn *was lower* with the Corn Laws in full operation when I was in England in '38 and '39, still more so I believe in '35 and '36, but I myself did not much *then* attend to it.

If all things come down equally we shall be as when my father said in 1798 often, that wheat ought never to be more than 5 shillings a bushel.

Many things *are come down*—not the 'fashionable', coachmakers,

milliners, tailors etc, but very good and respectable tradesmen, many
articles of daily use much dropped.

Our Poor have never been so well off as now, near me, with wages
at 8 shillings and employed, their families were starving on 12
shillings when corn was high and clothes etc, and 16/– per week
would never have made up the difference.

To all appeals for a surveyor Mrs. Frere had the same answer
—a lengthy treatise on economic matters with the facts twisted
to suit her own particular point of view. Her tenant knew from
his own experience that her conclusions were entirely unjusti-
fied. Her parting shot in the letter quoted above was that Miss
Forster had in her possession a letter from C.C.P. to her father,
Major Forster, in which he expressly stated that it was at his
son's wish that he had leased Bovills Marsh Farm. To persuade
a woman such as this to change her mind seemed hopeless, but
on the very next day he answered her arguments. Like her, he
took to underlining his main points:

Your rent is high, whatever might be the price of corn, but up to this
time, though I have got little out of the farm for myself, I have always
paid the rent *punctually*, if not *cheerfully*, and nothing but a sense of
real justice to myself would have led me to make the application I
have done.

He went on to say that, with rent and £1000 spent on
buildings, the farm had not paid its way, nor could it be
expected to do so. In good times he himself had volunteered
increased rents to landlords from whom he had leased farms,
and the abatements his father had had on Bovills Marsh had
been completely justified. (29 December 1849.)

Mrs. Frere replied two days later asking if he would like to
purchase the farm, and by giving an account of her losses on
her other property, the only exception being a farm of a
hundred acres which, with the newest methods, was doing well
in every way and yielding greatly increased crops (31 December
1849).

This implication that he, too, could make a farm pay if only

176

he improved his methods of farming, touched him on a very tender spot and brought forth an immediate reply. At this very time, he was recommending abatements all round, to the landlords for whom he acted, but he himself could not even get the favour of a surveyor's visit.

I thank you for your reply to my letter and for the offer of the purchase of Bovills Marshes, but I beg to say that I am not a purchaser and I should think them a *very bad purchase* at anything like the usual number of years at the present rent.

. . . It [the farm] is not worth the rent I pay for it, and I have only endeavoured to place this fact fairly before you and without any wish to *cajole* or '*compliment*' you out of your income. I have been obliged to reduce the rent of land belonging to myself at the present time. . . . The adjoining farm to yours is of the same size and *equally good in every respect*. I now hold it under a recent renewal granted according to the valuation of a surveyor with whom I had no communication whatever, at 40 per cent less than I pay to you. (1 January 1850.)

The next letter was from Miss Forster, who wrote:

. . . Mrs. Frere has written, and has said *exactly* what I would have wish'd to say. The share in that farm is by far the largest portion of my *all*, and I am quite sure Mrs. F. is as ill able as I am to bear any reduction. *Much* against my father's will it was miserably reduced by Mr. Frere on y^r father's constant plea of inability to go on, and after all, he proved how well he knew its real value by what he agreed at last to give rather than lose it because he had held it so long and because 'his son wish'd for it'. (10 January 1850.)

Mrs. Frere was sorry that he was unable to purchase Bovills Marsh, pointing out that if he paid £10,000 for the farm he would get it for what yielded only £300 a year in the funds. She then proceeded to treat him to another discourse in economics:

I do not consider that there is any real ground to suppose that the present is more a time of depression than has *often* been seen before, in the vicissitudes of prices which took place when Corn Laws were in *full force* and we are able to meet the present prices by the improved quantity of corn grown (we ourselves on poor heath land grow 9 coomb per acre where 5 or at the *outside* six was considered possible by the oldfashioned farmers, who still allow all the finest portions of the compost to evaporate etc etc)—then again as to beasts—by always keeping them warm and well-fed from the first we can sell ours (on the comparative small scale of 100 acre occupation I allow) to the Butcher a year younger than used to be thought of. I speak practically, therefore I am now estimating at £1 per acre for *my Rent*. . . . (11 January 1850.)

So the controversy went on, J.O.P. keeping back a portion of the rent and pleading with the landlords to send a competent man to look over and value the farm, while Mrs. Frere consulted her agent, L. Hotchkiss, of The Mall, Kensington, and others:

All have agreed in dissuading us from making any abatement *as up to Mich^s last*, at all events, and then to see what changes this current year may produce.

They consider that the *years* that a reduction of rent made to meet a *temporary* state of things having been *allowed by us to go on long after the reason for it ceased* ought to be balanced against the short period since prices were *exorbitantly* high etc etc. (20 May 1851.)

This letter produced from J.O.P. the most bitter observation, that

If the farm were in the hands of an ordinary farmer it w^d *inevitably be thrown up* [i.e. by the tenant] but because I happen to be in a different position and am supposed to be capable of meeting the obligations of the lease, you hold me to the bargain and refuse any sort of enquiry into my statement. This hardly comes within my interpretation of fair dealing and certainly is not the sort of treatment that either in my own case I sh^d accord to a tenant of my own, nor sh^d I feel justified in acting, as the agent for other parties. (23 May 1851.)

His plea seems to have met with partial success, for, after a second letter, written on 14 April 1852, not a surveyor but Mr. Hotchkiss himself came down from London to see the farm. His visit resulted in a 10 per cent abatement for a limited period, and very grudgingly given.

. . . we have decided to throw off for this once, from the year's rent up to Mich^s '51, the round sum of Forty Pounds, which is Ten per

Cent on the £400, but which ought rather to be considered as for the year from '49 to '50 than from '50 to '51 as both Mr. B. J. L. Frere and Mr. G[urdon] Rebow [her nephew] consider.

Mrs. Frere continued to enlighten her tenant on various interesting points of husbandry and agricultural history that tempt one to go on quoting from her letters. On the question of substituting general farming for the growing of wheat, J.O.P. would have agreed with her:

Depend on it *we* (that is we English) have been very unwise in so much giving up the breeding and rearing of *good* stock, (whilst the *Wheat Mania* was fostered by the laws) so that it will take some time to get good stock *plentiful* enough for the grazier to *buy cheap*, but if we can look forward to an abundant and cheap supply, I believe the *immense increase of meat eating* in the lower classes will bring agricultural affairs round again. . . .

She enclosed a short note from Miss Forster in this letter, which again puts their case against the tenant:

I will not delay any longer writing to say that if *you* think it right to *throw back* £40 off the rent to last Mich^s I am satisfied to do so, although I must say I do *not* think Mr. Parker has any claim to it at our hands, for the probable injury his speculation has permanently caused to 50 acres of our fine marshes by breaking them up, which he was only allowed to do in consideration of his paying a *good* rent and being a thoroughly responsible tenant. (29 April 1852.)

Though the abatement was granted for one year only, it seems to have been continued, for in 1853 he was paying £360 a year

which is really more than the farm is worth. I am not the person to grumble without good cause for it, but the lease of this farm is a stone round my neck. (To Miss Forster, 19 April 1853.)
. . . merely because I happen to be able to pay better than some people would be, I don't see why I should be denied the redress which must have been conceded to a common farmer. (To Mrs. Frere, 19 April 1853.)

Neither was he satisfied with these temporary year-to-year abatements:

I cannot avoid again repeating that if I had considered it a mere matter of 10 per cent abatement you never w^d have heard from me. I again say that it is a peculiar case which is not met by a reduction of this nature, and I am confident that the report of an indifferent person taken from actual view of the farm would even induce you to come to the same conclusion. You have mentioned Mr. Gurdon Rebow as one of the parties to whom you had mentioned the matter. I know him to be really a practical man of business and if he would undertake a friendly reference in the matter I should be perfectly satisfied to leave myself in his hands. If something of this kind was done in a fair spirit you would hear nothing from me afterwards whatever might be the result. (18 May 1853.)

He got no satisfaction whatever. The rent was put back to its former level, and he retaliated by withholding some of it. In May 1856 he received a letter signed by both Mrs. Frere and Miss Forster repeating the old arguments that he and his father had broken up fifty acres of 'beautiful pasture' and that the entire responsibility was his. Indeed, they said, they would never have allowed any farmer to have committed such an act had they not known him to be a man of substance whose rent they could be quite certain of receiving in full.

Thus, throughout the whole period of the lease, J.O.P. never succeeded in getting the landlords to send the surveyor he had continually asked for. In 1860 the lease came to an end and Mr. Frere's son at first intended to sell the farm. However, in September 1861 he changed his mind after paying a visit to the farm, and decided that if he could not let it he would keep it in hand. J.O.P. then instructed William Beadel of Chelmsford to negotiate for the farm, and he secured it for one year only at a rent of £400. J.O.P. was quite satisfied with this arrangement.

He will be able to look for a good tenant and I shall have time to arrange the selection and diminution of the flock etc.

At the end of the lease J.O.P. had considerable claims for reimbursement on account of buildings he had put up on the farm. In this too he met a disappointment. His solicitor, Fred

Chancellor, informed him that he was not likely to get everything to which he thought himself entitled:

I have had Mr. Clark with me to-day in reference to Bovills Marsh but I have not yet been able to come to any satisfactory arrangement with him. The first point raised was that he was only bound to pay for those buildings actually named in the lease, for instance the lease described a 4-roomed cottage; a double cottage has been built and he proposes to pay for about half the value of the double cottage. He declines also to pay for the 2 sheds, also for the chaff and harness house in connection with stable, also the walls and fences all round and the formation of yards.

I argue that the spirit of the Covenant was that you were to put up a homestall and spend not less than £800 in its erection, and after the manner in which the work has been done, I consider it very ungracious on the part of the lessors to cavil at the arrangement of the buildings. I told Mr. Clark that I must ask him to refer back to his Principal before we proceeded in the matter, as I could not on your behalf admit the justice of the basis of his valuation, and I thought upon consideration his clients would agree with me that they should pay the value of the buildings as they are.

Have you any evidence of the Lessors or their agents at any time expressing their satisfaction with the buildings? (28 September 1861.)

No complaints on the part of the tenant could move Mrs. Frere's son to pay more than was stipulated as a minimum figure in the lease. On 4 November 1841 J.O.P. received a letter from Frere's solicitor:

My clients are willing to waive the wording of the lease according to my construeing, if we limit the extreme amount to be paid to £800. i.e. they will not pay more than the £800 of the value if the buildings walls and fences exceed that sum but as much less as our valuation comes to; on receiving your reply in the affirmative, I will proceed to a final valuation.

The amount he finally received was £730 5s. 6d. Chancellor described the whole proceeding as 'rather shabby', Beadel as 'very ungentlemanly'.

He was now taking the farm from year to year. In February 1863 he offered £370.

It is clear that we differ in our opinion as to the value of the marshes, but I am quite willing to test my estimate and am willing to continue your tenant from year to year at such rent as two indifferent persons shall set upon them. (2 February 1863.)

He could at first get no satisfaction. It was only a firm notice to quit in March that persuaded the landlord to accept his terms. He then consented to keep the farm, stating:

I have no wish unduly to depreciate your property, but I have throughly satisfied myself that it is not worth my while to retain the occupation at anything like the present level. . . .

So far as regards the owners, I think you are greatly mistaken in this matter. It was taken with great expectations of the result of breaking up a portion of the land. This was not fully realised, but the owners all the same for more than 20 years have received an excessive rent. . . .

In March 1865 he was given the first offer of the farm for £10,000.

Pray do not think of me in the matter [he replied]. I should not entertain the idea of purchasing for a moment. I have always given Mr. Frere to understand that the rent that I pay is beyond the value of the farm, and I believe the result of the sale will prove it. I shall be surprized if the farm sh^d realize more than £8,000.

In 1866 his prophecy was proved correct. The landlord could not sell.

In Mr. Beadel's opinion the rent is 20 per cent beyond the value, and now that you have tried to sell it, you must know that the public are of the same opinion.

For ten years longer he held the farm. There is no indication in the diaries that he paid less than £370. In 1877 he declared that he would no longer pay more than £300, as farms of a like value in the same district were being let at £275. (4 March 1877.) Two years later the owners engaged a surveyor who reported that the farm was worth £300 a year, the tenant paying the tithe. J.O.P. accepted the report, as he had always promised he would, and continued to hold the farm at that rent. In 1884, however, when he sent his cheque, he accompanied it with the following note:

You may consider yourselves exceptionally fortunate in getting in this rent as you do. I can't get my own!

The next year he asked for a reduction owing to the agricultural depression:

Some abatement ought to be allowed at the present time, and if I should be permitted to go on at £250 a year I will try it for a time, but otherwise I shall be obliged to give it up. (10 February 1885.)

The landlord does not seem to have been willing to consider this, and on 23 March he gave notice to quit at Michaelmas unless the rent was reduced. The reply was characteristic of the people with whom he had to deal.

Your tenancy being a yearly tenancy from Michaelmas, under the Agricultural Holdings Act, you have to give a twelve months' notice ending at Michaelmas in order to determine the tenancy so that your letter of the 23rd March last cannot possibly be a notice to determine before Michaelmas 1886.

Thus ended a correspondence lasting over half a century. There is no note in the diary as to the exact date on which Bovill's Marsh Farm was vacated.

One cannot but feel that he was very shabbily treated.

CHAPTER XII

RAILWAYS

IN THE AUTUMN OF 1830 Christopher Comyns Parker spent his second honeymoon touring, by private carriage, the main beauty spots and historic towns of the south of England. At the same period his son made his regular journeys by coach to and from Oxford. C.C.P.'s letters to his friends coming to visit him always instruct them to catch the Tally Ho coach from Gray's Inn coffee house in London. This passed his drive gate on the way to Maldon. Twelve years later, J.O.P. records in his diary:

March 1st, 1842. Started by G.W. Railway to Totnes, quartered at the 7 Stars.

Within that twelve years had begun the most stupendous social revolution that has occurred in England at any time. The coaching age, the age of Sam Weller, Mr. Pickwick and his cronies, ended before the steam-driven monster. In 1829 George Stephenson had won the Manchester to Liverpool prize with his 'Rocket'. Slowly at first, but then with increasing momentum, steam overwhelmed coaching. Up to December 1835 there were five private railway acts; in 1836–7 there were thirty-nine. The railway mania had begun. By 1850, £230,000,000 of private capital had been invested in them, and thousands of miles of line had been laid. Towns which had done all they could to keep the hated railway out were now petitioning the companies to have the lines brought into them. Landowners and country gentlemen now wanted the railway to come in their direction, though kept invisible from their terraces or mansion windows by means of tunnel or cutting. Money was attracted from all classes of society. Much was gained by the few, more was lost by the many, and new personalities rose, typical of the Railway Age.

The problems of creating a railway were many. Before a single turf was cut, surveyors and engineers had to be engaged and valuers had to accompany them along the proposed line. Then the interested people in the district had to be canvassed and as much support as possible obtained from them, even to the point of giving some of them a seat on the Board of Directors. Prospectuses had to be written giving details of the projected line, the amenities the promoters hoped to provide, and particulars of numbers and value of shares. Support had to be got for the Bill which had to go through Parliament, and, once passed, the long and complicated business began of settling claims for payment for land required for the line. Sometimes direct negotiation between company and landowner was sufficient to do this; if that proved too difficult arbitrators were appointed, and if they failed to agree the matter was referred to an umpire.

Christopher Comyns Parker and his son had little to do with the promotion of railway companies, but they assisted in some measure in settling claims for land. Sometimes they acted on behalf of a company, sometimes for their old clients when they made claims on a company, and occasionally J.O.P. acted as umpire.

The first entry in the Parker diaries with regard to railways is dated 20 September 1837:

Wrote to Mr. Robertson in relation to the Eastern Counties Railway Company.

In 1836 this company had obtained parliamentary sanction for the making of a line from Shoreditch through Romford, Brentwood, Chelmsford, and Colchester to Norwich and Yarmouth, and notices had been served on the owners of property over which the line was to run, informing them of what land would be required, and of the steps that were to be taken to procure it. The letter from J. C. Robertson, who was secretary to the company at the time, asked C.C.P. to give, together with eight other 'professional gentlemen', his opinion on certain matters which were in dispute between the Company on the one hand and Lord Petre and Mr. Peter Caesar Labouchere on the other. This involved seven to eight miles of the proposed line.

It appears, from the instructions given to these nine professional gentlemen, that before the passing of the Act an agreement had been entered into by which the company should pay Lord Petre £20,000 for the value of the premises to be taken, and £100,000 as compensation for injury done to his estate, and that Mr. Labouchere of Hylands, near Chelmsford, whose son Henry was a Privy Councillor and Vice-President of the Board of Trade at that time, should receive £5000 and £30,000 as similar compensation and 'to induce him to withdraw his opposition to the Act'.

The validity of these agreements is intended to be contested by the Company on the ground among others of the sums conditioned to be paid Lord Petre and Mr. Labouchere being enormously disproportionable to the real value of the land which will be taken from them, and to the actual injury they will respectively sustain.

The grounds of the claims of Lord Petre were clearly stated in the surveyors' instructions: that the projected line was to pass through the Thorndon estate within a short distance of the mansion built by Lord Petre's grandfather at a cost of more than £250,000, in which he, Lord Petre, was then resident for more than nine months out of every year, and that 'it would inconveniently cross and intersect the road and principal approach thereto from Brentwood and within view from the windows of all the principal apartments'.

that the construction of the Railway according to the route described would ruin the Mansion House as a family residence, that the privacy and retirement of it would make such an inroad upon His

Lordship's pursuits upon his Estate and on his enjoyment thereof that he must certainly quit Thorndon Hall and seek a residence elsewhere.

Lord Petre also claimed that his most valuable farms would be severed in a most injurious manner, particularly that of Margaretting Hall, where the railway would pass within a few yards of 'an excellent residence standing thereon on the one side and the Parish Church on the other'. Mr. Labouchere stated similar grounds for his claim. The surveyors were asked to say whether the facts given by the two claimants were true in every detail. One interesting question follows:

Supposing Lord Petre were actually forced by the Railway to seek another residence elsewhere, for how much his Lordship might build such another Mansion as Thorndon Hall (deducting the value of the present house as old materials).

The directors, however, probably deeming such a question might lead them into too much expense, had it ruled out, and there is a note in the margin, 'not to be estimated'. The final question asks how much the two gentlemen ought to be paid, 'taking a large and liberal view of the whole circumstances of the case'.

On 26 September C.C.P. met the eight other gentlemen at Brentwood, and on 4 October he went over the proposed route, giving his opinion in writing on the following day. The unanimous verdict of the surveyors must have been a great disappointment to Lord Petre. They stated that the railway would pass Thorndon Hall at a distance of more than a mile, that it would not be in view of any of the principal windows, and that where it cut the road of approach to the Hall it would not pass through land belonging to Lord Petre. The riding and recreation of Lord Petre and his family would not be adversely affected. The soil through which the railway was to pass varied considerably in quality and the surveyors could give no answer on the question of severance until they knew the existing letting arrangements. Thorndon Hall would not be ruined as a residence for a nobleman accustomed to live there for nine months of the year, nor would the estates of Mr. Labouchere be more seriously affected.

Taking a large and liberal view of the whole circumstances of the case, it will be proper for the Company to pay Lord Petre by way of price for the quantity of land required from His Lordship the sum of Three Thousand six hundred pounds and Sixteen thousand four hundred pounds by way of compensation for the injury he will sustain.

And . . . taking a like view of all circumstances it will be proper for the Company to pay Mr. Labouchere Four thousand pounds.

. . . The advantages, however great, to the large and contiguous property, farms etc., belonging to the Claimants, of a rail road communication with the Metropolis etc., we have not set off or taken into our consideration.

Their concluding remarks as to the future benefits of the Railway Age are interesting:

The Railway, especially as it respects the views from Thorndon Hall, is by the Engineer's designed line and consequent deep cuttings, and from the natural circumstances of the intervening Country, as well as the distance, very much masked, and continues to be so for a considerable extent, and we do really believe will be found when executed to be little if at all objectionable to any resident Gentleman or Gentlemen, and to some we know, that a complete view, at such a remove, of the practical adaptation of Science to the purposes of national industry and prosperity would be highly delightful.

From that time onward, railway entries become more frequent in the diaries and letters. In June 1838 C.C.P. was again engaged on behalf of the Eastern Counties Railway Company when they bought some eight acres of land in South Weald from the Tower family. For this an award of £700 and a further £832 10s. for the value of severance was made by an umpire. He also seems to have been occupied in some cases on behalf of landowners, making claims on the company.

21st May, 1838. Attended at Mr. Edward Walford's, Chipping Hill to view his lands to be taken by the E.C.R. Company and consulted with him as to the proposed claim to be made for same and for his

lands at Boreham which I had previously viewed. Attending
Directors when I ultimately obtained £2350. Attending Mr. A.
Johnson to renew his claim when we obtained £1050. Attended for
Sir John Tyrrell and had from the Directors an assurance that the
line described in the 56th Clause of the Act should not be departed
from unless by consent. Agreed for Mr. Copeland to call at Boreham
to arrange claim for land.

May 5th, 1838. Attended Directors of E.C. Railway to make claim
for Mr. Spencer Phillips but not having particulars deferred to next
meeting.

In the same year he was concerned in the negotiations for the
purchase by the Railway Company of the Chelmsford lands
belonging to Lady Mildmay, consisting principally of the Town
Field, on which the present Chelmsford Station stands.

25th May, 1838. Looked over lands Lady Mildmay's for Railway
Claim.

Lady Mildmay obtained £10,000, not including any sum for
compensation. This was the largest claim C.C.P. was concerned
in with this company.

Meanwhile the construction of the line was progressing. The
work had begun in March 1837. On 18 June 1839 the line was
opened as far as Romford, and on 1 June 1840 it reached
Brentwood. While the extension to Chelmsford was being made,
land was being bought up on the farther stretches of the line,
and on 26 May 1838 C.C.P. was appointed umpire in a dispute
between Cowlin Everett, occupier and owner of Feering Mill,
and the Company. The award was made on 3 July 1840. The
claimant was very dissatisfied with it.

I will venture to state that there is not a parallel case in the whole
line where an individual has received such a scanty remuneration. I
do consider I am severely dealt with.

Nevertheless, three years later, when extra land belonging to
the same person came to be wanted, C.C.P. refused to alter his
opinion.

Being informed by Mr. Beadel that more land has been taken and that Mr. Cowlin Everett was not satisfied with the price stipulated by my award and that I be requested to review the same,

I have carefully inspected my minutes made June 22nd, 1840, and have inspected the premises and find the additional lands taken is in parallel lines with what was originally set out, therefore in no way injuring the property of Mr. Everett otherwise than by loss of quantity. I cannot see any reason to alter my former opinion of value and must still consider Mr. Everett liberally remunerated by being paid at the rate of £135 an acre.

All through the late thirties and the early forties schemes for making railways, many of them abortive, were being drawn up. Some of them reached Parliament and were embodied in Acts. One of these was the proposed railway from Romford to Shell Haven which we first hear of in 1838 in a circular to the owners of land along the proposed track, in which connection C.C.P. was engaged to act for Mr. George Spitty of Stanford-le-Hope, Miss Hanson of East Horndon, the Sir John Hawkins Hospital which held land at Stanford-le-Hope, and others. Four years later in connection with the same scheme he was acting for his old clients Thoyts of Barking.

In 1845, Oliver Hering, an old friend of the family and lessee of Heybridge Hall, wrote an interesting letter about the proposed 'abominable' lines which were planned to cut across his farm.

The Witham–Braintree scheme is bad enough as it necessitates the breaking up of Beales Meadow, the Hope, the Stone etc etc, but the Chelmsford–Blackwater Schedule is most atrocious, running through almost every field in the whole farm, through the garden, the lawns, over the cottages, and then the mill meadows and the other grass-lands. I don't know what my tenants may think of all this devastation, but I am determined to oppose it.

J.O.P., however, was interested in this line, for he had attended at the offices of the line on 1 December.

No meeting in consequence of the Solicitors being quite knocked up with preparing papers and plans for depositing at the Board of Trade.

In June 1847 Hering received his notice from the Maldon, Witham and Braintree Railway Company that some of his land would be wanted, and on 2 July the purchase of nearly four acres was agreed on at a cost of £1150. In August 1848 the line had been partly constructed and more land had been taken by the Company than had been agreed on. Additional compensation had to be arranged. In November J.O.P. went over the ground with Beadel:

November 10th, Attending at Maldon Station to meet Mr. Beadel and Mr. Douglas with reference to approaches to be given by Railway Company to marsh beyond the line in occupation of Mr. G. G. Ward, and as to alteration of crossing over line in Stone Meadow. Mr Beadel agreed to give a double-mouthed crossing over the line at the old pathway into Stone and Hope Meadow and to give to G. G. Ward a passage under the viaduct for cattle and along . . . the line from the causeway for carts. The compensation for non-fulfilment of original contract to be left for further consideration of Mr. Beadel and self.

On 19 January 1849 the following entry appears:

Asked for £200 but agreed to accept £150 as compensation for land taken for siding to navigation and further severance occasioned by proposed right of way from the Causeway.

At the same time as this was going on he was engaged on behalf of General Bourchier in obtaining compensation from the Stour Valley Railway Company for land taken from his estate at Bures. After two inspections of the line, on 10 and 19 March 1847, he put in a claim on 3 April for £1000. On 4 May he 'walked over the line of railway in course of construction' and found that the level of a crossing had been altered on Mount Hall Farm. He complained about this to the engineer, and on 6 June

Attending Mr. Fisher and had long conversation with him respecting crossing upon Mount Hall Farm and land taken by the Company in the formation of gangway to approach same. Agreed that I should have measurement taken of land actually taken by Railway including the bank or incline in question.

On the 13th he went again to Mount Bures and found a crossing nearly twelve feet high, with approaches taking up nearly a rood of land. For two months he tried unsuccessfully to get an interview with the representative of the Company. On 5 August he succeeded in seeing him at Colchester and registering his complaint:

Claimed archway over line . . . and payment for additional land taken pro rata with amount paid for original quantity. Mr. Downes did not admit that the level crossing . . . was not to be more than 4 ft high as stated by me to be the agreement with him, but allowed that he did not expect it to be 13 feet, and allowed also that the contractors have acted unwarrantably in taking the other land. Stated that I was willing to accept either an archway or compensation, but that unless a satisfactory offer was made . . . I should use the legal hold which the land taken without notice gave me upon the Company.

Only one letter with regard to this transaction survives. In it J.O.P. mentions a payment by him of ten guineas for a second opinion on the extent of the claim:

This you may remember was with your concurrence and I feel that the money was well spent as it quite put a stop to any opposition to the amount of the claim, and enabled me to substantiate the sum of £1000.

With regard to the further encroachment and the extra payment for it, he has this to add:

I cannot conclude without again expressing my regret and annoyance that you [Col. Bouchier] should have been put to so much inconvenience by the Railway Company. I am only sorry that I considered that I was treating with gentlemen who would not forfeit their word when pledged to me, whereas in spite of their most positive assurances, they have altogether failed to fulfil their engagements then made to me. In my last letter to the Solicitors I gave them fully to understand what I thought of their conduct. One of the Directors informed me on Friday that the cheque for £700 was drawn so that I now really hope there will not be any further delay in transmitting it. (13 November 1848.)

Essex, like many other counties, abounded in abortive

schemes for railways during this crazy decade. One of them, mentioned above, was the Chelmsford–Blackwater Scheme. Another was the proposed South Essex Railway which was to run over land in the Rochford Hundred for which he was agent:

March 4th, 1846. To Mr. Thomas Parker in answer to letter requesting me to attend at Eastwood with reference to land to be taken for South Essex Railway.

April 7th, 1846. Met Lord Wynford by appointment at the Carlton Club; had conversation with him as to proposed South Essex Railway.

A third was the proposed Gravesend Railway. This affected lands in Barking owned by the Thoyts family.

Attending Mr. Dean by appointment. Had long conversation with him as to conditional purchase of land at Barking for the N. Gravesend Railway Co. . . . Quantity 5a, 3r, 12p. Claimed £1200. Mr. Dean on behalf of the Company offered £1000. . . . (30 April 1846.)

In June 1852 the Act authorising the construction of a railway from London to Tilbury and Southend received royal assent. It was to leave the main line of the Eastern Counties Railway at Forest Gate and pass through Barking on its way into south-east Essex. The course of the line had already been planned, and within two months landowners received notices telling them what land would be required by the London, Tilbury and Southend Railway Company for their works. Among these were M. G. Thoyts (Barking), Sir J. H. Pelly (Aveley), Sir Charles Smith (Vange), the Rev. George Heathcote and the Hon. Payan Dawnay (Pitsea). All four engaged J.O.P. to act on their behalf.

The negotiations which he conducted with the engineers and solicitors of the new company lasted some three and a half years, and entailed innumerable letters, visits and attendances at meetings. Prior to any claims being made out on behalf of landowners, the requirements of the Company had to be

checked, and the interests of landlord and tenant had to be
ascertained. In some places where the line made awkward
severance not only had the landlord to be compensated but the
tenant too, and facilities in the shape of level-crossings, fences,
bridges, or archways through embankments had to be provided.
Where deviations from the original track were planned,
additional compensation had to be arranged. The work in
progress had constantly to be visited to see that the terms of the
agreements were kept, especially as far as a tenant's access to
his land was concerned; and where the line interfered with
farm buildings, others had to be put up at the company's
expense at convenient places. Where harvests had to be interfered with, or tenants had to remove corn from their barns that
had to be taken down, compensation had to be given.

In November 1952 M. G. Thoyts received £1400. His tenant,
T. L. Coppin, received in the following January £15. In
addition to compensation, his rent was reduced owing to the
railway having taken some of his land. This kind of thing
happened all along the line, and occasioned countless disagree-
ments between landlord and tenant. Coppin claimed a reduction of £20 in his rent. His landlord, on the advice of J.O.P., was
willing to grant him £5 and to agree to the erection of buildings
to the extent of £50 on the farm he rented.

I daresay that a good deal of inconvenience has been experienced
during the construction of the line and before the crossings have
become level, and solid, but he will soon *get used to it* and will then
think nothing of it. (J.O.P. to M.G. Thoyts, 18 May 1853.)

The claims of Major Thoyts and Sir J. H. Pelly were fairly
quickly dealt with. Those of Sir Charles Smith and the Rev.
George Heathcote took much longer because they concerned
not only the construction of a line but also a deviation from the
original plan in 1853, for which the consent of the justices had
to be obtained, and necessitated the construction of new farm
buildings.

August 8th 1853. Attending at Pitsea Hall to meet Mr. Norton to consult with him as to claim to be made for compensation at Pitsea Hall and form in which same should be delivered in. Went over land and buildings and decided to have estimate of reconstruction of house and such buildings as must be removed taken, so as to produce in support of claim. Claim to be for 'land taken, special severance of fields cut by line, damage to wharf and reconstruction of buildings'.

On 20 March J.O.P. visited Beadel of Chelmsford with regard to the compensation claims at Vange and Pitsea.

Stated that I would agree to settle Sir Charles Smith's case at £500 for landlord and £50 for tenant. Mr. Beadel stated that he would endeavour to come to my terms. Also offered to accept £2250 as compensation for land and removal of buildings at Pitsea Hall. Mr. Beadel said that he would report my offer and endeavour to come to terms.

These terms were apparently agreed to by the Company some four days later, and the owners of Pitsea Hall now had to erect the new buildings. The removal of the old ones was commenced forthwith.

At first it was proposed to make the station at Vange, in the lane leading to the wharf, on land owned by Sir Charles Smith. An entry in the diary for 29 May 1854, however, seems to indicate that farmers in the locality did not favour the choice of site:

[Called] in Mr. Fowler respecting station at Vange Wharf. Saw Mr. Bridgman and explained locality to him and informed him of meeting of farmers etc. at Wickford Castle, and proposal to memorialize the Directors.

J.O.P. seems to have favoured Vange as the best location, but on 22 July a meeting was held at Pitsea of all parties interested. The general opinion seems to have been in favour of Pitsea, for on 14 August,

at Messrs Crowder and Maynards and afterwards with Mr. Bridgman with respect to land required for station at Pitsea Hall.

He was now pressing the Company's solicitors to pay for the

additional land required for the station at the same rate as for that which they had bought for the line. An interesting entry in the diary for 25 September runs:

[Called] on Messrs Crowder and Maynard as to 'pro rata' price for land taken at Pitsea Hall—that it sh^d be calculated on the basis of the original price agreed for the land, £750 and not £600 as afterwards arranged for the sake of avoiding the Stamp Duty.

Actually the total cost at first agreed on had been £750 for the land and £1500 for the buildings. This had been changed to avoid duty to £600 for the land and £1650 for the buildings. After some hesitation they agreed to pay £150 instead of the £135 they had originally promised, £100 for the land and £50 for the expense of making a fence.

Other questions arose. The tenant of the Hall was required to move his corn out of the barn which was to be taken down, and received £20 compensation. Then there was the question of access to the new station. There had been a bridle-path running to the boundary of the grounds of Pitsea Hall. Now it was necessary to continue this to the railway. It transpired that the former had been kept in order by the parish. The latter, after some altercation, was taken over by the Company, and J.O.P. consented to fence it, planting quick or thorn with a temporary fence to protect the trees while young. By the middle of 1856 all major questions concerning the railway had been settled. In March of that year the original single line was brought into use, and the doubling of the line was completed in June.

Up to this time J.O.P. had often acted either for a company or for a landowner, or as valuer or umpire, but he had never taken a principal part in the promoting of any railway venture. Nor had he ever had any intention of so doing, until, on the 15 March 1858, he received a telegraphic message from a certain Mr. J. Oakley asking for an interview at Woodham Mortimer.

Answered that I would await his arrival in the morning.

Oakley came down by the first train from London bringing

with him news of a scheme originated by Sir Morton Peto, one of the foremost railway promoters in the country, to make a line from Tilbury, through Maldon, to Colchester,

and desired that I should undertake to see parties along the line and obtain consent to the proposal.

There is no indication that J.O.P. knew anything about this proposal before Oakley, who was Sir Morton Peto's surveyor, broached it to him. He was certainly the right man to approach, for besides being a landowner at Woodham Mortimer, through which the line was planned to pass, he was agent for many acres in the Barstable and Dengie hundreds and a personal friend of most of the men who were likely to be interested in furthering or preventing the construction of this line.

The proposition seems to have struck him immediately as worth while, for later the same day he went with Oakley to see Lord Rayleigh at Terling Place, and afterwards to Colchester to see G. Round, who was not at home. He therefore gave Oakley a letter of introduction.

After that he flung himself with enthusiasm into the task of getting support for the proposed line from all the gentlemen through whose districts it would pass. On the next day he wrote to Squire Kemble of Runwell and the Rev. George Heathcote, with whom he had had much business in connection with the London, Tilbury and Southend Line at Pitsea. On the 18th he went round the Woodham Ferrers District and obtained the consent of all he met to the proposal. On the 19th he was at Maldon where he made six visits, and later, at home, wrote six letters on the subject. On the 20th he visited four persons in the district round Birch. On the 22nd he was in London to convey to Sir Morton Peto the result of his enquiries.

Met Sir M. Peto and Mr. Whiteman respecting the proposed railway. Reported interviews with various parties and received instructions to see landowners, obtain consent and do all that is possible towards the furtherance of the scheme.

On the 23rd he went to see the owner of property in Berechurch.

Mr. White stated that he sh^d offer no opposition provided the line did not interfere injuriously with the House etc. at Berechurch and proper compensation was made for land taken etc.

The letter he wrote after that visit has been preserved:

I had a very satisfactory interview with Mr. White yesterday. He expressed a hope that the line might be so constructed as not unnecessarily to interfere with the Maypole Farm, and the appearance of the approach to Berechurch Hall, and in case it did so, if no engineering difficulties presented themselves, a slight deviation of the line might be arranged, but beyond this he wished to offer no objection nor to seek more than might be considered fair and reasonable compensation for land taken and injury sustained. I have promised that as soon as I am furnished with the tracings to let him see the proposed line as laid out on the Parish Map.

On the 25th he was again in London, 'and received instructions to go over the line with Mr. Oakley'. This he did the next day, attending a meeting at Colchester, going over the Town and Hythe with reference to the position of stations, branch to the Hythe, etc. The next day, the 27th, he went to Marks Hall to see Mr. Honywood who promised him an answer as to his attitude to the proposed line when he had talked it over with his steward. He went to London again on the 29th to report progress.

By this time the plans of the line were complete, and on 8 September J.O.P. went over the whole course of the railway from Pitsea to Woodham Mortimer with Oakley. On the next day they went as far as Tolleshunt D'Arcy and the 10th was spent in the Colchester district. Within two days he had prepared a report on the value of the land along the proposed line.

Public interest was by this time awakened. The inhabitants of Wickford sent to J.O.P. a memorial urging that the line should pass through their town instead of through Rawreth as had been planned. On the 19th, Sir Morton Peto was himself in Maldon to see the Mayor, and in Colchester, where he met the Mayor and corporation. At Colchester there was 'unanimous vote of approval of Sir M. Peto's explanation of the project of proposed railway'.

On the 20th, after a fortnight of intense activity on account of the proposed railway, J.O.P. went for a short holiday at Sharpham. Up to this time he had acted as adviser and propagandist, but on the 22nd he received a letter from Sir Morton asking him to take a seat on the Board of Directors:

I am aware that from the reckless way in which projects were 'got up' during the Railway Mania that many Country Gentlemen suffered severely from misplaced confidence; in fact, direct lines not wanted and schemes of impracticable character were suggested in all directions, the parties who projected them knowing well that the persons whose names were on the prospectuses were liable. . . .

Now in the line which has brought us together I may fairly assume it is one which will benefit the county and meet with general support from the Landowners.

To the offer Sir Morton added that, to guard the proposed directors against loss in the event of lack of subscribed capital, he proposed to deposit with the bankers of the Company money which would cover any possible loss.

J.O.P. was lukewarm.

I feel most desirous to forward the proposed object by every means in my power, but it is a great question with me whether I should not be able to serve you more efficiently in an independent capacity than as a member of the Board of Directors.

You have thought fit to engage me at present with Mr. Oakley as one of your advisers with reference to the value of the land etc., through which the proposed railway is intended to pass. I do not feel that it would be compatible for me to retain this office if I were to accept your kind proposal, and as a man of business I do not pretend to be indifferent to the consideration that though the one may be the more honorable position the other would be more remunerative. I am quite of opinion that the course you intend to adopt with reference to 'deposit' for the purpose of covering the preliminary expenses etc., must be satisfactory to any one taking a place on the

Board, and I therefore wish you to consider that in making these suggestions I am really desirous that you should turn your mind how my time could be most advantageously employed towards the success of the object in view. (25 September 1856.)

In his reply on 4 October, Sir Morton pressed J.O.P. to accept the seat on the Board for the time being, as it was most important that influential local men should be recruited as directors. Then, when the Bill had been passed, the capital obtained, and the line was certain to be constructed, he could resign from the more influential position and accept the more lucrative one.

Throughout the month of October J.O.P. was engaged answering the many queries which came to him from various landowners, and dealing with the memorial from the people of Wickford. The deviation of the line through that town would, according to estimates, cost some £7500, lengthening the line by nearly three-quarters of a mile, whereas if the line were made as originally planned, the station nearest to Wickford would not be more than a mile from the town.

Under these circumstances you will at once see we should place in serious peril the whole line by adopting the deviation, as it would be truly alleged against us that we were sacrificing the general interests of the public for the sake of a trifling increase of local convenience. (John Fowler to J.O.P., 6 October 1856.)

Fowler does not mention that the mile mentioned involved the climbing of a long if not steep hill. Some twenty-five years later Wickford got its station, and a direct link with London through the London and North Eastern Railway.

In the same month, October 1856, J.O.P. acceded to Sir Morton's request:

I shall be ready to what on consideration is thought best for the success of the project, and as to directors etc, I should be glad to see you and talk over the parties whom it may be advisable to invite to take places at the Board. (15 October 1856.)

On 27 October J.O.P. was again in London,

attending appointment with Sir Morton Peto. Found that I had mistaken his letter, having read Monday for Tuesday, and that he was gone to the Victoria Docks. Went there to dejeuner on board the 'Istamboul' steam clipper. Home by ½ past 6 train. Had conversation with Sir Morton Peto respecting Directors etc etc., and agreed to meet again on a future day.

November and December were taken up with compiling the list of directors and writing the prospectus of the Company. A letter from Oakley on 5 December gives the proposed list, and states:

As far as you are concerned [i.e. on his being a director], he [Sir Morton] puts it very strongly, and that you shall not thereby lose your fees as Surveyor. . . . Sir Morton will deposit such sum as will remove all chance of loss to the Directors.

His friend Squire Kemble also gave his consent to be appointed to the Board.

I wish every success to the Colchester and Tilbury, and in consenting to allow my name to be added to the list of Directors I do so with the hope that my name as a Landowner and resident in the country through which the line will pass, may be of service in promoting the wishes of Sir M. Peto. Should we be successful in obtaining an Act of Parliament, it would be a matter of consideration whether I should continue to act as a Director, as I should not like to undertake the Office unless I could resolve to work at it with the best of my power. . . . (T. Kemble to J.O.P., 8 December 1856.)

The prospectus, dated November 1856, appeared later in December. £700,000 was asked for in subscriptions, and the fourteen provisional directors, a very strong body of local gentlemen, included the mayors of Gravesend, Maldon, and Colchester, five more Colchester gentlemen including George Round, two Maldon gentlemen, Thomas Kemble, J.O.P., and two London businessmen. The line was designed to join Kent and Essex by the steam ferry at Tilbury, and

The line traverses one of the most highly cultivated districts of England, and the moderate cost for which it will be constructed will enable the projectors to offer such a tariff of fares as will secure a large local traffic as well as that to be derived from the East Suffolk railways.

The work, like that of the L.T.S., would be done by Peto, Brassey and Betts, and the line would be leased at 6½ per cent of the profits to Sir Morton Peto for twenty-one years, he depositing £100,000 security for the rent.

In the early months of 1857 Essex became the centre of conflicting railway interests. The proprietor of the *Railway Times*, who was a director of the rival Eastern Counties Railway Company, published in his journal a pamphlet with the title of 'Petovia',

. . . a review of the Scheme for a Railway from Pitsea to Colchester, and an exposure of the motives which prompted it, the absurdities which characterise it, and the inevitable failure which awaits it.

This pamphlet was an attack not only on the projected railway but also on the directors of the London Tilbury and Southend Line which had just been completed. A reply was published and circulated to the shareholders of that line attempting to refute the various charges in the pamphlet. Everything possible was done to rouse interest. From 13 to 15 April J.O.P. was in the Battlesbridge, Latchingdon, and Southminster areas seeing parties whom he thought would be willing to give evidence in support of a Bill for the railway. On the 16th he was at Maldon, and on 4 May he went to London to consult as to who should be called. On Saturday, 9 May, however, a paragraph appeared in *The Times* intimating that the Eastern Counties Railway Company was to take over the East Suffolk lines which Sir Morton had himself hoped to control in his effort to link Gravesend with East Anglia through his new line. The very next day, J.O.P. wrote to C. R. Tyerman, who was to represent the Company in putting the Bill before Parliament:

I have a letter from a brother director intimating that 'our railway scheme is at an end', and that we ought to be reassured that we are not to be called upon for any of the preliminary expenses, etc etc. The understanding has all along been that the Directors would not be called upon for a farthing and I believe that the promise will be fairly and honorably kept, but I want to be able to answer those who apply to me, and therefore shall be glad for a note from you to tell me the meaning of the above rumour, and that no fear of any responsibility need be apprehended.

On the 11th, Tyerman wrote that Sir Morton himself had been surprised by the course matters were taking, 'which has been shaped by a third party largely interested in the Eastern Union'. He reassured J.O.P. that Sir Morton would scrupulously fulfil his financial engagement to the provisional directors. On the 15th the provisional directors met in London when Sir M. Peto announced that in consequence of the state of the money market, the paucity of shares taken up and the proposed arrangement of the Eastern Counties Railway Company to take the East Suffolk lines, the Tilbury and Colchester Bill must be abandoned. Adjourned to the 22nd.

Before the adjourned meeting J.O.P. furnished himself with as full details as possible of the complaints of the people of Maldon and Colchester of the lack of good railway services. Following the meeting, he went with a deputation to the Chairman of the Eastern Counties Railway to put these grievances before him and to argue that another line was necessary. The deputation had little result, for at another meeting on the 25th at Sir Morton Peto's office, after full examination determined to abandon line.

Five days later he met Oakley at Colchester Station and had long conversation with him as to the abandonment of T.M. and C. Railway, and as to bill for survey etc. Stated that I should not make out any Bill myself, but shd leave it to him to see that I was paid for the time and trouble given to the business, but not in any such way as to lead to the supposition that I had taken up the line except as a bona fide scheme.

On 29 July the last meeting of Directors was held and the repayment of deposits was ordered.

J.O.P. received £200 for his services. Six months later Oakley asked for his support in a scheme for extending the London Tilbury and Southend Railway from Southend to Burnham, across the Rochford Hundred. His reply, sent from Sharpham, shows his disappointment at the failure of the former scheme:

I feel quite the advantages of the proposed line, and in a *quiet way* shall be most ready to help you and those with whom you are associated, but as a matter of personal interest it does not touch me like the previous scheme, and I should not therefore be disposed at once to take a prominent part even if I were not deterred from doing so, by the fact that wherever I go I find the disappointment of the late failure so fresh that as soon as a new scheme is mentioned, some such observation as, 'No, we're not going to be done again', is sure to follow. With my own friends I don't mind communicating upon the subject, but under the circumstance I can't put myself forward in a public manner. With regard to the landowners etc, they must be blind to their own interest if they don't see the advantages of it, but all the same, as soon as you begin to talk about getting the land at *agricultural* prices and *taking shares* in payment for it, it is astonishing how few are ready to acquiesce in the proposal. . . .

He had no more correspondence with Sir Morton Peto, although three years later, in October 1860, when an attempt was made to revive the Tilbury Maldon and Colchester scheme, he went so far as to attend a meeting at Latchingdon where a resolution was passed in favour of it. Nothing more seems to have been done.

The age of railway speculation has long since passed by, and now Essex is served by two main lines running across the county, roughly from west to east. Since that time other small railways have been made, some of which have gone out of use through the development of road transport. North–south communication in Essex is still very bad, and much remains to be done to connect, by public transport, the places which the Tilbury–Maldon—Colchester line would have served.

CHAPTER XIII

THE SEA

NOBODY COULD HAVE KNOWN more in their day than did the Parkers, father and son, about the struggle of the Essex marsh farmer against the force of waters. It is a grim paradox of nature that in coastal Essex the friend is also the enemy. The rain, without which no crops can grow, must be controlled and guided into marsh ditches and thence into the sea or it could in a day turn a fruitful field into an impassable and barren quagmire. The sea, which for generations has been an additional source of livelihood to the Essex man, must be kept at a distance by high sea-walls, or, spilling over the land at high tide, it will spread death and destruction, leaving behind a bleak and poisoned country-side on which no crop will grow for years.* Thus the ceaseless duel has gone on for centuries, the coastline continually changing shape, with here a lost marsh or a swamped island visible now only at low tide; and there, a brand new wall where man has taken the offensive and wrested a few acres from the sea, while continually the endless process of drainage and ditching has gone on within the walls.

Christopher Comyns Parker and his son, who were able to travel extensively and to see farming conditions in all parts of England, must many times have envied the upland farmer on light soil who could clean out his ditches and then put the subject of drainage out of his mind for many months. For the men in the hundreds bordering on the sea it was an ever-present problem, and never a year passed without a crisis in one form or another, arising from overflowing ditches, heavy clay

---

* For a vivid account of disaster in our time, see *The Great Tide: the Story of the 1953 Flood Disaster*, by Hilda Grieve. Essex County Council, 1959.

land parched and hardened by hot sun after floods, or broken sea defences. From the Tendring Hundred to Barking the Parkers either owned or managed lands which were constantly in peril. Woodham Mortimer was happily out of the way of sea encroachment, but they also owned Eastlands in Bradwell, leased Bovills in Mayland and were agents for over half a century for such estates as Heybridge Hall (the Dean and Chapter of St. Paul's, O. Hering and Lady Milbanke Huskisson), Down Hall, Bradwell (T. T. Clarke), Dengie Hall and Bridge Wick (the Fanshawes), the Mildmay lands in Burnham, Plumborough Farm, Hockley (the Otte family), Wallasea Island (Lord Wynford), Potton Island (Archdeacon Wilberforce), Pitsea Hall (Rev. George Heathcote and the Hon. Payan Dawnay, Vange Wharf Farm (Sir Charles Smith), Court Wick Farm, West Tilbury (the Governors of Chelmsford Grammar School), the Barking lands of the Thoyts family, and many others. They were also Commissioners of Sewers for the Dengie and Foulness Levels for long periods.

Crops on the heavy clays of south-east Essex are the first to be parched and caked hard by too much sun and drought, the first to be drowned by excess of rain. Thus, yield depends to a large extent on the attention which is given to them at times when they are not bearing crops. Lime, chalk, the plough in autumn, and, above all, constant attention to drainage are necessary. This involves ditches well cleaned out and fields tile drained or mole drained. There is nothing inspiring to the layman about the draining of heavy clay soil. It is part of the seasonal routine which has to be regularly done and made good like the spring-cleaning of a house; and the accounts of these operations, or rather the operations needed, are written down in the minute books of the Commissioners of Sewers. A presentment of Thomas Schreiber, Rector of Bradwell, for Parsonage Marches, and of C.C.P. for Land Farm in 1826, runs:

That the outfall between Parsonage Marshes and Land Farm in the Parish of Bradwell is grown foul and muddy and not sufficient to carry off the water running thereto, and that 120 rods of the said outfall ought to be scoured and cleansed and made six feet wide at the bottom and kept open and cleansed at all times during the winter season and at all other times when necessary.

In 1843 J.O.P. received a letter from a Scottish farmer asking him for particulars of what he called 'Essex Drainage'. His reply, which dealt not only with the heavy London clay of the south-eastern lowlands but with the gravel of the higher levels, the boulder clay of the north and north-west and the chalky soils of the Cambridge border, is a summary of all that was then known about the subject. Of the antiquity of the practice of land drainage in Essex, he says:

With respect to the antiquity of draining or land ditching, as it is more generally termed, in this county, I am unable to arrive at any definite conclusion, but from all that I can gather on the subject I should be inclined to believe that the system has prevailed as a necessary adjunct to good farming, and as far as the cutting of parallel drains filled with wood and straw is concerned, for a good century past. The removal of superfluous water from the land by surface drainage or land ditching appears to have been time out of mind an acknowledged principle of good farming, without which all applications of manure or other acts of husbandry would be rendered comparatively valueless and ineffectual. Indeed it seems to have been long regarded as the *sine qua non* of good farming, and in conversing with several old labourers for the sake of learning the practice of former times, I have found that they were accustomed to the work from their boyhood, and that their fathers had been in the habit of engaging in the same kind of labour before them. I am not led to suppose that the system was so generally adopted as at the present day, or that anything like the improved methods of drainage by tiles were adopted, but the draining of wet and squashy lands by ditches filled with wood and straw or stubble has been much practised in this County for a long period and has tended materially to improve the healthiness of the climate and increase the production of the soil.

He goes on to deal with the straightforward ditching processes of the north-east of the county, and the advantages of the new tile drainage where gravel and loam is mixed and where springs 'rise up and spew out upon the surface'. Over the tiles he recommends the use of stones, the smaller the better, covering them slightly with straw.

For this purpose the stones *cannot be too small*—the finest gravel well sifted, or sea shingle are both capital materials but better than all is the broken cockle shell occasionally to be procured on the sea shore. If when first done a layer of straw be placed on the top of such material to prevent the first sediment from the upper soil sinking, the superincumbent earth forms a crust on the top of the drain which does not fill in or mix with the stones or shell and the drains appear after many years as clean and free from soil or obstruction as when first laid down, and would seem to give good promise of lasting for ever.

The soil with which he and his father were most concerned was the heavy clay of the south-east which becomes so heavy and sticky in rain, and which dries out if undrained and unworked into great unbreakable clods in which nothing but weeds will grow well. Here,

Land ditching by covered drains has only been partially adopted, and many of the best practical farmers, and men not too blinded by prejudice to a fair consideration of the subject, doubt whether the system can be generally practised with advantage on such soils. Where the soil is uniformly composed of that stiff and impervious texture which does not admit of the water soaking below the top surface moved by the plough, it is thought better to lay up the land in ridges or stitches, from which the water is taken by intervening furrows, and by them at certain intervals into cross furrows drawn by the plough at a greater depth and afterward dug or *spitted* by the spade so as to convey off the water freely and rapidly by surface drainage. If drained at all in such land the ditches are seldom cut deeper than 14 or fifteen inches below the plough, and they are necessarily placed at frequent distances very commonly 1 rod apart, from the circumstances of the impervious subsoil only allowing the water to find its way into the drains by perpendicular fall, instead of the oblique and gradual percolation by which it is carried off in more porous strata.

In his development of the subject he adds one very true comment:

I cannot speak from my own observation, but in all that I have read of the drainage of heavy lands I have never been able to conceive that the heavy lands to which the effectual drainage has been applied are equal in stiffness, in tenacity, in stubbornness, to our own.

Owing to this, it was generally acknowledged that the efficient management of the heavy land farms necessitated greater capital outlay than that of any other. Those which were in addition liable for the upkeep of sea-walls were the most expensive of all. Where, as in Foulness and the Dengie Hundred, commissions of sewers were functioning, they were subject to the periodical assessment of marsh 'lots' or rates for common expenditure as well as the costs of the upkeep of their own sea-defences.

An interesting glimpse of such work in progress is to be had from the diaries of 1843–8, and the correspondence with Lord Wynford on the condition of the walls round Wallasea Island. On 2 February 1843 J.O.P. wrote:

At Wallasea Island to look over Shearwood's Farm—Lord Wynford's. Mr. Allen [the tenant] not there on account of the weather. Went over land, found same in improved state of cultivation. The wall in good order—1 man and 2 boys replacing chalk and stone—abt week's work. Requires one load of Piles, and Ld of Stone and one Ld of Chalk, dropped along the wall where wanted and laid in with judgment to make same in most substantial condition.

Before the end of the month much of the repair work had been undone by a high tide, and a great deal of other damage had occurred. On the 22nd he visited the farm again,

to look to repairs of sea wall and damage done to same by tide and gale.

On the 2 March he was there again examining the injury to the wall with the tenant. He gave directions to procure immediately two freights of chalk and 1500 piles, and gave the men who were to work on the job instructions as to how to proceed. On the 3rd he wrote to Lord Wynford:

On examination I found it scarcely possible to make an estimate of the work as the repair will principally consist of manual labour in relaying materials displaced from the front of the wall. Your Lordship's tenant has employed men on whom he can depend to do the work and will superintend them during the progress. I shall also go over myself and see that the work is properly done. . . .

A special meeting of the Commissioners for the Island of Foulness has been called (in consequence of the late damage) for Wednesday the 15th inst. Of this district Mr. Gepp is Clerk, and knowing him to be thoroughly conversant with the law relative to sewerage I have requested him to look into the question of 'damages sustained by extraordinary tides and winds' so as to give me his opinion upon it, and having been summoned as a Commissioner to attend the meeting I will make a point of attending that I may be able to gather any information likely in the present case to be of service to your Lordship.

A contractor named Gardiner was engaged and gave an estimate for the repairs to the wall of £895 4s. 9d. It was sent to Lord Wynford on the 21st. On the 27th J.O.P. went to town, saw Lord Wynford at the Carlton Club, and received instructions to stone the wall.

stated that I would not insure the expence corresponding with the estimate, but wished to place the work under Gardiner's superintendence.

On the 30th he was again at Wallasea, taking Gardiner with him. On the same day he wrote to Bensted & Higgins of Maidstone Quarries stating that he would want a large quantity of stone, probably about 1000 tons, to be brought to Foulness regularly during the process of the work, and asking for their lowest price.

They offered him the stone at 5s. 6d. a ton on twelve months' credit and at 5s. a ton on six months' with 2½ per cent discount for quarterly payments. At first he refused to accept this and ordered stone from another firm named Clay, but

May 22nd, 1843. At Wallasea to look to repairs of Lord Wynford's wall and to examine quality of stone sent by the respective parties, Clay, and Bensted and Higgins. Found the latter superior and told

Mr. Clay that I could not feel justified in taking an inferior article at the same price, and that I would allow Messrs Bensted and Higgins to supply part of the stone.

All through the summer the work of repair went on. J.O.P. did not find it necessary to pay frequent visits to the island, but left the work entirely to his contractor Gardiner in whom he had great confidence. On 7 February 1844 Lord Wynford wrote to him asking for information as to the state of the sea-wall, to which he replied that

as far as regards the heavy work upon the most exposed and dangerous parts of the wall, it is now completed in a very satisfactory manner and bids fair to stand the test of any boisterous weather. The amount of stone for which I had contracted has all been supplied and the last freights are now being laid down. The men will be some little time longer employed in finishing off their work, when the wall will be placed in most secure condition, and I trust the outlay will not exceed by more than a very slight amount the sum which I had calculated.

On 12 March J.O.P. set out, intending to go to Wallasea, but the weather was too rough to cross the Crouch. On the 20th he paid a visit and looked over the work.

found same nearly completed and new work in no way injured by recent easterly winds.

He wrote to Lord Wynford to tell him that the men would finish all that was proposed to be done except for a small piece of chalking, by Saturday the 23rd. The final letter announcing the completion of the walls was not sent until 17 June, when J.O.P. wrote to Lord Wynford to say that the expenditure had been within a very few pounds of the estimated outlay.

Thus, in 1844, the walls were restored to a condition which was deemed satisfactory, but another high tide in June 1845 caused damage which was estimated at £20. Again, on 12 December 1845, the sea-wall was breached and considerable expense incurred in making it good. In August 1848 Gardiner was asked to quote again for the repair of the walls and produced an estimate of £698. On 6 September J.O.P. met Lord Wynford on Wallasea Island and received instructions to have the walls repaired according to Gardiner's estimate. This, however, does not seem to have been done, for in October the farms were inspected by Joseph Gibbs and a long report made. For many years so much expense had been incurred in protecting the island from the sea that Lord Wynford had contemplated selling it. In February 1849 J.O.P. wrote in his diary:

To Lord Wynford with rent a/c and informing him that I had been obliged to give orders for such repairs of the walls as were absolutely necessary.

Thus the gruelling fight against the sea went on. Landlords, Lord Wynford among them, had the utmost difficulty in getting their rent from tenants who farmed lands which were subject to inundation, and repair covenants were often left unfulfilled, as in the case of Wallasea Island. The tenant, Stephen Allen, was described by J.O.P. as being a slovenly and negligent farmer, but one marvels, in face of such difficulties, how either landlord or tenant could carry on and make a farm pay its way. The explanation is that it is rich land, and in a favourable season the farmer reaps a large profit.

Such were the conditions along the whole of the Essex coast. Wealthy landowners could afford to keep their walls in order; the poorer could not. At the same time as Lord Wynford was restoring the walls of Wallasea, Archdeacon Wilberforce was doing the same on Potton Island, and having trouble with equally awkward tenants. Some farms on the mainland were in almost as precarious a position as those which were on islands. One of these was the Wash Farm at Clacton, owned in 1849 by John Round. Though the farm had only 140 acres, it had a frontage of about two miles to the sea, with a long sandy beach. In the following year J.O.P. found the wall of this farm

in most dangerous condition, the wharfing much decayed and broken away, and several serious cavities in the face of the wall.

Here the tenants were so discontented and the trouble with neighbours so serious that J.O.P. advised that steps ought to be taken to have the level placed under a Commission of Sewers. The wall was repaired in 1851.

The bursting of a sea-wall on any of the estates he managed was always the signal for a period of intense work. On 12 December 1845 he was called up in the night by special messenger to inform him that a high tide had caused a breach in Lady Mildmay's wall at Burnham. He went there, found two breaches, 'took measures for stopping same', then went straight to Wallasea where the water had flowed over the whole length of the north wall but had not breached it. The next day he went to Marsh House and to Bridge Wick, Dengie, and visited Hyde Marsh, Wymarks, and Down Hall, Bradwell. He noted the state of the wall and land on all these and got emergency measures in progress. To the end of his life he was never free from such alarms. On 29 October 1882 he wrote in his diary:

Received letters from Philip Smith and Robert Page reporting serious damage to sea walls at Clacton and Bradwell. Wall of new enclosure nearly broken through in several places and facing carried away throughout nearly the whole length, and 20 men engaged in making good the damage, to be kept at work through Sunday to prevent further mischief. Wrote to Mr. Philip Smith that I would come to Clacton on Thursday. . . .

The damage done by overflowing was ruinous to many an industrious farmer. Landlords often felt themselves compelled to assist on such occasions by abatements of rent. In 1876 a farmer called Knights on a farm in Latchingdon sustained the losses of crops on his arable land for two years, besides what extra he had to pay for feeding his cattle away from home. On J.O.P.'s advice he was allowed by his landlord £50.

More serious was the plight of a farmer named Faux who had come from Huntingdonshire in July 1872 to farm Lady Milbanke Huskisson's land at Heybridge. The walls had been topped in 1870. A letter written by J.O.P. on 4 May 1874 describes what happened to them:

I enclose a tracing from the Parish map by which you will see that the farm is in great part bounded by river wall, and the Chelmer and Blackwater navigable canal passes through the whole length of the farm. The walls, at the time of the flood, were as high, and generally in as good condition as I have ever known them to be for the last 30 or 40 years, and was of a height to keep out all ordinary tides, but the tide of the 20th March came up the river with a wall or bore, rose to many inches higher than any one on record and overtopped nearly all the walls of that part of the river, and rising some 9 inches above the stone coping of the sea lock of the canal, drove back the waters of the canal upon the adjacent lands. This latter cause may have added something to the depth of the flood on the north side of the farm, but the south side was entirely submerged by the tidal water, which overflowed the walls, a great part being flooded to the depth of 5 feet, and the water remaining on it for 2 or 3 days. The crops were looking extremely promising, and the effect has been utterly to destroy them, and to soak the land in such a way that it has been impossible to do anything with it. Besides the loss of the present crop, the salt water has a very prejudicial effect upon the soil, and injures its productive quality for many years. . . .

He went on to enclose all the correspondence indicating the extent of the damage and concluded with a note on the character of the tenant:

Mr. Faux is a most respectable tenant, and is farming the estate in a very spirited manner. There is no doubt that he is the loser to a very large extent, and he deserves to be very liberally treated. In conversation he has stated that unless he obtains full compensation he will throw up the farm. . . .

In the hope of settling the matter, Faux was offered compensation of £250. This he rejected as 'next door to an insult, this being less than a fourth of this year's damages, setting aside the future. (9 May 1874.)

On 18 May J.O.P. visited Heybridge Hall and went over the farm with Faux. He found that the crops on the flooded land had not in the slightest degree recovered, and the tenant was trying, with little hope, to get mangold wurzels and turnips to grow. It turned out that both landlord and tenant had had legal advice. J.O.P. told Faux that the landlord was not legally liable for the damage, and though Lady Milbanke Huskisson would be willing to take into fair consideration the loss he had sustained, no legal claim could be acknowledged. Faux replied that his loss must be liberally and fully met or he would take legal proceedings.

For a while the question of litigation hung in the balance. On the 21st, Lady Huskisson's solicitors wrote:

It only remains for Mr. Faux to decide whether he will make a legal or a moral claim. If the former we must do the best we can, and if the latter you must bear in mind that Lady Huskisson would be quite as innocent a sufferer as Mr. Faux and would naturally feel any loss of income.

Faux's valuer estimated a loss of £1142 in the current year and a further £515 owing to the check which had been caused by the flood to the productive power of the land. On 24 June J.O.P. saw Faux's legal adviser and offered an abatement of £200 from the rent of the current half-year, £200 from the half-year ending at Michaelmas, and £100 a year for four years from that time.

This, though it was not accepted by the tenant, at least saved the expense and inconvenience of going to law and opened the way to the process of dogged bargaining which followed. J.O.P. on his own responsibility offered £200 for three half-years and then £100 for four years. The tenant's representative asked for £250 for three half-years, £100 for four years, and the free occupation of a recently stubbed wood rent free.

The course of this bargaining, the juggling with deferments of rent, the pressing appeals to accept, the holding out of threats for non-compliance, the bringing in of extraneous considerations such as the repairing of the farmhouse as makeweights, the freely conceded appreciation by the landlord of the tenant's difficulties, followed by the great BUT, the threats of the tenant to quit forthwith if not satisfied, the occasional recrimination, the impatient rejoinder:

I cannot agree to any payment present or future beyond what I offered in my letter to you of the 3rd of August. If I thought that I could do so with any sort of justice to my clients I should not stand out, but I feel that I have gone to the utmost reasonable limit, and if I had not had a high-minded liberal lady to deal with (who chose to put thorough faith in my representation of the case) and considerate and sensible legal advisers to act with me, no such terms could have been obtained. As I have said before, I believe that you too must honestly admit that Mr. Faux's case has been fairly and liberally met, and I trust that you will not only allow me to report that the matter is finally settled, but that Mr. Faux is as satisfied as any man under so unfortunate a visitation can reasonably be expected to be. (J.O.P. to J. A. Eve, 29 August 1874.)

The financial terms were settled by 31 August but the argument still went on. On 8 September Faux's adviser wrote:

I think now I have the pleasure of being able to settle the matter. *Terms:*
£200 for 3 half-years, and £100 per annum for 5 more; the roof of the house to be repaired and the barn as well: the question of woodland need not be imported into it. Mr. Faux will not give more than 30/– per acre; if you do not like to let him have it for that he will decline it; by leaving the point out of the question we are enabled to come to a settlement.

Thus the matter was concluded. If, as Lady Milbanke's counsel held, Faux had no legal claim, he was very well treated. J.O.P. had gone to the utmost lengths to satisfy him. Lady Milbanke Huskisson was not so pleased about the outcome.

Mr. Faux seems to think only of his own inconvenience and not at all of mine when I am making him an offer which I can very ill afford, and every one to whom I tell my story considers it very liberal for my means, for my rents do not ever bring me in more than I require or enough to enable me to lay by. (Lady Milbanke Huskisson to J.O.P., 12 September 1874.)

A few years after the flooding had occurred J.O.P. added a comment that is of great interest. It was that if he had suspected that the land would recover so rapidly he would never have agreed to terms so favourable to the tenant.

(It is interesting when reading the above to recall what happened after the great inundation of 1953. In that year the Lord Mayor opened a fund for the sufferers, and millions of public money were spent in compensation and repair of sea-walls. It was not left to landlord and tenant to retrieve the situation.)

In the latter years of the eighteenth century, farmers began to be interested in the value of marsh land as agricultural land, and there was a renewed interest in reclaiming it from the sea. Already private enterprise had added to the quantity of farm-land, and in the Dengie Hundred, the Quayles and Henry Bate Dudley had made the locality famous (*The Great Tide*, pages 32–4). The Parkers themselves, owning land at Bradwell, were no newcomers to marsh farming, and it was the prospect of obtaining marsh crops that induced Christopher Comyns Parker to enclose seventy acres outside Eastlands Farm, Bradwell, and to lease and farm Bovills (see above, page 174). On one occasion, at least, J.O.P. as agent came into direct contact with a private embanking project. Captain Fanshawe, who owned Dengie Hall and Bridgwick Farms, decided at the end of 1843 to enclose additional acreage. After a dispute with a neighbour who wanted compensation for allowing a new wall, if built, to join his own, the line of the wall was set out (29 February 1844) and estimates were obtained. The work was finally entrusted to Gardiner who was at that time also employed on the repairing of Lord Wynford's walls on Wallasea Island. On 10 April J.O.P. went over the line of the proposed wall with the wallers, and the work was begun. In May it was in full swing and a second gang was set on. J.O.P. visited the site on the 23rd, and again on 19 June after some of the men had downed tools.

found that some of the men had struck the work and others were requiring more wages than originally agreed upon. Afterwards saw Mr. Gardiner upon the subject and told him that he must do the best he could to keep the men at work and make the most of the present fine season.

He was there again on 15 July, on 22 September, and on 19 October, when the work is definitely referred to in the diary as 'Bridgewick Enclosure', and again on 24 October as 'Bridgewick Wall'. On 8 November he was paying money to the contractor and giving him directions as to the disposal of planks. In December he was inspecting the work in progress clearing the outfall from the new gutter. In January he was considering the division of the new level between the tenants and adjusting rents, and on 22 February he paid the contractor off. On 8 March he again visited Bridgewick:

also looked at new wall and found same to be in satisfactory condition.

At the beginning of the following year the walls were heightened and the enclosure made more secure.

In 1851 an ambitious scheme was drawn up for the reclamation of some 30,000 acres between Great Wakering and Bradwell, to be achieved by the construction of a sea-wall some twenty miles in length. Most of the local landowners were opposed to this as it involved considerable interference with their farms and would involve their making claims for compensation. On 19 March 1852 J.O.P. entered in his diary:

With T. Gepp as to opposition to South Essex Estuary Bill.

He took a leading part in this opposition. On the 22nd and the 23rd he was at the House of Commons; several times he went to Bradwell to observe the rise and fall of the tides; he visited many other landowners to help to organise the opposition, on 17 and 19 April he was with T. M. Gepp framing the petition. On 14 May he visited Counsel and went through the evidence and the brief. On the 17th and 18th he attended the House of Lords. Finally, on the 20th,

Received telegraph from Messrs Bloxam respecting terms offered by South Essex Estuary Company, and went to Town by 3 o'clock train,

and afterwards with Mr. Bloxam at Mr. Badeley's chambers arranging terms of agreement, the Company agreeing to give all saltings as defined on deposited plans and £200 costs whenever enclosure should commence—further opposition to be withdrawn.
May 21st. Morning to London. Attending Committee House of Lords. Agreed with South Essex Estuary Company to withdraw all opposition on the terms stated above. Committee passed first reading of the Bill.

In evidence given twenty-six years later, J.O.P. tells what happened as a result:

On a previous attempt made by the South Essex Estuary Reclamation Company to enclose lands under the Act of 1852 they commenced these works in front of my land. They proposed to enclose the whole frontage but in consequence of the difficulty of doing so they only enclosed about half the frontage. In the original Bill they proposed to enclose as they do in the present Bill 2/3rds of the way down to low water mark. They abandoned their original intention and only enclosed down to 300 yards to seaward from the existing wall. I purchased the land so enclosed from the Company, but the soil of which the embankment was composed is of so loose a material that it is very troublesome to maintain the wall and I have had to expend over £600 on strengthening it from time to time. Several breaches were made by the tide before I came into possession of the enclosed land and two breaches have been made since.

The complete scheme fell through, and little more was heard of large-scale enclosure for another ten years. On 21 November 1862 he received a letter from Batty & Whitehouse intimating that another company might be set up.

On the coast of Essex bordering upon Dengie Hundred between the rivers Crouch and Blackwater a considerable tract of land has been as you are doubtless aware, formed by the peculiar set of the tide which might be reclaimed and converted to a profitable use by the judicious outlay of capital.

The expense will be great but some gentlemen are willing to incur the risk of obtaining an Act of Parliament and making the subsequent enclosure provided the persons having claims upon the land in question will assist the undertaking and agree to the following terms.

The letter went on to say that the applicants would bear the cost of enclosure, the owners assisting and giving evidence in favour of the undertaking. When enclosed, the land would be handed to the foreshore owners at a rent of 7s. 6d. per acre, the owners giving access to the part to be reclaimed.

The above ground rent is insignificant when it is considered that the promoters incur all the risk and expense, that the land will be worth at least £40 per acre and will be free of tithe and land tax which alone exceed upon the adjoining properties the amount to be imposed.

To this J.O.P. replied that there had been a similar scheme which had been opposed by the landowners, and before making a definite reply he must consult them. He then submitted the letter to T. M. Gepp who replied with a caution:

Term No. 3 stipulates that the land *found* to be the property of each foreshore owner be handed over to him subject to a rentcharge of 7/6 per acre. Now my impression is that such will never be so found. The Government, I fear, will claim it. (3 November 1862.)

On 14 November he attended a meeting of the trustees of the Dean Clark Charity whose lands were also affected by the proposed enclosure:

Mr. Robert Page reported as to quantity of saltings etc. Decided to oppose.

On the 16th he wrote to the Rev. Charles Fanshawe in reply to a query as to the extent of the land affected. Fanshawe was interested in Bridge Wick, on which his uncle's enclosure had previously been made.

On a former occasion I was a party with your uncle and several others to a petition against the Bill, and our opposition was so far successful that had the scheme been carried out we should have obtained a far better arrangement than is now proposed. We were to have as our share and free of all cost ¼th part of our enclosed frontage. . . .
I consider Mr. Batty's proposal far too equivocal to accede to it. They say 'that the Company will be willing to hand over at 7/6d per acre to each owner so much as will be found to belong to them'.

Now one of the tests of possession has been said to be 'previous enjoyment or use'. If this be adopted each owner would only have that which is already fit for grazing, and in your case, the grassy saltings having been enclosed some 20 years ago, little but mud remains outside, and you would be found to have nothing.

The negotiations went on for five months, and then on 21 April 1863 the following entry appears in the diary:

At Messrs Woodruffe's office to give evidence for Committee. Bill withdrawn.

It seems that the enclosure under the old Act of 1852, which did not expire until 1867, was still going on, for on 31 October J.O.P. claimed £1000 for Eastlands saltings. The diary goes on:

November 2nd. Long interview on the evening with Mr. Beadel as to compensation for right of way to Chapel and shore. Stated that I would demand £1000 and £250 for right of way, and I would write to him to that effect.

November 13th. Had long interview with Mr. Beadel as to compensation and eventually agreed to accept £1050 and wrote letter to him to that effect containing conditions on which I w^d accept same.

On 20 November he signed the agreement accepting £800 for the saltings and £250 for the right of way. On 18 December he was consulting about the road to be set out from the Chapel gate to the new enclosure, and, on the 22nd, fixing the boundary line between Eastlands and the new enclosure. In May of the following year he negotiated with the Company for letting to them St. Peter's Chapel, probably as a storehouse. On 4 June the following entry appears:

Home and to Bradwell. Inspecting works of S.E. Estuary Company. Men engaged in constructing new wall near the Glebe outfall, but the more distant enclosure abandoned, and the quantity about to be enclosed merely the solid salting lands—about 200 acres. *Parturient montes!*

On 9 July he found that the Estuary Company's contractor was taking soil from the foot of Chapel Hill and from the roadway across Chapel Hill for which no agreement for compensation had been made. The diary for the 11th went on:

Met Mr. Liman, Mr. Beadel and Mr. Hutchings. Stated that I considered that the excavations made by the Contractor were quite unwarranted and that I required compensation for all spoil earth taken, for the land enclosed by me many years ago, for the soil taken from the road way and for the turf taken from the site of the huts, that I protested against its all being done without my consent, but that I did not wish to hinder the works, and would agree that everything should be left to be settled between me and my tenants and the Company by Mr. Beadel. . . .

He visited the site on the 16th and the 23rd and made his protest on the spot.

One interesting result of the works at Bradwell was the renewed interest that was taken in St. Peter's Chapel, which was then being used as a barn or a shed for cattle. On 30 August he was there with the Secretary of the Essex Archaeological Society 'examining the foundations of the Roman Walls near the Chapel, etc.' This led to the excavations of 1864 and 1865.

The rest of the story of the South Essex Reclamation Company is told by J.O.P. in the evidence he gave against the promotion of another Bill to reclaim the Dengie Flats in 1879:

I entered into an Agreement with the South Essex Estuary and Reclamation Company with reference to my saltings on the foreshore at Bradwell. The Company were to pay me £1000 for giving up my rights to such saltings and foreshore. They never paid it to me but on the contrary they disputed my right to the saltings or foreshore and leaving enclosed 70 acres in front of my land, I was compelled to purchase it from them and pay them £1000 for it and this after long and expensive litigation in Chancery. The Company made such an ineffectual wall to enclose the 70 acres that I have since been obliged in great measure to reconstruct it.

I believe the old Company was formed of persons of no position or pecuniary means and mere speculators. No person in the neighbourhood supported it in any way and it was composed wholly of strangers. The old Company obtained their Act in 1852; this expired in 1866 when their powers were renewed for 5 years. Since they obtained this Act in 1852 the Company have enclosed about 70 acres of land near Bradwell and this land was so badly and imperfectly enclosed that for a long time and until sold by the Company to me it was absolutely useless for agricultural purposes. From that time until the expiration of this Act the Company enclosed about 240 acres more.

The sea constantly broke thro' the seawall and flooded the enclosed lands. The company being wholly without means to carry out their Scheme were ordered to be wound up in Chancery in the year 1868, and I believe the Creditors of the Company have never received any payment of their debts. [Note. The purchase of the land—69 acres, after litigation was made on 2 February 1870.]

Still the efforts for reclamation went on. On 26 June 1871 the House of Lords threw out another South Essex Reclamation Bill on the preamble, after concerted measures of the landowners to oppose it. During the time the Bill was under consideration the new Company were actually working on the embankment.

Again, in December 1878, another notice was sent out by a new South Essex and Dengie Flats Reclamation Company to all landowners of land affected by a proposed reclamation. During the early part of 1879 new measures were concerted between them to oppose it. J.O.P.'s evidence before a Committee of the House of Lords gave a brief history of the attempts to carry out this enclosure:

By the proposed works a very large tract of land and seashore to seaward of the existing wall in front of my land and the land of the adjoining owners will be taken by the Company and the existing means of discharge of such waters from my land which are of a costly character will be destroyed and rendered useless if not properly provided for, and it will be impossible for me properly to drain and keep drained my land. . . .

I believe from my knowledge of the nature and value of this salting land that the Scheme of the Company will turn out a failure and will never be carried out, but in the meantime if the Company obtain their Bill, adjoining landowners who are willing to enclose are prevented from doing so.

In my opinion it is impossible that the scheme of the promoters of this Bill can turn out a success. From my experience the cost of enclosing these saltings and foreshore is equal to the value of the land when enclosed, and there is no margin of profit left. . . .

On part of my farm there is an ancient building known as St. Peter's Chapel which is very interesting in an historical point of view; there is also the site of an old Roman encampment and I strongly object to the interference by the Company with this building and site.

In March 1880 the enquiry was held by a Committee of the House of Lords. J.O.P. was in London on the 8th, 9th, 10th, and 11th. On the last day the promoters of the Bill gave their evidence, and it was thrown out without those who opposed it being called.

It was apparent that further enclosures would be both risky and unprofitable; it was indeed as much as could be done to hold the sea back from land that had already been won. In 1897, ten years after J.O.P.'s death, the ill-fated seventy-acre enclosure on Eastlands Farm was completely inundated in the worst tide Essex had ever known. The whole of the badly constructed embankment was torn away and the light barley stacks on the enclosed land were floated up to the old wall and left there 'as shapely as when they started on their voyage'. In other parts of Essex 30,000 to 35,000 acres were under water (*The Great Tide*, pages 42–5).

Only in this century, and after two wars has it been completely realised that defence of the land against the sea is something that should no longer be left to the individual farmer or land-owner to cope with. Land is a national asset and therefore the nation as a whole must take the main responsibility of defending it. As a result of an Act of 1930, the Essex Rivers Catchment Board was set up. By the River Boards Act of 1948 this was supplanted by the Essex River Board, obtaining part of its income from the County and County Boroughs and grants of 85 per cent of the cost of new approved works on tidal defence from the Government. No longer, as in John Oxley Parker's day, is the marsh farmer left to struggle, virtually unaided, against the encroaching sea.

The history of land reclamation on the Essex coast seems a story of constant failure. And yet across the channel considerable success has attended the work undertaken by the Dutch. Is it something in the tides that renders work on the Essex coast doomed to failure, or have the Dutch some knowledge of sea-wall construction not yet attained by us?

CHAPTER XIV

TRUSTEESHIP

IN A BUNDLE OF LETTERS left by Christopher Comyns Parker is one, apparently addressed to him, and dated 11 November 1842. It runs as follows:

My dear Papa,

I am told there is no infection in paper or I would not address you. I must have your counsel and advice. Mr. Phillips says the sooner I take myself off the better. To part with my children would, I fear, not kill me but drive me mad, and if I remain here, as Miss Phillips declares, on *sufference*, I shall go mad too. Had I not better make up my mind to take my allowance and go somewhere? As my trustee you ought to know how I go on. . . . If I leave my husband am I entitled to my dear children? As this is only on business and to be burned as soon as read, I shall only add my affectionate love to all . . . and believe me, dear Papa,

Aff^{tly},
Your daughter,
Julia.

. . . I have left off taking the Sacrament having hatred in my heart.

Christopher Comyns Parker had no daughter named Julia. Later in the series it appears that Julia was the daughter of a certain Rev. Mr. Marriott who seems to have been the incumbent of one of the livings in the Dengie Hundred. Both he and C.C.P. were trustees of Julia's marriage settlement, and the only reason why it appears in the Parker collection is probably that one day, in great turmoil of mind, Mr. Marriott brought it to him as a fellow-trustee and, after talking about Julia's suggestion, left it behind. The settlement in question had been made in 1826 when Julia was to be married to the Rev. Howell

Phillips, who was also probably a friend of the family and later became a fellow-student of Oxley's at Oxford.

Previous to 1842 there had been a great deal of trouble between Julia and her husband, who seems to have been both unbusinesslike and improvident, probably a weak though rather likeable character. A puzzling entry in J.O.P.'s account book at Oxford for the Michaelmas term 1830 suggests that he lent Phillips £5, but there is no indication as to whether or not he got it back. In 1842 Phillips was already married, and had borrowed £2000 of his wife's marriage settlement in return for his bond and an insurance on his life which was to cost him £53 1s. 8d. a year.

He and his wife never seem to have agreed. Her letters show signs of chronic mental and nervous illness, his of a complete lack of ability to suffer anybody who could not concede to him complete virtue, wisdom, and right.

Temperamental differences revealed themselves in money matters. In 1842 Mrs. Phillips was left £5000 by an uncle, but apparently only the interest could be touched. Mrs. Phillips's brother Marriott, who acted as her trustee in this connection, apparently paid over the principal of this legacy, unaware that at the same time he should pay the legacy duty. He was therefore fined a percentage of the money left (£200) on top of the duty of £150. There seems to have been a longstanding ill-feeling between the two brothers-in-law, and when Marriott paid over the legacy he probably did it in such a way as to give Phillips the least possible benefit. In September 1842 C.C.P. repaid Marriott, on Phillips's account, the £150, and advised Phillips to repay him the amount of the fine. In advising Phillips of the £150 he would have to repay his brother-in-law, C.C.P. wrote on 10 September 1842:

I am aware it is by no means pleasant to reimburse money spent, but I hope the business will be amicably settled and family feuds and litigation avoided.

There was every justification for the anxiety he expressed. The reply and the letters that followed are a revelation of the hatred that existed not only between the brothers-in-law but also between husband and wife.

Mr. Marriott having infringed an Act of Parliament and incurred a penalty of 10 per cent by payment of his sister's legacy without first paying the duty thereon, and the penalty for that illegal act having been commuted for a payment of 4 per cent, I do not see how I can be called upon to pay the commuted penalty. . . . The mode in which he thought proper to pay the legacy was not only illegal as regards the Government but intentionally uncourteous towards me and my Trustees—by it I lost half a year's dividends, a sum fully equivalent to that Mr. Marriott has recently paid. His unkind act has recoiled on himself, and has been the instrument of reimbursing me out of his own pocket, that £100 of which he had previously so improperly deprived me. . . .

This was doubtless the trouble which led to Mrs. Phillips's pathetic letter of 11 November. We do not know whether Mrs. Phillips left her husband at the time, but we do know that she succeeded at a later date in depriving him of all control over her personal income.

This may have led to his petition in the Bankruptcy Court presented in October 1849, and J.O.P. after the death of his father, was concerned in this because, as a trustee of Mrs. Phillips's marriage settlement, he was partly responsible not only for the payment of that settlement but also for any moneys Phillips may have borrowed on his life insurance policy, for at some date he had gone surety for the payment of the premiums on a life assurance policy. Thus he was interested in the prompt payment by Phillips of the premiums on that policy.

You are aware [wrote Phillips] that the income under my marriage settlement amounts to about £600 a year, 3 of which belongs to me and 3 to my wife. My professional income is about £200.

I have proposed in my petition to set apart the *whole* of my moiety, together with the *whole* of my professional income, to pay my debts in full—that portion arising from the marriage settlement to liquidate the debts of creditors *holding securities* and the £200 professional, to pay the others. . . . I do not wish Mr. Marriott to know it, and have only told my wife, to whom, poor thing, all the misery I have suffered is owing, that I am arranging my affairs by paying the by-gone debts by instalments.

It must be assumed that because he was a trustee of the marriage settlement J.O.P. had bound himself as surety to the Albert Life Assurance Company for payment of the premiums on Howell Phillips's life policy. On 31 August 1850 J.O.P. received a letter from them requiring immediate payment of £55 12s. 10d. 'for the punctual discharge of which you have made yourself liable under the terms of the bond executed by you'. Howell Phillips must have expected such action by them for it is amusing to find a letter from him to J.O.P. dated two days after that from the Assurance Company which runs:

If the Albert Insurance Office write to you will you be so good as to forward their letter to me and in reply to them say you have done so, requesting me to attend to the matter immediately which you have no doubt I will do. You need not make yourself uncomfortable about the matter. I will prevent any burthen falling upon you and Mackenzie, though the difficulties against which I have to struggle are very great.

He goes on to blame his wife, saying:

This inconvenience is entirely due to a want of an accommodating spirit in my wife, who acts in a way which would have completely sunk anyone but myself. (23 August 1850.)

At another time he is promising payment and hoping for better days:

I hope notwithstanding the awkward position in which my poor wife has placed me, to be able to keep up my payments without in any way involving you, even temporarily. (20 April 1850.)

In July 1851 J.O.P. received an almost threatening letter:

If you have written anything to the Albert Insurance Company which may affect my credit, I shall not be able to manage them, and they will only become more peremptory as regards their claim on you.

It was followed by one two days later apologising for the earlier one and stating that his troubles were largely occasioned by his illness and the obstruction by his wife.

Later we find him referring to his creditors as scoundrels, and that the conduct of the Assurance Office has been most unjust. This peculiar gentleman died in September 1852. His last letters to J.O.P. show increasing evidence of the mental strain he was going through, not caused entirely by his circumstances but partly by his own instability and his inability to manage his own affairs. Mrs. Phillips complicated things by putting herself into the hands of a legal adviser whom the trustees considered unsatisfactory, then, by making a will they considered impracticable, and finally by herself dying in April of the following year.

... she sank under illness of mind and body, the former I think has been long coming on and the last 2 or 3 weeks showed much violence. I fear from what I hear that she not very long since executed a will under the power the settlement gives her of appointing the trust property amongst the children in what shares she pleased, and by this she has left the two eldest girls very little. This will I fear lead to trouble, and compel us as trustees to be very careful what we do. (Alfred Turner to J.O.P., 5 April 1853.)

Mrs. Phillips's death was not to end the problems of the unfortunate trustees. On 25 August of the same year J.O.P. received a letter from the solicitors of the two elder daughters asking if he could remember any circumstances from which one might conclude that Mrs. Phillips had been mentally incapable:

The morbid hatred which was entertained by the deceased against her husband and two eldest daughters for many years of her life has been carried out as you are aware probably by the will of this poor lady in question, and unless we can set aside that will, the two youngest children instead of half the property will engross the greatest share of it to the prejudice of the two elder girls who did nothing to deserve the ill-usage in question.

In support of their case they investigated the life history of

Mrs. Phillips and produced what they considered evidence enough to prove,

that the deceased was actuated by an insane hatred of both her eldest daughters whom she appears to have treated with the most systematic cruelty, cruelty indeed which only insanity could excuse, while at the same time with the cunning so often seen displayed in like cases, she by her wilful but unfounded complaints induced many people to believe that she really was a very ill-used person. . . .

To the request thus addressed to him, J.O.P. replied that he considered Mrs. Phillips to be strange, wild, and eccentric in manner and conduct, but could bring to mind no circumstances which would cause him to conclude that she was mentally incapable.

From this date for over thirty-one years neither diaries nor surviving letters give any significant facts about the Phillips inheritance, but we know from odd references that J.O.P. was occupied with the other trustees in matters concerning the property, which consisted of a house in Southwick Crescent near Hyde Park. It also appears from a letter of 3 May 1885 that the claim of the two elder Phillips children was upheld, and the estate inherited in four equal parts. By that time two of the four children had died, leaving two surviving sisters,

Mrs Rundell and Mrs. Garrett; the former, having become possessed of the 2 one-fourth shares belonging to her sister and brother who died, is now the owner of three-fourths, Mrs. Garrett having the remaining one-fourth. (Sharon Turner to J.O.P., 30 May 1865.)

The house in Southwick Crescent should, according to the will, have been sold in 1864 when the lease ran out. If this had happened, the trust would have been wound up and J.O.P. would have been relieved of any further responsibility. In deference, however, to the wishes of all parties, the house was re-let on a new twenty-one-year lease, and at the expiration of this in 1885 the trustees were again faced with the problem of sale. Turner had the house surveyed and the dilapidations valued, but did not wish to proceed without knowing that the other trustee agreed with him.

J.O.P. would have been glad to see the whole affair ended, but he reminded Turner that everything must be done without exceeding the trustees' powers, as Mrs. Rundell was 'a somewhat litigious person'.

In July 1885 J.O.P. received a letter from Mrs. Rundell who had acted on her own.

In March last, hearing it [the house] was to be empty I took the dilapidations in hand. . . .

She also engaged an agent, received offers for the tenancy, sent for the key from Turner, and then learnt that the trustees had decided to sell the house. She now engaged a solicitor to challenge the decision.

I maintained that as an interested party things cannot be completed without me, especially as the representative of my father and family and Mr. Turner is aware that through kind friends and my own brain I shall certainly never allow myself to be wronged in any way by any adviser whatsoever. . . . I refused to allow Mr. Turner to act for me and now I hear he 'advises a sale'. Whether or no a sale can be carried out without my consent in the many positions I hold as representative, time will show. . . .

The trustees were advised that under the terms of the marriage settlement the house should be sold, but Mrs. Rundell was opposed to a sale. She was a lady whose views could not be ignored with impunity. So the trustees applied to the Court for direction as to how they should act.

Permission to relet was granted, and though Mrs. Rundell continued to be obstructive and refused to give her approval to any course proposed by the trustees, they decided with some trepidation to spend the £150 received for dilapidations from the old tenant in modernisation and repairs. As J.O.P. wrote in March 1886:

With the number of unlet houses now standing empty in London we shall be lucky if we obtain a tenant even when the Southwick

Crescent house is put in order; but it is quite certain that no one would go near it in the neglected state in which it has been.

In July J.O.P. received a curt post-card from Mrs. Rundell to say she had changed her solicitor. This was the fourth time such a change was recorded in letters, and is an eloquent comment on the nature of the trusteeship. But good news was at last in store. In December came a letter from his co-trustee that a tenant had been secured at £220 a year, who wished for a seven-, fourteen-, twenty-one-year lease.

As far as J.O.P. was concerned the trusteeship was at an end, for he died in the following year. It had lasted sixty years in all, the whole of the time covered by the diaries. Many a time in the days when, in the early 50s and late 70s his own business worries were increased by agricultural troubles, he must have regretted ever having accepted such a harassing commitment as this.

CHAPTER XV

PERSONAL

ONE CANNOT FOLLOW the story of the business relations of a man without gleaning some facts about his character. The mere reading of Christopher Comyns Parker's diaries shows us something of the intense activity in which all his life was spent, and the fact that he took the trouble to record this so minutely reveals his industry and attention to detail. Had we merely had his diaries, however, we should have missed much of the real quality of the man, for in a cold and factual account of a succession of business transactions, personal feelings rarely show themselves. It must be realised that the diaries were kept solely to enable him to render an account to clients in respect of work done on their behalf. Luckily they are supplemented by the letters, from which we have so rich a store of information. In the long and long-suffering friendship with Charles Fanshawe, for instance, we see something of the lengths he was willing to go to give advice and service even to an undeserving friend. The capacity for preserving a friendship was a common trait of both father and son, and one cannot help feeling that John Oxley Parker throughout the whole of his life was strongly influenced by his father's example, so much had they in common. Both possessed the industry which made for success in life, together with the integrity which brought respect from all quarters. Both had the good nature which endeared them to their tenants, and not only to their friends but also to their clients. The kind of service C.C.P. gave to Miss Shaw in the sale of Fen Farm, Woodham Ferrers (see page 93), was repeated by Oxley in the efforts he made for Mrs. Orpen's welfare when her Birch farms became too much for her to handle.

Indeed, there seems little doubt that Oxley knew, consciously or unconsciously, that his father's character and attitude in life were worthy of emulation, just as at a later date he found that his business methods were the best that could, at that day, be employed. That is why in some respects when we pass 1843, the year in which C.C.P. died, we might, as far as business is concerned, be dealing with the same man. It is only in the more intimate concerns of personal and family life that certain differences appear. Even these are only the differences which naturally exist between a father who has founded and has had to work up a business, and a son who gets all the advantages of education, social life, and training that a conscientious father can give him. Oxley had a great capacity for enjoying life. As a young man he felt deeply and had a keen sense of beauty which he kept for as long as he lived. His diaries—over thirty of them— are prosaically labelled *Business Day Book*, but they are much more: they are a personal record of his enjoyments, his keen and lively observations, his loves, especially of nature, and to some measure of his sufferings. In them he could write volubly of the virtues of his friends as he lost them one by one, despairingly of the passing of his near relatives, with real artistry of the beauties of Wales, Devon, or Scotland, and at great length on the best holiday he had, when he was seventy-one years of age, in Italy. The account of this tour is given with as much enthusiasm and appreciation as could be written by any young person. Then, at home again, he records in brief notes, among the minutiae of business deals, the familiar sights and sounds of the countryside. In the last six months of his life these follow each other with such frequency that one might well believe it a premonition of his parting from the world he loved so well.

April 8th, 1887. Good Friday. Slight frost—bright all day with very cold NE wind. Everything very backward. Horsechestnuts just showing, gum on the buds. Peach trees in blossom—hope they won't be cut off.

April 19th, 1887. Thought I saw a cuckoo flying along a hedge at Sandon.

May 1st, 1887 (Sunday). Fine and bright, but very cold wind. Blackthorn out in hedges.

May 5th, 1887. Saw first swallows on Baddow Lane.

His father had never entered such things in his diary but his letters show the same warmth of character and richness of observation. The affection between father and son comes out very clearly in them. In August 1829, when Oxley's mother was gravely ill, his father wrote to him at Arkesden where he was staying with the Griffenhoofe family:

Your dear good mother has been gradually sinking during the whole of to-day. and was not able to keep up more than two or three hours, and there is too much reason to fear we shall very very soon be deprived of one of the best of wives and kindest of mothers. Mr. and Mrs. G. Gepp are here and were very kind and attentive. Your uncle Gepp and Tom came over in the middle of the day. The scene has been most affecting, for nothing can exceed the calmness and pious resignation of your ever dear mother. The firmness and precision with which she gives instructions about the most minute things is astonishing. I wish you not to lose any time on the road, but do not ride very fast for fear of accidents. I felt confident you would return to-morrow but I thought it best to adopt this arrangement, that you may avoid stopping anywhere, and I shall prefer your coming home by Boreham.

In December 1829 Oxley matriculated at Oriel, and early in 1830 C.C.P.'s letters take on an admonitory tone:

You are now, my dear Oxley, launched into a new sphere, and much of your future happiness and prosperity depends upon the choice of your associates and in a proper employment of your time, not allowing pleasurable pursuits to improperly interfere with the duties you have to perform. Remember the time, though long in anticipation, is really short, that you will have the assistance of others, to gather that store of useful knowledge which will render you capable of selecting that line in future life that may best suit your taste and inclination, whether in business or profession. I repeat now what I heretofore mentioned in conversation, that I do not wish you at present to fix on the line in life you intend to pursue. You are yet very young and circumstances may alter your opinions. It will be my duty to give advice if I think you are in error, but it has not, and I hope never will be, my inclination to dictate that which may make you uncomfortable. I have great happiness in the reflection that up to the present time you have never intentionally caused me a moment's uneasiness. Anxiety I have often felt, but I have always been rewarded by grateful results. I feel confident the same good disposition which has hitherto governed your actions will continue to influence your conduct to the lasting comfort and happiness of us both.

His progress during the first two years does not seem to have been entirely satisfactory to his father, for on 30 January 1832, after he had arrived at Oxford from the Christmas vacation, he received a disturbing letter reminding him that time was passing and he could not afford to waste it:

You are now at a time of life when every temptation is daily exciting you to join in pleasures and dissipations, many venial, but others that may injure your health and for ever ruin your constitution, and I regret to say, in many instances, lead to premature dissolution. God grant that you may by your own prudence escape danger and you may continue a blessing to me while living and a hope for protection to others when I am gone. Certain circumstances decided me in writing to you soon after you left home, but the collect of the day made me resolve not to allow a day to pass away without carrying my intentions into effect. Pray, my dear Oxley, do consider that others feel more interest in your prosperity than you can be expected to feel yourself at this period of life. I did not during the last vacation teaze you by remonstrances for your neglect of books. Too many temptations were daily cast in your way to induce me to hope that my reproofs might avail, but do not think that it was unobserved, and I assure you, painfully so. Resolve but to recover lost time and the end is accomplished. If one idle companion laugh at you, the praise of the more discreet will be tenfold. You have ability, you want nothing but exertion, and pray indulge me by its use.

Oxley replied with a promise to try to do better, and an avowal not only that he was not a good student but that the praise of his schoolmasters at a former time might have been given more to please his father than to justify him:

You will not be surprized to receive a letter from me following so quickly upon my last, since yours which crossed it on the road claims at my hands the most heartfelt and grateful acknowledgment. Never did father write or son receive a letter more replete with the most gratifying marks of sincere and fond affection in the lively interest and anxiety expressed no less ardently, I am sure, than is felt by you for my present welfare as well as future happiness. . . . I have begun this term with the intention of making some little use of the time between now and Easter—not that I can make up for lost time, but I must not quite lose that which is before me. It is right to give the D***l his due but I always think and cannot avoid confessing that I have generally received more credit than I could lay claim to. I have often been considered even studious, which title, Heaven knows, I have little deserved. I never was fond of study or any sedentary employment, and I do not flatter myself that I have used much exertion to conquer a naturally indolent disposition. I have been accused, too, of having ability, but have never yet discovered good ground for the charge. . . . The favourable letters you used frequently to receive from Dr. Burney were, I know, much more gratifying to you than to myself. I could not but consider them made up of a kind, but exaggerated mixture of humbug and flattery, and derived little gratification from them save in the boyish hope of increased indulgence at home, from the report of such good behaviour at school. Dr. Hawkins' letters have, too, borne the same favourable reports, and this combination of creditable opinions has, I fear, raised hope of results which will never be accomplished, and of expectations which will never be gratified. More will be required of me, I fear, on this account than I shall ever be able to attain. (2 February 1832.)

His father's reply, satisfactory though it was, had to conclude with a warning note on the question of over-spending:

You must be aware that feelings of sincere affection prompted my admonition and recollections of early life act as a mirror in exposing the temptations and dangers to which young men are exposed. Your frank and candid reply was most grateful to me. Your own happiness materially depends upon self-exertion. Providence has been bountiful to you although your modesty induces you to undervalue your endowments. . . . You mentioned your pecuniary resources are nearly exhausted. I was in hopes you would not have required any further advance this term. You are aware of the defect of the last year's produce or I should not say a word. Let me know what you really want and I will send it. You state a wish for an allowance. Give me a reasonable hope that it would be beneficial to you or myself, and you shall have it, but between father and son, I at present cannot allow its utility. With guardians or trustees it is necessary to justify them and throw the blame of excess in expenditure upon the ward who, when of age, has his debts to pay and feels, by embarrassment, the folly of his youth for the remainder of his life. Pay ready money for everything you have, and keep an account of what you expend, and I have no fear that you will injure me or yourself by your expenditure. I will correct the last word. [C.C.P. had written 'by your *extravagance* but had scored this out and inserted '*expenditure*'.] (13 March.)

In the following term Oxley's determination to work harder seems to have borne fruit, for after he had left home for college in June, his father wrote:

Let me first advert to my joy at the comfortable state of body and mind in which you appeared during the whole of your last vacation, compared with what I regretted to observe on the former occasion. I assure you it gave Frances [Oxley's stepmother] as much pleasure as it did to myself, and made us both happy. I hope you find your mare useful, and that Oxford shoeing will improve her feet. It must add very much to your comfort having the opportunity of a daily ride without hazarding your limbs upon a variety of hacks. (4 June 1832.)

He concludes with the usual reminder to Oxley to persevere with his studies, and:

I have received Mr. Crickett's account of the wine he sent; he pronounced it very good. I hope you and your friends will find it so and not pour it out lavishly.

Thirty-three years later J.O.P. was writing letters to his own sons, Christopher (whom he always addressed as Cris) and Oxley. They were at school, first at Worthing, then at Oxford, and were much younger than he had been when he received his own father's letters. Nevertheless, the father–son relationship worked out very much to pattern:

I daresay that you feel a little unsettled for the first day, but go to work like a man, and keep at the top of the class and bring home a good steady working character when the holidays come round again. (Dated 'Tuesday morning', probably in September 1863.)

Cris was evidently fonder of study than his father had been, for J.O.P.'s comment on his report runs:

From Mr. Wickham's report and from what you have told Mama, you seem to have been trying to do your best, and I hope will carry it on . . . and then you will deserve to enjoy your holidays all the more for having made the most of your time at school. (25 November 1863.)

Only once in the boys' schooldays do we get a hint of reproof, and that is in a letter to Cris dated June 1864. Even then, the boy was still top of his class:

I have this week received Mr. Wickham's report and it gives a tolerably good account of what you are doing. I think you deserve to be told I am pleased with it. There is one flaw in the report, and as it seems to come like an old story of an old fault in the schoolroom at home, you ought to be reminded of it, and the sooner you get rid of it the better. Mr. Wickham says that you 'would do better with more attention at your desk'. Now this is the old story of 'playing at lessons'. Miss Brunswick [his former governess] used to call it silly, and so do I, and so, you see, does Mr. Wickham, and I daresay if you ask Miss Billing she will tell you the same—'a place for everything and everything in its place' is a very good maxim, and never more true than in the case of lessons. Play hours for play and school hours for lessons—stick to them well while you are at them and enjoy the play the more afterwards. I am very glad you held your place at the top of the class so far through the half and I hope that you will manage to retain it to the end. (8 June 1864.)

In his youth J.O.P. was taught, in common with all other young men of his day who were considered well educated, to write ornately. In his Oxford days when doing a theme he appears never to have used a short word where a long one could be found, and rarely to have made a direct statement where he could find a circumlocution. Here is a fragment from one of his themes on the subject of *Possunt, quia posse videntur*.

Few things, indeed, will eventually be found invincible to the frequent endeavours of sagacity and perseverance. Apprehensions of ill-success, or at least fears lest the object of pursuit should not equal the expectations of its goodness, often deter men from the prosecution of any meditated design, but confidence that the object of their wishes is worthy of their exertions leads to the boldest experiments. To this end it is requisite that they should acquire a just and lively apprehension of the value of the reward, for no one earnestly strives and hopes to gain that which he does not long to possess, and no one can vehemently desire to be in possession of that which he has not first learnt fully to appreciate.

A lifetime of business correspondence caused him not to unlearn this early style but to gain that habit of short and direct statement which came later. Contrast this with the simple letters written to his son at the child's own level and full of sincere affection. When Cris was nine years old he was taken by his father to Dr. Wickham's school at Worthing. (2 February 1863.) In his diary for that day he wrote:

To London and Worthing with Cris to school at Wickham's. Rained all the time I was at Worthing; unable to go out. Cris behaved very well. . . .

Immediately on his return to town that day he penned his first letter to his son:

Monday evening. My dear Boy—I was very much pleased with you to-day. Considering that it was your first separation from home you behaved manfully. I could plainly see that your heart was full, but you bore yourself bravely through, and a little overflow at the last was only to be expected. When we parted I think Papa shed nearly as many tears as you did, but he was glad to feel that you were left in kind hands and that you would soon forget your troubles in the bustle of unpacking your things and the novelty of making new acquaintances. I daresay that you will find many nice companions among your new school-fellows, and I hope that you will soon be very happy amongst them. You may be quite sure that nothing will make school happy so much as trying to do all things well, and trying as much as possible to please Mr. Wickham, and this I hope you will do to the utmost of your power. It was very unfortunate that the day was so wet. I thought that I should have a nice walk with you and should be able to show you about Worthing. I arrived here in time for dinner and have had a pleasant evening with Grand-papa. . . .

Owing to their father's business activities, the boys received most of their letters from their mother, but at intervals J.O.P. found time to write. When he did, he filled his letters with news about family and friends, about hunting and coursing, the places he visited and the people he met.

I came from home this morning and have chosen a miserable day for getting about through the dirty streets of London. It has been raining all day just fast enough to stir up the mud without washing it away and the streets are in a filthy state. It is only half past four but I am tired of going about in the dirt, and as there is time to spare before dressing for dinner I will send you a letter. (29 February 1864.)
On Monday I was in London and in the afternoon went to see the cattle show. There were a great many very splendid animals and the place is so large and airy and so clean and well-arranged that it is a very fine sight. The new tenant at Hazeleigh Hall, Mr. Taylor won the highest prize with a very beautiful animal. Mr. Kemble was shooting with me in Hazeleigh Hall Wood. After we had done shooting and it was getting quite dark we had it led out and looked at it by *lantern light*. We then thought it would be very difficult to find anything to beat it. . . .
Our shooting to-day will be in pretty fir plantations along a fringe of cliffs skirting some meadows. It is pretty ground and I always enjoy a day there. We shall dine with the old tenant after our sport. He always places me in the post of honour by his side at dinner, but it is rather troublesome. He is so deaf that he cannot hear a sound, and everything must be written on a little slate at his side. (Written at Redgrave, Suffolk, 8 December 1864.)
Beddgelert is a very curious old town. The cottages are built all up the face of the mountain so that the inmates of one house look down the chimneys of their lower neighbour. There are also great sand-banks along the shore which are sometimes drifted very much in

windy weather, and some of the houses in the lower town are almost buried in the sand. (Written at Barmouth, 29 September 1865.)

On Thursday a deer was turned out at Latchingdon with Mr. Gale's harriers. The deer was turned off in the same field as last year, and strange to say went almost the same line, in some cases going through the very same fields. The ground was so terribly heavy from the rains and snow that I kept mainly along the roads. The hounds went so fast that very few could really live with them, but your pony went capitally and kept a good place all through the run. The heavy ground told upon the deer too, and it was taken at South Hanningfield having gone about nine miles in just under an hour. . . . A deer was turned out near Maldon the week before but the poor thing was a tame one and would not run. I did not go as I thought it was only a sort of 'Cockney Day' for the Maldon people. (Written from Woodham Mortimer, 24 March 1867.)

I have been away since Friday, having come down to Norwich by the afternoon express and then early on Saturday morning on the other line to Brandon to breakfast with Mr. Wilson who had driven across country the night before. The young squire is thinking of selling a property which he has there and Mr. Wilson wanted me to meet him there and talk it over. It is in a strange country of *sand and rabbits*. There are thousands of acres of land, good for nothing else, and which are devoted entirely to rabbits. The surface is covered with nothing but short grass and moss, and is as full of holes as a honeycomb, so that you see the rabbits popping up and running about and disappearing again in all directions. On Mr. Wilson's warren they usually catch about 30,000 a year, so you may fancy what a number there are.

For all their love of outdoor life, both father and son knew how to write good letters and in them gave of their best to their children. The above examples of J.O.P.'s writing is more than equalled by the delightful letters Christopher Comyns Parker sent between 1826 and 1831 to his youngest daughter Elizabeth. Though few letters survive, they appear to be part of a much larger series. Elizabeth, born in July 1814, was at school first at Bromley, Kent, then at Ewell and Notting Hill House. She was studious, thoughtful, and tender-hearted. Her nephew, Oxley Durant Parker, writes of her:

Our Aunt, Elizabeth Oxley Parker, the only surviving daughter of Christopher Comyns Parker, was very well educated and extremely well read. On December 8th, 1848, she had the misfortune to have a serious fall from her horse when riding, and injured her spine, so that she was rather short and slightly deformed, but she was very good-looking. As her mother was rather an invalid, she was sent to school like her brother Oxley, at an early age. . . . She used to sketch well, was a good botanist and a great lover of bees. She always had a lot of hives and seemed to have a great deal of honey from the bees. She had a special garden near the hives and filled it with flowers which the bees were fond of. . . . All through her life she took a very keen interest in the education of the Woodham Mortimer and the Cock Clarks village children, and was at the National Voluntary Schools there constantly . . . and she held night classes for young men at the Grange during the winter months.

The letters C.C.P. wrote to her, which are the most delightful in all the Oxley Parker correspondence, are genuine historical documents, full of pertinent observations on the social life of the day. His answers to her perplexed questions on politics and society are well thought out and must have been helpful to a girl passing through the most impressionable period of her life. One can only quote a few choice fragments from them. In October 1826 C.C.P. records in his diary:

From 6th to 23rd, engaged on Mr. Tufnell's property and journey to and from York and Northumberland.

The tour was the subject of a long letter which he sent to Elizabeth. In it he described how he endeavoured to see all he could of the two counties while his companions amused themselves coursing and shooting. He visited Alnwick Castle and park, dined with the Duke and Duchess of Northumberland, stood on the pier at Sunderland while ships passed in full sail, visited a cloth factory in Leeds, and on the way home by coach,

. . . Perils by night and day prevented us reaching London before five o'clock. The fog was so intense in the night that . . . the guard walked by the leaders to prevent our coachman overturning, which we two or three times feared as we got off the road, and fifty-eight miles from London we encountered a very severe tempest which accompanied us nearly the whole way to the Metropolis. I never was so wet for so long a time. I was an inside passenger but unfortunately had, a little while before the storm came, requested a gentleman to allow me his place outside, and I could not be so uncivil as to turn him out.

Travel enters a great deal into the letters. In 1829 C.C.P. lost his first wife, and the following year was writing to his daughter:

I feel as you may suppose very dull at home, day after day by myself, but business calls me very much from home and that is a relief to me.

At that time he was treating for a new 'chariot', but the finest conveyances could not prevent unhappy accidents on the bumpy and imperfect roads of those days:

Mr Baker has unfortunately broken his leg by a fall from the Maldon coach on Wednesday week going down Danbury Hill; he is going on very well. I unfortunately was passing that way just after the accident happened and I saw the poor man in a cart and Miss Baker in great distress.

On 24 March 1830 he was in town for the purpose of drawing lots for the four divisions of the Caswall Estate, and he wrote to his daughter from the Gray's Inn Coffee House:

The valuation of the Caswall property has drawn largely on my time and this day the parties meet to take their chance by drawing lots for the four divisions which I flatter myself I shall present finished in good style. Mr. Driver was with me on Saturday and I have taken advantage of his ability and experience upon some knotty points, and he kindly offered to assist in drawing out the particulars. I have been very fortunate, and if the parties interested are but satisfied with the result of my exertions I shall be highly gratified, as it is a property of nearly £80,000.

In that month the important election which was to result in the introduction of the first Reform Bill had just taken place, and C.C.P. had been busily engaged on behalf of the Conservative candidate for Essex:

My heart and soul were in the cause of our friend Mr. Bramston, and most zealously do I devote my time in his service, and triumphant was the result. I started a subscription to defray the necessary expenses, which was met with the greatest marks of liberality, and we raised about £9000 of which little more than a third will be required to discharge all demands, for many friends sent the voters free of all expenses; every day's contest brought fresh supporters.

In September he was commenting on the erection of the new Danbury Place:

The first stone of Danbury Place is to be laid on Tuesday next. I was busily engaged with Mr. and Mrs. Round planning the new approaches to the house one day last week, and I am to give them my time all Wednesday next for the same purpose. They mean to enter the park by lodges from both roads. By the plan the house will be a great ornament to our country. I think I have been very instrumental in preserving that beautiful spot from destruction. I sadly feared it would have been sold to be converted into a common farm. Now it will be daily improved in beauty.

There is no more striking illustration of the way in which C.C.P. kept personal affairs out of his diary than the two weeks' gap which he left from 20 September to 4 October 1830. He never mentions his second marriage or his honeymoon, which he spent touring the south coast of England. His letter to Elizabeth of 13 October, however, tells the full story: his visit with his bride to the dockyards at Portsmouth; the New Forest, Poole and Wareham; Weymouth and Corfe Castle:

The bay [at Weymouth] is well protected by the high ground and Portland Island from which the Portland stone used for building is taken. The principal street at Weymouth is a crescent with a good parade, secured by stone wharfing. Although I have called the place Weymouth, strictly speaking, it is Melcombe Regis, and Weymouth is in the back settlements over a bridge, uniting like Chelmsford with Moulsham, but a different sort of river. This place only required an evening and morning's walk to carry all away in the mind's eye. As we were starting, the French Royal Family from Lulworth Castle came to our hotel to a breakfast ordered for sixteen at twelve o'clock. They appeared very cheerful and continually showed themselves at the window. Had we stayed we might have joined them on the parade where they frequently walk for an hour or two at a time.

They vainly flatter themselves that they will be soon called back to resume their royalty in France. So are kings imposed upon by fawning sycophants!

From Weymouth they went to Salisbury where they attended a service in the Cathedral, then to Winchester, where they saw the Cathedral, the College and the Chapel Library. Then, by way of Windsor, they made their way home. In the last few sentences of his letter C.C.P. comments on the consideration his young daughter has shown him on the occasion of his second marriage:

. . . Need I assure you how gratifying your whole conduct has been in endeavouring to promote my happiness in the change it has pleased Providence to allow me to make, to soothe past woes and to cheer my future prospects. I may with confidence look forward to domestic comfort, blessed with wife and children whose principal study in their worldly concerns appears to be such as cannot fail to make us an united family. I really do feel one of the happiest of Beings, and God grant that we may all long continue so.

About Christopher Comyns Parker as a person no more is known than has already been written in this book. His son, however, emerges as a much clearer figure, partly because of the diaries and partly because Oxley Durant Parker, the younger brother of 'Cris', has left a brief memoir of him. He was a tall handsome man in his youth and retained his good looks in later life.

Father wore white buckskin breeches, like the Life Guards wear, and long Wellington boots; he was 16 stones in weight, and rode rather big hunters. Later on the buckskins and Wellington boots were superseded by white Bedford cord breeches and butcher boots. . . . . . . [He] was of a most genial nature and most sociable, and the result was that he was a general favourite wherever he went, no matter whether it was in the hunting field, on the election hustings, or at the agricultural meetings, where he always showed horses, cattle, sheep and pigs, and the sheds at Woodham Mortimer and elsewhere were full of prize cards, and the herdsmen were proud of what they won.

Father drove great distances with his horses and thought nothing of 30 or 40 miles a day. In my very early days he used to drive a pair in a mail phaeton, and thought nothing of driving over to Laindon Hills Farm and back, about 24 miles each way, and to Birch and Plumbro Marshes, and Mother would go with him.

. . . Certainly Father was in appearance a typical country squire in all his ways, and dressed up in his large white top hat and light coat.

To have lived as he did one must have had to be tough, for an open-air life in the nineteenth century was one long endurance test. He was often soaked to the skin in rain-storms, and accidents on the road, even in those days, were not infrequent, and were far more likely to happen to the horseman or the driver than to the pedestrian, in spite of the absence of pathways along the sides of the roads. We wonder, on reading the select list of mishaps which happened to J.O.P. during his career, how he managed to survive sound in wind and limb:

March 21st, 1844. In driving from Steeple to Southminster, Ludlow horse shied and jumped over hedge into field on Welsh Farm. No mischief to gig but lamed herself slightly.

March 27th, 1850. Met with accident. Mare frightened and ran away. . . . Escaped, but cart upset and broken.

24th July, 1854. Also to Margaret Woods Farm with Mr. Tufnell junr. Irish horse fell down, broke both shafts, threw us out, but no mischief except to shafts.

28th December, 1861. Upset at Rettendon by coal cart in road.

15th December, 1862. Upset at East Tilbury by front wheel coming off.

24th May, 1866. Returned to Battlesbridge with Will. Tufnell in his brougham. Pole broke in descending Hamborough Hill.

13th November, 1867. Shooting Hazeleigh Hall; 98 head. Shot in the cheek.

19th July, 1877. Night so dark that John had to lead the mare up the hill at Danbury. Sitting in the cart could not see man on the horse. Backed into ditch and upset at gate; no mischief done.

28th January, 1879. Between Chelmsford and Baddow a man pulled wrong rein and drove the shaft of his cart through the brougham and broke off the step.

7th January, 1881. Thrown from cob galloping after trespassers in Wilderness Wood. No mischief.

19th December, 1882. Rode to Hazeleigh Hall. Pony bucked and jumped in galloping across meadow. Lost my balance and came on my back.

1st April, 1886. Had a fall—knocked the back of my head. Rode quietly home.

Add to the above a fall down the stairs at Portland Road Station on 9 July 1880, and one wonders at the miracle of survival. Yet he had enough energy to set off walking home from Chelmsford (seven miles) in February at the age of sixty-nine and from Fambridge Ferry almost all the way to Rochford (nearly the same distance) on 2 June 1886, at seventy-four.

Beyond the very rare colds, some of which lasted for several weeks and were complicated by bronchitis, he had little illness. In 1871–2, and on two other occasions, he suffered from inflamed veins in the legs, probably owing to his being for long periods either on horseback or on his feet; but very rarely was he compelled, either summer or winter, to remain indoors for more than a few days.

The holidays he took were few and far between, and most of them were business-cum-pleasure trips. While his father was alive, that is, in October 1842, he visited his Dutch relatives, and in March of the same year he was occupied for several weeks at Sharpham measuring and valuing the timber on the estate for Mr. Durant, later to become his father-in-law. Every two or three years he enjoyed a short stay at Sharpham, usually after the harvest was over at Woodham Mortimer, and he went frequently to Canons, the Hertfordshire residence of his in-laws, and enjoyed a couple of days' shooting. When the family were small he found it convenient to hire apartments at some seaside resort (Dovercourt in 1855, Suffolk in 1861, Eastbourne in 1863, near to Cris's school at Worthing). Here he went some week-ends, returning to his business in Essex Monday or

Tuesday of each week. In 1865 he spent a week at Malvern, in 1866 two weeks in Scotland, a holiday which must have brought his honeymoon vividly back to his memory. In the summer of 1869 he went with Sir George Pechell on the memorable trip to visit his friend's Irish estates, and this lasted from 15 May to 7 June. The most memorable holiday of all was the one which came almost at the end of his life—a month's trip through France and Switzerland, to Italy. Of all these breaks in life's routine he left some record in his diary; the more remarkable sights he recorded faithfully:

19th August, 1866. Sunday. Mr. Clitton read service in the dining-room. In the afternoon, wandering over the hills—so clear that I could trace the whole shores of the Moray Firth, the hills of Ross and Sutherland with snow on many of their peaks and on the west as far as Ben Nevis and the adjacent hills.

12th May, 1884. Up at six, and after cup of coffee with . . . by steamboat to Monte Tresa and enjoyed the splendid view of the lake and mountains in the morning light. Returned in time to join the rest of the party at the hotel and then started at 11 by the same steamer to the other end of the lake. . . . Lovely scenery throughout the journey and splendid view of the lake of Como as we descended the zigzag road. . . . To Villa Carlotta. The gardens such a sight of choicest roses and other flowers as can scarcely be described. One magnolia tree sixty feet high, the trunk eight feet round. . . .

The paucity of good holidays, and of times when one's mind could be completely free of care, taught him to mix business and pleasure judiciously and made him an adept at snatching the odd moments of enjoyment. Often when in Chelmsford for the day he would dine at the 'ordinary' and follow up his dinner with a smoking-concert. When in town he would take advantage of a business trip to meet his family and go to a show in the evening. His taste in the theatre was catholic. In 1849 he attended the Egyptian Hall in Piccadilly to see the famous Albert Smith give one of his noted entertainments; in 1846 he heard Jenny Lind sing, and in 1852 saw Fanny Kemble in a recital from *A Midsummer Night's Dream*. His taste for the real thing did not stop his enjoyment of *A Midsummer Night's Dream* when in 1857 it was made into a pantomime. Probably Leotard on his newly invented trapeze (11 October 1862), the melo- dramatic *Colleen Bawn* (29 August 1862), the thrilling *Ticket of Leave Man* (4 April 1864) or *Jim the Penman* (12 April 1886) were quite as welcome to him as the more classic *Birds* of Aristophanes, *La Somnambula*, or *La Traviata*. He attended the Handel Festival at the Crystal Palace in 1857, and, ten years later, crammed the *Messiah* and *Don Giovanni* into one glorious day. On odd occasions he saw the year's exhibitions at the Royal Academy and, in 1874, went to the memorable show of Doré's and Hoppé's contemporary drawings.

His greatest delights were, however, either in the open air or in places where one was not entirely a spectator. He loved to be part of a review or a show, and seems to have taken a special delight in animal or flower shows, and in rural fetes at Maldon and other places

. . . when a rural fete took place, generally every other year at Woodham Mortimer Place. . . . Father was in his happiest mood. There was always a great crowd of country people from all around. Steam engines and roundabouts, Aunt Sallies, and coconut shies and races were going from morning till night, and I daresay little political gatherings, and Father walked all amongst the people; he was glad to see them, and they were delighted to see him and his family moving about 'natural like' amongst them. But there, those happy days have gone, and you must be careful, and no corrupt practices must be!

Occasionally he would attend the illuminations in London or the Lord Mayor's Show; on five occasions at least he was present at the Derby (1864, 1867, 1868, 1872, and 1875), and he saw the boat races of 1870 and 1871 between Oxford and Cambridge Universities. He was a good singer in his youth, but seems to have performed little in public in later life, the only entertainment on his part that we read about being his render- ing of 'Winter Garden' at a penny reading in Danbury (6 February 1868) and his reading of 'John Gilpin' at a similar

THE OXLEY PARKER PAPERS

function at Woodham Mortimer (14 February 1879). He continued to love dancing until late in life, though in his later years he often came home early. In the 60s and 70s, amateur theatricals became popular, and he accompanied many family parties to yeomanry and rifle corps theatricals and to performances at Braxted and Belhus.

Sport always occupied a prominent place in his diary. After about 1860 he regularly recorded the bag at each shoot:

25th November, 1863. Afternoon shooting, 7 guns, 389 head; 145 pheasants, 30 hares, 208 rabbits, 2 partridges, 4 woodcocks.
26th November, D⁰. 120 head, 17P, 30H, 70R, 3 Partridges.

The same guests were invited to Woodham each year to open the partridge shooting on 1 September and there were numerous half-days shooting, especially when his sons were growing up. He went frequently to his in-laws at Canons in Hertfordshire, where much larger bags were obtained than at Woodham, and it is clear that these were red-letter days. And the diaries tell of a drive to Alresford Hall for breakfast (about twenty-four miles) prior to a day's shooting there. Whether he drove home that evening is not recorded.

His favourite sport was the hunt, and as the years passed by he described the success or failure of the day, the 'ringing runs' and the lost quarries.

11th February, 1863. E.U.H. [Essex Union Hunt] Purleigh Wash. Long day. Short burst from Hazeleigh Hall to Beeleigh. Second fox from Mundon Furze, twice round to Norton and then away through Althorne and to ground at Hill Farm Latchingdon.

Later, one can almost feel the regret of the old man as he follows the hunt in his carriage, or leaves it half-way through the course.

31st January, 1885. Morning home. Rode to Bonham House thinking to fall in with E.E., the meet being at Springfield. Fox found in 15 minutes before I got there. Followed, but, heavy rain coming on, turned home. Did not see the hounds.

24th February, 1886. Stag Hounds at East Hanningfield Tye. Drove Louisa to the meet in the dog cart with young mare, followed them and saw the run by Hyde Hall, Gibcracks, Rettendon Common. Lost sight of them over the Hill and drove home.

16th December, 1886. E.U.H. Latchingdon. Tile Hall and Althorne Grove blank. Brace of foxes from field of cabbages. Chopped one in the cabbages and the other after short run killed in lower Grove. Found another brace in Snoreham Hall Grove and after a run by Marsh Tile Hall ran to ground at Tile Hall Grove—dug out and killed. Found again at Fambridge Hall, very good run. I went home from Stow and only saw the first part of the run.

On 15 April 1865 he took his two sons to the hunt for the first time, and this gets a deserving mention in the Diary:

E. E. Terling, Rayleigh Arms. Very quick run from Sandy Wood to Langleys Park Lodge, and killed. Cris and Oxley. Cris rode well.

Oxley Durant Parker tells an interesting hunting story:

The meet was at Hazeleigh Hall Wood, a sure find—but that year not so sure, of which father's great friend, Squire Tom Kemble, of Runwell Hall, probably had some knowledge. So the old squire drove over in his dogcart and arrived just outside the covert just as the hounds were arriving, but he drove right up to the Keeper's hut, and as the hounds drew the covert a view 'Holloa' was given and a fine old fox broke away and gave the hounds and the field a splendid run right back in a straight line of nine miles to Kemble's Gorse, and nobody was any wiser for Old Squire Kemble's ruse!

One of his friends was Sir Claude Champion de Crespigny to whom he refers in odd places. Besides being thrown over his horse's head on two successive days (see above, page 144), on 10 June 1882 he attempted a balloon ascent and had his leg broken by the basket of the balloon coming into contact with a wall. He had to be taken out of the car and his companion Simmonds made the ascent alone, coming down at Arras one hour and forty minutes later. Again, in August 1883, he tried another ascent, this time with success:

Did not go to see him off, but watched the balloon rising majestically over the bottom of the town [Maldon] and so quietly that there seemed to be scarcely any swinging of the car. The balloon was in sight for nearly an hour bearing NE. Heard the next morning that they had landed safely at Flushing and come off at once by boat.

J.O.P. was very regular in his attendance at the Chelmsford Beefsteak Club. It was founded in 1768, his grandfather, John Oxley Parker, being an original member. Membership of the Club was limited to forty and included some of the most prominent men in the county. It met once a month on market-day, on the Friday nearest to the full moon; the thought behind this being a light night for the drive home. It had then, and continues to have, its own cellar at the 'Saracen's Head', and is well known for the quality of the wine supplied with the dinner. The attendance was never large. At the anniversary of 1847 only eight dined. The dinner of 1861, at which twenty-five were present, was described as very well attended. At the Centenary Ball there was a very good company.

27th November, 1868. Beefsteak Club Centenary Ball. . . . Most successful Ball—270; all arrangements satisfactory, music, supper, wine etc., all first rate.

In the high noon of the nineteenth century new sports came to be popular, with the increase of leisure among the working and middle classes. By this time cricket had become a national institution. J.O.P., being a sportsman of the old school, never took part in the game, but nevertheless he came to like it and to support his village team whole-heartedly. Probably, being a family man and socially inclined, he realised, if unconsciously, the value of such an organised game as this in bringing together all elements of society. Cricket is first mentioned in the diaries on 26 June 1856:

T. Gepp's boys, cricket etc.

In the very next month he went to Danbury Palace to a cricket match and to see the grounds.

The speed with which cricket gained ground around the

middle of the century may almost be measured by the frequency with which it figures in the diaries. Two years after the Danbury match, the Woodham Mortimer team is first mentioned:

June 19th, 1858. Cricket Match. C. Durant, Gepps, William, etc, against Maldon Club. Woodham Mort^r one innings 110, Maldon 1st innings 32, 2nd innings 79.

This entry indicates that local teams had sprung up all over Essex. In the same year J.O.P. attended a county match at Braxted:

August 19th, 1858. Morning at home. Afternoon to Braxted. Cricket match, Essex and Cambridgeshire. Essex more than 40 ahead 1st innings.

At the time this game was played Cris was five and Oxley three. The boys therefore grew up in an atmosphere in which cricket was an institution, and probably admired the men who made up the local teams very much. Oxley, in his book, mentions the regular matches that were played when he was young:

For cricket we had a very good ground. There was an annual match against an XI brought over by Messrs Robert and James Page, our tenants, from Bradwell-on-Sea. Then there was a boys' XI that played against a Home team made up of cousins—three Durant boys, three Gepps, Pearsons from Springfield, Ridleys, Chelmsford, Charles Burney etc, and others of the Essex Calves' Club; Frazers, John Powell, James and Frank Round, Claughtons, Adys [Abdys?], Rowland Wilson etc.

Many of these names are recited in J.O.P.'s accounts of memorable matches (e.g. 10 August 1860).

For some twenty years, in the middle of the century, archery was in vogue, and there are notices of archery parties between 1846 and 1870 at various places in Essex. Later came lawn tennis, of which there is an early mention in 1877. When the game started it was customary to have school-children to collect the balls from long grass at the back of the court. Then, as play

THE OXLEY PARKER PAPERS

improved, fish- or wire-netting was put up. But at Woodham Mortimer Place the change was never made and until late in the 1930s children were still employed to collect the balls. By 1882 it was evidently well organised in the county, for the play on 5 August that year was for the Championship Cup, and J.O.P. describes the play as 'first rate'. The trains, incidentally, were crowded on that day with Bank Holiday passengers. August Bank Holiday, as we understand it, came into being after the Bank Holidays Act of 1871 and is first mentioned in the diaries in 1877.

On 19 September 1849 J.O.P. had a remarkable piece of good fortune. The story is again told by his son:

I must tell of an interesting day's shooting, and which proved a profitable day for father. He went to the Eastlands Farm at Bradwell-on-Sea, and it happened to be the day of the sale of the contents of the Bradwell Rectory by Mr. Shreibers, so he walked up there to attend the sale. He found the sale room full of dealers, and the two portraits by Gainsboro' of Sir Henry Bate Dudley and his wife Lady Bate Dudley, in 1849, were put up; they were full length pictures and each time anyone bid, father bid £10 or £20 more. The dealers soon put their heads together and audibly said: 'Who is that bidding; they are not genuine?' but father kept bidding as before, and finally they were knocked down to him for £300.

At the time he bought them he evidently did not realise the importance of this transaction. There is a brief mention of it under 19 September 1849. The amount paid for them was not £300, but 130 guineas. If only the dealers had known!

They were so large that Mother decided that Woodham Mortimer Place was too small for them, and father lent them to his brother-in-law, Mr. Richard Durant jun., and they hung for some years in the Billiard Room at High Canons, Hertfordshire.

The story of the pugnacious curate of Bradwell—playwright, duellist, eccentric, and reformer—has been told elsewhere (see *Essex Review*, XL, 70–2, and the Rev. E. Brown, *History of*

Bradwell), and though Sir Henry in the course of his tumultuous career had much to do with the improvement of the roads in his hundred of Essex, the portraits have certainly turned out to be much more important than the man.

His portrait, and that of his wife, by Gainsborough, show him as a handsome, and rather cynical, beau of the Regency period, and his wife as an ornamental and rather languishing woman. (*Essex Review*, XL, 74.)

In June 1863 the portraits were exhibited at the Colchester Town Hall. In September 1863 he was offered £400 for them but refused to accept it. In 1867 he was asked to send them to the National Portrait Gallery Exhibition at Burlington House, together with an account of the subject's life, which was later to be incorporated in a series of 'Eccentric Biographies' for the editor of the *Gentleman's Magazine*.

In December 1863, says Oxley Durant Parker, the two pictures narrowly escaped complete destruction by fire:

With four other large Gainsboroughs they were at Henry Graves' in Pall Mall, and they were all going to be engraved, when a fire broke out next door which destroyed Her Majesty's Theatre. . . . They were all saved and carried into the Senior United Club in Pall Mall, which is opposite Graves'. . . . It is a wonderful account of how they were saved, and we shall never know who were the strangers who helped to save six such valuable pictures. Mr. Graves said he never knew, for the stranger disappeared after the fire.

A letter in the collection, however, seems to date the fire at the end of 1857, and Mr. Graves certainly seems to have known who saved them, unless of course he is transferring the credit for the deed to his own firm:

D. Sir,

In dragging out your two Gainsboroughs the frames got injured and I have had them regilt and now send them by . . . train to you. . . . There was only 5 minutes to remove 8 Gainsboroughs and the fire consum'd £50,000 of value in 15 minutes.

Mr. Graves's postscript runs.

My son aged 22 saved your two while I saved my ledgers etc.

The pictures were again on view in January 1884, for on the 5th the diary reads:

To London by the 12-30 train. Louisa joined me at Chelmsford, for private view of the Exhibition of Old Masters at Burlington House. My Gainsborough Portraits of Sir Henry and Lady Dudley in prominent position in the principal room and attracting grand admiration, the pictures both looking well after their recent cleaning.

Oxley Durant Parker continues:

... eventually, I think, our father thought that one had some reason in drawing his attention to the fact that they should be in some house of his own . . . so after some Exhibition they went to Woodham Mortimer Grange, and though the house is small, they looked very well there.

By this time their value had been realised by all connoisseurs. Visitors began to arrive at Woodham Mortimer with offers to buy them:

... [wrote] to Mr. Beck that I would take £10,000 for Gainsborough pictures. (7 June 1885.)
Mr. Wertheimer and his nephew came down to see Gainsborough pictures . . . to the Grange. Met them there. Gave them luncheon and drove them to Chelmsford to the 1-27 train. Wanted me to sell the pictures to London, which I declined. Said he could not offer more than £6000. (26 June 1885.)
Mr. Beck and Mr. Deschamps came down to look at Gainsborough Pictures. (10 November 1886.)

Oxley Durant Parker continues the story:

Eventually, just before father died, in 1887, he [Wertheimer] bought them for £10,000 for Lord Burton, the rich brewer, living in Chesterfield House, Mayfair, where I went to see them by kind permission of Lord Burton, taking my wife and my sister. Lord Burton met us on his doorstep and greeted me, 'Glad to see you, Mr. Oxley Parker; now go and see the pictures, and I won't come with you, and then you can say how badly they are hung; but see the rest of my collection.

The story of his life would be incomplete without reference to his unfailing support of the village church, and his efforts to lead others to regular attendance. He was most regular in his attendance at both morning and evening service, and should some villager be absent in the A.M. the squire assumed it was due to ill-health and probably called at the house after morning service to enquire. The story goes that the verger sat at the back of the church with a long stick and this he used to tap on the shoulder anyone seen to be asleep during the sermon.

Thus through the diaries and letters of John Oxley Parker and through his son's memories of him, we see the Victorian gentleman going about his daily business and taking his pleasures: planting rhododendrons in his garden (5 April 1856), unpacking and bottling his wine (26 February 1845; 21 December 1852; 11 July 1858), distributing largesse to poor villagers (14 September 1848), sitting for his portrait (April–June 1880), keeping a careful watch on his weight (12 April 1869, 15 st. 6; 17 June 1870, 14 st. 8; 30 April 1879, 15 st. 8), observing the Aurora Borealis (10 March 1861; 14 December 1862; 24–5 October 1870; 12 October 1882), the total eclipse of the moon (23 August 1877), and the approach of a comet (5 October 1857), being forced to don a puggaree when the weather became intolerably hot (11 August 1871; 30 June 1883), visiting the dentist in London (31 August 1846; 23 February 1857; 23 April 1861), joining in sing-songs with Admiral Johnson of the *Victory* and Charles Burney, enjoying apricot and green gooseberry tart (6–8 May 1882), stopping the mail train to get a lift home (3 February 1861) or uncovering the foundations of the old Roman fort of Othona on the family farm at Bradwell with members of the Essex Archaeological Society (October–December 1864). Sometimes the entries have a touch of humour:

16th June, 1865. Home and to grass cutting party at Boreham House. Lord Macclesfield, Lord Raglan etc etc. *No Grass.*

22nd April, 1871. Dined with boys early at Mr. Wallis (Southminster), Wonderful bottle of old port. Brought away cork for T. Kemble.

8th July, 1885. Went on to St. Mary Abbots, Kensington. Marriage of Janet Woodham and Walter Grimston at ½ past 10. Bride in morning dress and no breakfast.

A note of regret creeps in as he records the growing-up of his children:

Christmas Day, 1870. Maria and Alice in Devonshire. First time any of the family have been away at Xmas.

Towards the end of his life he never omitted to record a note of thanks on his birthday for his continued good health:

January 16th, 1885. My 74th birthday. Thankful to be as well as I am. Never thought to outlive RD. [Richard Durant junior, his brother-in-law.]

January 16th, 1887. My birthday. This day I enter on my 75th year, and again thank God for continued health.

The long series of diaries end on 15 May 1887, at the end of a volume, with the entry:

Sunday. Fine bright day, cold N. wind.

John Oxley Parker, one of the most notable and typical of Victorian Country Gentlemen, died suddenly, lamented by all, on 8 October 1887.

CHAPTER XVI

PUBLIC SERVICE

IN 1837, the Maldon Board of Guardians, of which Christopher Comyns Parker was the Chairman, were in trouble with the Poor Law Commissioners. The new Poor Law had been passed by the Whig Government some three years earlier in an attempt to remedy the social evils which had been corrupting rural society ever since the beginning of the French wars. The Maldon Board of Guardians were not enforcing the provisions of the Poor Law Amendment Act as rigorously as they should.

The story of English Poor Law reform has its place in books of social history. In an earlier period of agricultural distress, a group of Berkshire county magistrates had decided on the principle of making up the wages of the farm labourer out of the parish poor-rates. This 'Speenhamland' system, called by the name of the place where the J.P.s met when they decided to put it into practice, rapidly spread over a large part of rural England, and brought increasing evils with it. No longer need the large farmer worry about paying his labourers a living wage; no longer need the shiftless type of labourer worry whether or no he was out of work, whether or not his work was well or badly done, for he received his meagre 'pay' just the same, and was doomed for ever to live on the verge of destitution. Meanwhile all those who paid rates at all were subject to the unfair burden of a rate which supported one class only—the employing farmer.

In 1832 the Reformed Parliament came into office pledged to introduce a series of Whig measures aimed at allaying this and many other social evils. Two years later they introduced the Poor Law Amendment Act, by which outdoor relief was almost completely abolished, and anybody who was able-bodied could only get help by going into the Union Workhouse. This institution was designed to be less attractive than work, and was cold and heartless compared with the relative comfort and homeliness of the old-time Parish Workhouse. The 'Union' came to be dreaded, and many respectable labouring families preferred to live in a state of semi-starvation rather than be subject to the rules, privations, and indignities of the dreaded 'Bastille'.

Woodham Mortimer was within the Maldon Union, whose workhouse, like many others, was rapidly filled up to over-flowing with workless during the years 1835 and 1836. There was nothing left for the Guardians to do if suffering throughout the country-side was to be alleviated, but in some way to get round this troublesome measure by small acts of clemency towards labourers with large families, indigent old people, and other deserving cases. For this they were admonished by the Poor Law Commission. An undated letter to C.C.P., as Chairman, illustrates this:

. . . If the workhouse is filled, outdoor labour of some sort must be found. The Comm\[rs] cannot permit relief to the A[ble] B[odied] in any shape, in aid of wages, and I must at once say that in my own opinion were they to do so at this moment they would destroy the whole benefit the Act is intended to confer on the labourers, and be guilty of the most cruel injustice towards them. Have we not a right to expect that as the price of produce increases, he who tills the ground and whose bread is dearer because of the gains of the farmer, sh\[d] be permitted to participate in those gains, and will wages rise if we again have recourse to the allow\[ce] system in any shape?

The Whig legislators were excellent theorists, and it was in the confidence that, in the long run, wages would rise, that they performed this 'operation without anaesthetics' on rural society. What the labourer *ought* to have according to the letter quoted above was one thing; what he *got* was another. Few happenings in English history can equal the suffering undergone by the rural labourers in the grim days after the Act of 1834. Unfortunately the Parker correspondence on this topic is incomplete, but we gather that C.C.P. must have written asking for some temporary relaxation, for he received a letter granting a very minute concession—the admission of one or two children of a large family into the workhouse rather than all, in preparation for the thorough application of the Act at an early date.

My dear Sir,

I regretted exceedingly that I was not so fortunate as to meet you neither at the Board nor at your own house on Thursday, as there were many points on which I wished to converse with you . . . particularly touching 'Out Door Relief'. You are aware that this must cease, and the sooner the better in my mind, for certain I am that justice never will be done to the labourer until the employers distinctly understand that there can be no relief, no matter in what shape, but by receiving the *whole family* into the Workhouse. The resolutions which I read to the B^d and herewith transmit, will by restricting all relief to the Ab[le] B^d with a large family of children all too young to work, to the admission of one or two of these (as the case may be) into the W. House, prepare them for what is to follow, viz, the absolute Rule, which will certainly be issued in the Union in a very short time. These resolutions have been adopted in many of my Unions and I earnestly request y^r assistance in introducing them in yours, and most particularly urge that 'Clothing' be altogether discontinued, even to the *Aged and Infirm*—give them any extent of Allow^{ce} you deem necessary to enable them to provide for their wants, but neither clothe them *nor allow them to work*—no *part* allowance, *part* wages—take them off the labour market, and place the whole of the work to be done at the disposal of the Ab. Bodied. I shall be very glad to hear from you on all these points. . . .

These two letters, both written in 1837, show the official view. What correspondence followed during 1838 we do not know, but a letter written by C.C.P. to Colonel Wade, who dealt for the Commissioners with the Maldon Union, shows not only his attitude to the New Poor Law but reveals the mainspring of those political beliefs which animated both him and his family throughout the whole century. He speaks of the undoubted necessity of applying the law, and of withdrawing outdoor relief from the able-bodied, but pleads that it should be done gradually, not only for the sake of the suffering labourer but also to avoid losing the services of many good men who, having been Guardians, have tried to carry out the Act, but cannot conscientiously be parties to inflicting further suffering on the labouring classes:

Woodham Mortimer Place
Decr 10th, 1838.

Dear Sir,

I am obliged by your letter of the 8th. I assure you that no-one can possibly be more anxious than myself that no relief should be given to make up wages. I remember arguing the point more than 40 years ago with the late Mr. Strutt then Member for Maldon, and foretelling the effect which would inevitably result from such a system which would prove a premium to the idle and worthless labourers and a disadvantage to the industrious and provident. We have seen the ill effects of this system woefully exemplified in the *mal*administration of the Poor Laws, but the working of the New Law is daily tending to the correction of those abuses.

With regard to the question now before us, I have read the letter transmitted by the Commissioners upon the subject of relief of the same kind to able-bodied poor addressed to the Guardians of the Fareham Union, and you also give a most decided opinion against such relief in any shape and in any case. Yet *when full* wages are given I cannot satisfy myself as to what is best to be done with very large families of which none of the children are able to assist in providing maintenance. Nothing reasonable in the shape of wages can meet the case. Wages in this neighbourhood have risen with the increased price of farm produce, and if flour continues at its present price a further advance will be no less necessary than just, but to afford sufficient maintenance without any other means of assistance for a man, his wife and six or seven small children, a more than reasonable advance must be made. Single men are clearly entitled to the same remuneration for labour as married, and an extravagant excess in the amount of wages to them would lead to idleness and dissipation at the Beer Shop, already sufficiently the resort of the vicious and dissolute.

In working out the new Law we have been anxious to carry out its principles to the fullest extent but at the same time by a gradual transition from that system to which the labouring class had become habituated, to do so without unnecessary hardship to them. We have discouraged as much as possible all applications for outdoor relief to the able-bodied, and have discontinued it so far as to give it in scarcely any case in any other shape but that (to which I am decidedly friendly where absolutely necessary) of receiving a child into the schools of the workhouse; and even this the Guardians are most of them as well as myself only inclined to do in special cases.

It will be said that should such cases be refused, increased thrift on the part of the labourer and the assistance of private charity, will be the means of mitigating the severity of destitution. As to the hand of private charity affording a partial relief to these necessities, this is all very well in those districts where resident gentry or other persons of opulence are found with incomes sufficiently ample to indulge in such liberality, but where this is not the case, and where from circumstances of locality or from the unhealthiness of the district the majority of farms are even held offhand, where then is the hand of private charity?

I cannot but consider it impolitic that an order so rigorous should be issued at the commencement of winter, and I am fearful it will create dissatisfaction. I am also fearful that it will cause considerable dissatisfaction amongst the Guardians, and if insisted upon that I may be deprived in consequence of the presence and assistance of many who are most useful as Guardians and anxious to carry out the working of the Bill so as to benefit to the utmost the permanent condition of the labouring poor. But many of those who now go to the full extent to which we have at present carried it will be quite unwilling to go further.

If the Commissioners knew the reluctance with which the parents in most cases submit to the separation from a single child when an offer is made to take it into the House, they would see that there is little fear of such a practice being carried to excess; the relief is only accepted where the necessities of poverty urge a compliance.

Another winter passed, and the minds of the poor would be prepared by gradual restriction of relief to receive with less discontent its entire abolition to able-bodied out of the House in any shape whatever, which at present is considered a course of undue severity and hardship.

I have been led on to much greater length than was my intention at the commencement of my letter, but the wish to express my own feelings on the subject has induced me to protract it. I am only sorry to trouble you with so much. I regret that you cannot attend our Board next week. I am particularly engaged the Thursday following, but if you can postpone your visit for a week (to the 27th), I will make a point of being in attendance.

I am, Dear Sir,
Yours very faithfully
C. Comyns Parker.

The letter of the Commissioners to which I have above alluded speaks of 'a somewhat diminished consumption on the part of the labourer' —this is really seeking in the lowest depths a deeper still, and looking for an argument in a quarter that will not afford it. Such expressions publicly made use of will do more than can easily be imagined to alienate the friendly feeling of many who are favourable to the general principle of the New Law.

This letter, which shows pity, toleration, and great humanity, is purposely quoted in full, for it is Christopher Comyns Parker's political testament. Politics in the 30s was mainly concerned with domestic questions, and in this he was a Tory of the Old School and of the best type. He loved the common people around him; he hated to see them suffer through inhuman Whig precision and he believed that the working-classes were on the whole 'loyal and well-disposed', as he put it in another letter. But,

when we reflect on what has so lately passed on the Continent (the Revolution of 1830) and the still disturbed state of other Nations, it must be right to use every prudent endeavour to meliorate the condition of the working classes who are in many parts of the Kingdom in a most deplorable state of poverty and privation of all common comforts and in many instances in a state which no change can make worse. When such is the situation of our poor Country, every thinking and benevolent mind must wish for the adoption of such measures as are expected to grant relief. (To his daughter Elizabeth.)

This was just as true in 1838 as on the day he wrote it in 1830.

While not denying, therefore, and indeed being eager to further the process of social reform, he saw society not as a number of units to be dealt with by an administrative machine, with blind impartiality, but as persons, each with his own rights and dignity, poor though some of them may be. He was not therefore willing without protest to administer the 'operation without anaesthetics' designed by Edwin Chadwick in 1834. He believed each locality should be allowed to work out its own aids to the implementation of the Act so as to avoid the suffering which he considered unnecessary. A large landowner himself and agent for several others, his business still made him see England as a land of small farms where every man had his own problems and his rights to every form of aid that could be thought of to help him solve them. Where industry existed he believed it should be rewarded; where ill-fortune struck, it should be as far as possible minimised; where the law entered into human relations that law should be wisely administered and decisions made according to it tempered to the needs and circumstances of those it was made to serve. This was the mainspring and spirit of his Toryism. For it he worked unceasingly.

In the election of 1830 T. G. Bramston was returned with 1840 votes against the next candidate's (also a Tory) 661, but the Reform agitation later in the year brought the Whigs more into favour, and in the first Reform election one of the successful Essex candidates was the Whig Charles Callis Western. The following year, both successful candidates, Western and Wellesley, were Whigs. The Maldon elections, with which C.C.P. was intimately concerned, showed the same tendency, the Whig candidate, Sir Thomas Barrett Lennard, coming out on top of the poll in 1832. In the elections of 1835 and 1837, however, the Tories regained the ground they had lost, for Essex was normally a Tory county and was represented by men like T. W. Bramston and George Palmer of Nazeing for the southern constituency, and Sir John Tyrrell for the northern. Maldon, too, turned conservative, electing Mr. Quintin Dick in the three polls of 1835, 1837, and 1841. Though there are no lengthy references in the diaries to the work C.C.P. did in these electoral campaigns, the Purleigh Tithe letters show that he was active. Possibly illness prevented his taking part as he would have liked in the campaign of 1841.

In 1826, when he was Mayor of Maldon, C.C.P. took part in a memorable election, not as a supporter of the Tory candidate but this time as the returning officer. The poll was taken on 7 June and the fourteen following days. The candidates were the Hon. G. M. A. W. A. Winn of Warley Lodge (Tory), Sir Thomas Barrett Lennard of Belhus (Whig), and Quintin Dick of Layer Marney (Tory). The first two were returned. It is said that more than £50,000 was spent at this election, and that 'one of the candidates [Winn] was so appalled at the serious incursion it had made upon his fortune that he soon afterwards sickened and died'.

Besides being Chairman of the Maldon Poor Law Union and Mayor of Maldon, C.C.P. had filled other public offices. In the height of the Napoleonic Wars, when England was relying largely on her landed gentry to captain her militia and volunteer regiments, he was commissioned by the Lord-Lieutenant as Captain of a company in the 2nd battalion of the local militia. He also served on the Bench in Petty Sessions and Quarter Sessions and was a Deputy-Lieutenant for the County. He was deeply mourned in 1843, and his passing was commemorated in the local Press in sincere, if banal, terms. The writer of the verse, extolling his philanthropy and his public spirit, says:

The Halls of Justice, the Manorial Court,
The Shire assembled for its Country's Good
Will miss his smile, shrewd Councel, manly Port,
And many a Gap wherein he nobly stood.

A more entertaining type of verse is political satire, from which no public man, whatever his virtues, can be entirely free. In 1835 the Municipal Corporations Act was passed, and, according to this measure, all boroughs were given a uniform system of government in place of the old close corporations which had formerly governed them. According to the new law, the ratepayers and freemen were entitled to elect the councillors, who, in their turn, were to co-opt aldermen, and councillors and aldermen were to elect their mayor yearly. For a long time C.C.P. had been a member of the Maldon Corporation. Now, when the government of the town became elective, his office of Alderman came to an end. In December 1835, when the first lists of candidates for the Council were issued in Maldon, C.C.P. was disappointed to find that they were party lists. He deplored the incursion of the party struggle in local politics, and in a circular to the people of Maldon he said so. This to him was a novelty, and something to be feared.

Of the two lists now in circulation in your Town, I cannot but express my decided disapprobation. Each of these exhibits to the Electors, in the names of those proposed to their notice, an exclusively party list; and should either of these suggestions be followed up by the election of those named, the good intentions of the Legislature would be defeated. With these views, and under these impressions, I cannot refrain from expressing the hope, that in the appointment of the body of Town Councillors, by whom your Mayor and Aldermen will be chosen, the greatest caution will be observed to select those, and those only, who, from the prospects they possess—the stake they have in the welfare of your Town—their general intelligence and acknowledged respectability—are really the most eligible men to have this important trust confided to them. Let this be done without reference to politics; let the animosities and bickerings of party be, for a time, acknowledged by all who view the subject with impartial and disinterested feelings.

Thus, C.C.P. was probably one of the first men ever to deplore the eclipse of the independent candidate and the rise of the all-powerful 'party ticket' in local government. The triumphant Whigs traced his disappointment to another cause and published a good-natured lampoon which far surpasses in quality the dim eulogy of 1843. Even through the mild satire may be sensed the townsmen's admiration of the former stately alderman:

269

The magic dreams of Tory times, alas! are waning fast,
The stout and lofty Alderman is put to bed at last,
No longer o'er his jovial face the hallow'd halo plays,
That glow'd upon bold Comyns' phiz—the phiz of bygone days.
The daring look that once adorned his fair and open brow
Is vanish'd like a summer's cloud; 'tis tinged with yellow now.
The heart that once beat high in place, and brav'd the Borough storm
No longer throbs for civic fame;—it shudders at REFORM!
Oh! I remember well the day, and so do many more,
When Comyns and his sky-blue boys set Maldon in a roar;
Great Comyns then, with chain and mace, and corp'rate honours
    drest,
Threw dignity into the May'r; ev'n Rads his power confess'd.
Now where alas! oh lackaday! is all his glory flown,
That aw'd the men of Whiggish hue, and kept the Liberals down?
'Tis gone for ever, like the sands o'er Afric's deserts driv'n,
And wither'd like the Woodham Oak, by lurid lightnings riv'n.
Oh! who can envy such a fate, forsaken and forlorn?
Forgotten, smil'd at, then walk'd out, and all his titles shorn.
I would not change for any change, whatever it might be,
To live my Borough honours out, and pray at last, like thee!
But paralyz'd poor Comyns dies, not Alderman nor Mayor.
Lord Melbourne's Municipal Bill has eas'd him of this care.
The day that follow'd Christmastide, his work was fairly done,
Then he was going, going, going, going, going,—GONE!

True, after 1836 the old Aldermanic days were past, but there
was still plenty that an energetic party man could do in political
work. John Oxley Parker followed his father in this. In July
1847 he was busy with the forthcoming elections:

July 26th. At home farming, and canvassing Boro' [Maldon] voters.

July 30th. Nomination of candidates, Maldon election.

July 31st. Maldon election. Messrs Dick, Waddington and Lennard.
Mr. Dick losing by 14 votes.

The result was a resounding victory for the Liberals and
Independents:

David Waddington (Independent)   461
Thomas Barrett Lennard (Liberal) 443
Quintin Dick (Conservative)   427

Among the collection of papers is a bill for this election for
£25 11s. 6d. It includes supper for 62 freemen at 2s. 6d. each
(£7 15s.), breakfast for 29 freemen at 2s. each (£2 18s.). The
rest of the bill, apart from a minor item of 15s. 7d., is for beer,
wine, porter, brandy, grog, gin, tobacco, cigars, and cheroots,
and adds up to £13 2s. 11d. This, which appears a very liberal
sum for drink and tobacco, was really minute when compared
with the fantastic amounts consumed at some other elections.

At the beginning of August J.O.P. was present at the
nomination for South Essex:

August 3rd. Drove to Skreens to breakfast with Charles Durant, and
accompanied Mr. Bramston and Mr. Smijth to the nomination. Sir
Edwd Buxton proposed at the hustings by the Whig party.

August 4th. Through Dengie Hundred, to see persons in the different
parishes to apprize them of the opposition and to arrange for
bringing up the Voters. Evening Committee at Maldon.

August 5th. Morning to Chelmsford, afterwards attending Committee
at Maldon.

August 6th. South Essex Polling. 1st day. Smijth 37 majority.

August 7th. D°, 2nd day. Sir Edward Buxton returned by majority of
35.

August 9th. Declaration of poll. Mr. Bramston and Sir Edward
Buxton returned. Dined with Mrs. Bramston.

The results were:

T. W. Bramston (Conservative)   2158
Sir Edward North Buxton (Liberal) 1729
William Bowyer-Smijth (Con.)   1694

Five years later, in the 1852 elections, he was again present at
the nomination meetings and at the declarations of poll both
for South Essex and Maldon, and spent long hours in the
committee rooms.

All the elections from 1847 to 1886 are mentioned in the
diaries, sometimes accompanied by significant remarks and by
descriptions of the scenes during the campaigns. In 1859, when
a conservative candidate lost by four votes only, J.O.P. noted:

April 30th, 1859. Maldon Election. Peacocke and Western elected. Col. Meyrick losing by 4—and mainly through the stupidity of some of Mr. Peacocke's strongest partizans persisting in plumping for him late in the day and when he was perfectly safe!!

Had it not been for this, the Tories would certainly have had two members in 1859, for the results were:

G. M. W. Peacocke (Conservative) 503
T. S. Western (Liberal) 431
Lt.-Col. Meyrick (Conservative) 427

In 1865 J.O.P. went to London to talk over the question of Conservative candidates with Benjamin Disraeli, and three days later he introduced Mr. Ralph Anstruther Earle, the candidate they had agreed on, to the members of the Conservative Party at Maldon. Earle contested the seat for Maldon and was returned on 12 July with G. M. W. Peacocke, who had sat for the Borough since 1859. Then, for South Essex, we have the note:

Met Lord Eustace Cecil, who had declared himself the Conservative candidate for South Essex in conjunction with Mr. Selwin. Meeting of Committee and speaking in the Corn Exchange.

H. J. Selwin and Lord Eustace Cecil were both returned.

In all the elections before the Second Reform Bill, J.O.P. was busy in two constituencies, Maldon and South Essex, besides having a vote in North Essex and East Surrey. In 1868 the constituencies had been further divided, and there was a sharp fight with four candidates, two Tories and two Liberals, in South-East Essex. J.O.P. campaigned for whole days on behalf of his friends James Round and Lt.-Col. Samuel Brise Ruggles-Brise, and was gratified at the declaration to see them top the poll with 2860 and 2815 respectively as against 2229 for Sir Thomas Western and 2234 for Sir Thomas Abdy. Though South-East Essex was Conservative, Maldon sent up two Liberals this time to join the ranks of the Gladstonians who made 1868–74 the Age of the Second Reform Ministry.

He does no more than record the election of 1874, but in 1880 and the days which followed the first Disraeli Ministry, electoral battles were fought with greater verve throughout all Great Britain between the supporters of the two political giants of the day. At this time the working-man was becoming politically conscious in a way that he had never been before, for he was aspiring to the vote and knew that he was very soon to have it. Disraeli had created the new Tory Party and was already making a bold bid for the support of the working-classes. Conservative clubs and Liberal clubs were springing up in villages which before had seemed remote from political strife, and the labourer who up to this time had been a noisy partaker in events in which he could wield only a second-rate influence, was now on the verge of political power, and was a force to be reckoned with. The Education Act had been passed in 1870 and the English ruling classes had begun to 'educate their masters'. Thus, in 1880, 1885, and 1886, political enthusiasm rose to fever-heat, and this is reflected in the diaries. J.O.P. flung himself with vigour into committee meetings, canvassing, and public speeches. He was a first-rate speaker with an excellent voice, and these were the days of Oxley Durant Parker's memories,

. . . the good old times when refreshments played a great part, and every Christmas Day the yard was very full of freeman voters from Maldon, who came to wish him a Happy Christmas and to drink his health and receive 2/6 each, and probably have some food besides. His wagons were loaded up with voters, drawn by four horses all dressed with blue rosettes, and every man, too, was given a blue rosette, and a large blue flag was fixed to the wagon.

In 1883 he flung himself with enthusiasm into the work of forming the new Primrose League which was designed to attract the new working-class voter to the Conservative Party, and many of its functions are recorded. On 16 March 1885 his friends Round and Brise were again adopted for East Essex. On the 23rd he took the chair at a meeting of their supporters. The

Liberal candidate was Charles Page Wood, who had made use of the agricultural crisis to declare himself the Tenant Farmers' Candidate. J.O.P. was angry and considered it as a sort of false pretences. He was tempted to visit one of Wood's meetings:

Inclined to go and speak against [this]. . . . Tired and afraid of evening East wind.

Wrote . . . that I had great fear that the depression of the times would induce a number of ignorant Farmers to split for Wood, to give him a chance.

He had no cause for fear. East Essex again voted strongly Conservative, both candidates being returned. In the Maldon election a Liberal came out at the top of the poll.

Times were bad, labourers were sullen, and, what was more serious, the Acts of 1884 and 1885 had given them power to do great harm, so J.O.P. thought. Something had to be done to stiffen the ranks of the Tory party. On 12 May 1885, though by this time he was seventy-three years of age, he took the chair at a meeting in Maldon to form a Conservative Association for the Dengie Hundred, with himself as President. The Gladstone Ministry, accidentally defeated over a clause in the Budget, had resigned, and a caretaker government under Lord Salisbury was in office until a General Election could take place on the new register.

With the passing of the new Act, his main interest now came to be in the South-Eastern Division of the County for which the adopted candidate in 1885 was Lt.-Col. William Thomas Makins, whom he accompanied almost everywhere in this electoral campaign. The entries in his diary show well enough the changed political climate as a result of national crises:

November 12th. Attended meeting of electors in Mr. ——'s barn; not so numerous as I had hoped, and a silent, unappreciative audience. Mr. Wills, the Liberal Candidate, had had a large meeting in a tent on Mr. Owen's lawn the previous evening. One or two questions asked . . . and show of hands in favour of Col. Makins.

November 13th. Meeting in barn near the Feathers [Bradwell] Noisy.

Interrupted by constant questioning by the Primitive Methodist Minister and Mr. Jopling and others. A chemical stinkpot of asafoetida or something of the kind brought in by roughs which nearly drove us out of the barn—held our ground through the noise and had the show by a few hands.

In the district round Woodham Mortimer where he lived they had a more friendly reception.

November 17th. Col. and Mrs. Makins arrived in the afternoon. Had tea and cold meat and went off to meeting at 6 p.m. in a barn at Purleigh Hall. Good meeting of farmers and residents in the parish and neighbourhood and large assembly of labourers. Everything went off most orderly and with what appeared to be a thoroughly good reception of Col. Makins. . . . Obliged to leave in time to go to Mr. Garrett's barn. Good meeting and large number on the platform. . . . Very fair reception but boys noisy at the far end of the barn. Favourable show of hands at both places. Home to supper at 10.

November 18th. Col. and Mrs. Makins at meetings at Latchingdon and Steeple; the first very good, the other noisy. They got back by ½ past 11.

On the day of the poll, 4 December, J.O.P. was busy with his friends taking voters to and from the station. On the following day he wrote:

Received telegraph of Declaration of Poll at Southend. *Col. Makins' majority only* 207. Makins 3707, Wills 3500.

Colonel Makins did not represent South-East Essex for long. Early in the following year Gladstone was defeated on his first Home Rule Bill. He dissolved Parliament and another General Election was held. This time Makins was adopted for the Walthamtsow division of Essex and we find the following entry in J.O.P.'s diary:

July 1st, 1886. Evening meeting of Rasch's supporters at Woodham Walter. Oxley took three wagons full from Woodham Mortimer. Good meeting—Rasch and L. Beadel spoke well. Vote of confidence carried.

This was the new Conservative candidate, Major Frederic Carne Rasch. Oxley Durant Parker had indeed cause to remember those lively election meetings in his memoir on his father, when he had been their transport officer!

On the following day, J.O.P. went to hear Rasch's opponent, W. H. Wills, and this is probably one of the few occasions when a man has put himself out to keep order in the meeting of a rival political party:

July 2nd. In the evening drove round by Hazeleigh White Hart to meeting called by Mr. Wills. Thought that we sh^d hear him. Only Mr. Brightwin and Mr. Bull addressed the meeting. Did not reply to any of their statements—only listened and kept the meeting quiet —very few attended.

On the 5th he attended one of Rasch's meetings at Orsett and another at Stanford-le-Hope:

Both went off well. A few roughs at Orsett, threw bags of flour at the carriages, and at Stanford-le-Hope, boys threw road grit at carriages.

On the 9th he was at Belhus, and to another meeting which was chaired by Sir Thomas Barrett Lennard (grandson of the Sir Thomas of 1836, see above).

Rasch spoke well, and enthusiastic meeting in his favour. On to Rainham. Meeting in the open shed at Mr. Circuit's farm. Good meeting and favourable reception, but some dissentients and questions, but large majority for Rasch. Returned to Belhus. Dinner at 11!

The next day he attended meetings at Prittlewell, Southchurch, and Great Wakering, 'all good-tempered and unanimous'. Afterwards he enjoyed a quiet week-end at home. On Monday, the 12th, he was distributing blue placards for posting. Polling day was Wednesday the 14th.

Weather fine. Men taken in wagons to Woodham Walter, Oxley driving the first wagon and other wagons from Hazeleigh and Cock Clarks to Purleigh. Voters all well disposed and very little display of yellow at either polling place.

What a fine sight it must have been. Several farm waggons driving up to the polling booth with horses, waggons, and men decorated with dark blue rosettes and ribbons, and the men enjoying what was so rare in those days—a holiday. We have, alas, no record of the thoughts of those individuals who were not Tory minded, but it is a picture that makes present-day polling appear very prosaic and sombre.

Thus ended his last election, one of the most memorable and most demanding of all. He forgot to enter in his diary the thumping majority gained by Major Rasch (3758–2916) though he recorded that of his friend James Round (4623–2322) in the Harwich Division.

It is to be expected that a man of J.O.P.'s standing should take part not only in political work but also in public service such as the magistracy and various county committees. In fact it seems true to say that little took place in the county in which he did not participate. He was made a Deputy-Lieutenant in 1852. He was a Justice of the Peace long before the Local Government Act of 1888 and was very regular in his attendance at the Petty Sessions for the Dengie Hundred, and was chairman of the bench for many years. Also he attended Quarter Sessions at Chelmsford regularly, and it is interesting to note how frequently his diary records a lunch or dinner with the judges when they were in Chelmsford for assizes, for such hospitality is rare today.

It was his practice to note outstanding cases at Quarter Sessions, or any that concerned him or his parish:

6th March, 1845. At home. Discovered robbery of wine etc. By cook [Susan Webster].

7th March, 1845. At home. Captⁿ Pattison attended at W. M. Place and committed Susan Webster for trial.

9th April, 1845. At Chelmsford attending trial of Susan Webster. Got the case brought on first in the morning. Prisoner pleaded guilty and was sentenced to 3 months in Colchester House of Correction. Remained in Court for the rest of the day.

4th July, 1849. Attending Quarter Sessions. Three boys from Latchingdon convicted of stealing eggs and sentenced to 7 days each and a whipping.

2nd January, 1856. Quarter Sessions. Boy . . . convicted of stealing coal from Viner's cottage. 2 years' imprisonment.

29th February, *1856.* Afterwards to Chelmsford. Attended examination of man charged with the murder of Sir John [Tyrell]'s keeper. Prisoner not further examined but committed on the coroner's verdict.

28th February, 1857. Morning home. Afterwards to Latchingdon to Petty Sessions (J. Jordan jun. 14 days for stealing faggots from the Grange).

December 1st, 1866. Home and Latchingdon Petty Sessions. Chas Reed and —— Allen charged with stealing tame rabbits from T. Royce and Richart Martin. Committed on their own confession to 6 weeks and hard labour.

One of the most interesting entries is that of 16 August 1867, which records a conviction under the old 'Red Flag Act', repealed after the first Brighton Race of 1896:

Had Messrs Sadd's man fined for not being at a proper distance in front of *his traction engine.*

On 3 April 1877 he proudly records the presence of his eldest son Cris at the Sessions for the first time, and, three weeks later, his son's first appearance on the Bench.

During his long period of service he was on many committees. Among these, his attendance on the County Rate Committee is recorded year after year, and there are mentions of the Licensing Committee, of which he was Chairman in 1873, the Turnpike Committee, the Sanitary Committee, the first Education Committee, the Committee for establishing Highway Boards, the Brentwood Asylum Committee, the Constabulary and Highway Committees, and many other *ad hoc* bodies. On 15 October 1850 there was a motion in Quarter Sessions to reduce salaries all round and to abolish the County Police. This was wisely negatived by a large majority of magistrates. Twenty years later he was sitting on a special Committee to deal not with the reduction or abolition but with increase:

December 13th, 1870. Chelmsford Committees—'Increase of Police Force', and 'Salaries of Clerks to Justices' and 'County Surveyors' Bills'.

He was as interested as his father had been in the welfare of the poor, and was a member of the Board of Guardians for Maldon even before his father's death. (29 December 1842.) In June 1848:

Attended Committee, Maldon Union House. Proposed various alterations of internal arrangements and new plan for wash-house etc., and instructed Mr. Bray to provide drawings for the same.

In 1870 a new workhouse was needed, and a field was purchased in Maldon on which to build it. In 1871 a selection of builders was made from whom tenders should be invited. On 1 August these tenders were presented:

Tenders for new Union given to E. Saunders—£14,700. Other tenders £15,000, £16,000, £17,000, £18,000, and Gozzett £22,000.

The building was started and in the following year two more gables and a clock tower were decided on. (25 June 1872.) On 30 September 1873 the first meeting of the Guardians was held in the new House.

In January 1856 a proposal was made that a reformatory school should be built for the county. He attended committees of people interested in the project, a subscribers' list was issued, and he served on the sub-committee which recommended a site for the school on land offered by Mr. John W. Perry Watlington. The school was established and was in existence for twenty-three years. It was dissolved in October 1879 by the decision of the subscribers.

One of his main interests was the volunteer forces. The popularity of these bodies reached a peak in the middle of the century, after the *coup d'état* of Louis Napoléon Bonaparte in Paris had embittered relations between Great Britain and

France, even to the point of preparing for a possible French invasion.

We gather'd our laurels and rode on our bays,

sings Sergeant Bouncer in Burnand and Sullivan's 'Box and Cox':

I mounted my horse in Her Majesty's Force
As one of the yeomen who'd meet with the foemen,
For then an invasion threaten'd the nation.

All over the land men were drilling, and their units were patronised by the country gentry:

14th September, 1852. Morning at home. Afterwards to Police Station, Latchingdon. Enrolled 16 men for volunteers for Militia. Also at Southminster for same purpose. Enrolled 8 more.

In February 1853 J.O.P. was again at Latchingdon and Southminster enrolling volunteers for the militia. On 6 May he dined at the Officers' Mess of the West Essex Militia. From that time onward the diaries contain frequent entries concerning the raising and equipping of volunteers:

December 6th, 1854. Drove early from Stanstead to Chelmsford. Attending with Capt. Skinner at the Office of the Clerk of the Peace to arrange proceedings as to the assessment of Boroughs and the expenses of the *Militia Armouries* etc.

By that time France was no longer to be feared, for in the summer of 1854 the Crimean War had broken out. In December, British and French forces, after having at Balaclava and Inkerman forced the Russians back on Sebastopol, had settled down outside the fortified city for a winter's siege. All over Great Britain domestic questions were now subordinated to the need for raising money and comforts for the war. In November and December J.O.P. was attending 'Patriotic Fund' meetings, and on 13 December his own parish of Woodham Mortimer sent up its subscription.

Now Great Britain and France were unnaturally close friends. On 16 April 1855 J.O.P. was in Pall Mall when the

Emperor Napoléon III of France and his Empress Eugénie passed in their carriage through cheering crowds. Men like Sergeant Bouncer, who had risen to their country's call, were going home again,

As there wasn't a foeman to meet with the yeoman,
And so no invasion threaten'd the nation.

but the volunteer movement continued throughout the 60s and to a lesser extent through the rest of the century. On 25 September 1858 J.O.P. was present when new colours were presented to the West Essex Militia. Rifle corps and volunteer corps were not merely a possible means of defence if the country should be threatened; they became a kind of men's social clubs and as much a phenomenon of the new age, when the labourer had come into his own, as the cricket club. In August 1860 he took part in the formation of one of these corps:

August 23rd, 1860. Evening attending meeting for establishing a *Rifle Corps* for ½ hundred of Dengie. After consultation a resolution was passed that I sh^d communicate with people at Maldon as to forming a corps for the whole district.

On the 28th he met the 'Maldon and Dengie Hundred people', and on the 30th was at a meeting at Southminster but business prevented him from attending the meeting at Maldon on 7 September. Nevertheless, after the meeting had been successful, he took on himself the bulk of the work of raising the corps. On 11 October he received a requisition 'numerously signed' from the Hundred to call a meeting with the object of forming a Mounted Rifle Corps. On the 13th he was at the War Office where he had a long interview with Colonel McMurdo on the question of dress, accoutrements and drill:

Learnt that it would be acceptable, and that it was not desirable that it sh^d be expensive in dress or saddling accoutrements.

On the 18th he took the chair at a meeting at Latchingdon Petty Sessions, when twenty-five men present put up their hands to signify that they were prospective members. On the 25th he wrote to the Duke of Manchester for guidance as to the rules of the proposed corps. A series of committee meetings followed and the draft rules were agreed on 20 November. On the 25th he wrote to Sir John Milbanke concerning the use of marshes on his property at Heybridge for rifle practice, and on the 27th he went through the list of persons to whom letters should be sent applying for subscriptions. On 1 December he was again at the War Office where he saw the Duke of Manchester in person.

In January 1861 the enrolments began, but the numbers were disappointing:

January 22nd. Meeting of 1st Essex Mounted Volunteers at Latchingdon for enrolments. Only 23 enrolled.

Concerts and dinners followed in an effort to make enlistment attractive but the results were not good enough. We hear very little of the corps throughout the summer, but on 23 August the following entry appears:

Meeting of Committee of *Mounted Rifle Corps* for the purpose of settling all outstanding accounts and arranging for the return of subscriptions to those who had paid them to the a/c of the intended corps. Also decided that application should be made to erase the 1st Essex from the list of corps in consequence of insufficiency of enrolled members.

This must have been a great disappointment to him, and considerably damped his enthusiasm for taking on responsibility of this nature. On 12 July he declined the offer of a captaincy in the Essex Yeomanry. Again, on 19 July in the following year, Colonel Palmer (George Palmer of Nazeing) pressed him to accept a commission:

. . . There ought to be more mounted men in that district. . . . It would occasion you no trouble as there would be an efficient sergeant placed under your command to do all necessary duties and who would be paid through me £35 per annum, and if you chose to employ his services in any other capacity you might find him a cottage and give him a trifle more—an efficient sergeant could be found who was good with pen and ink or in supernumerary agricultural or building affairs, as there are always men to be found in the

Blues and the Life Guards desirous of retiring upon their pensions who are glad to obtain a little military employment as Troop Sergeant-Majors of Yeomanry Cavalry. . . .

He was also given the opportunity of naming his own Lieutenant or Cornet, but again the offer was declined.

Never after this did J.O.P. play such a prominent part in the volunteer movement, though he was still interested in the Essex County Rifle Association, founded in April 1861, whose meetings he attended. In 1868 he received a letter from the Chairman of the 23rd Essex Volunteer Rifle Corps, together with a request signed by sixty-six officers and men, that he would take command of the Corps. There is no indication in the diaries that the offer was accepted.

The climax of his public career came in 1883:

March 4th, 1883. Learnt that my name had appeared in the Gazette last night as having been 'pricked' by the Queen at the Council at Windsor yesterday as *High Sheriff* for Essex.

March 6th, 1883. Morning to Chelmsford. Sharp frost, 7 deg. Sworn in as High Sheriff before Mr. Woodhouse. Appointed Charles Gepp my Undersheriff and their agents in London (Paterson and Co) as his deputies. Charles Gepp also executed bond of Indemnity to secure me against any losses from actions brought against me as Sheriff during my year of office.

March 7th, 1883. Received Her Majesty's Warrant of Appointment as High Sheriff.

On the whole, the year of his shrievalty was unexciting. On 28 May he attended the Levée at St. James's Palace and rounded off the day with a visit to see *Iolanthe* at the Savoy. But 23 June was an eventful day:

To London with Louisa and the Bishop and Mrs. Claughton, and with them from Liverpool Street in Saloon carriage to Chingford Station where Mr. Barclay's carriage was ready to take us to Knighton. The road from Woodford to Knighton thronged with people and carriages in expectation of the arrival of the Prince and Princess of Wales on the occasion of the Drill competition of the Metrop^n Board Schools. I was requested as High Sheriff to wait in the Hall to receive the Royal Party who then proceeded to the inspection tent. Splendid day and most interesting exhibition of Swedish exercises amongst the girls, and Company drill of the Boys for a Prize Banner. Afterwards an elegant luncheon for about 20, and glees sung by the School teachers. The Prince and Princess were accompanied by their 3 daughters and all behaved with the greatest ease and courtesy to all the company. . . . Left with the Bishop and Mrs. Claughton at 4 o'clock, and home before 8—very enjoyable day.

One item in his expenses list for the year carries a gruesome association:

Retaining fee to Binns—executioner.

The diary tells the story:

September 14th, 1883. Gouldstone found guilty of the murder of his 5 children and sentenced to death; brought this evening to Chelmsford Gaol. Saw undersheriff as to measures to be taken to appoint executioner.

24th November. Telegraph from Agents that a meeting for inspecting selected candidates for the office of Executioner would be held this day at the Central Criminal Court. Went up by 11-30 train with C. Gepp and on to C. C. Court. Sitting with Mr. Sheriff de Keysin and Mr. Sheriff Savory, to inspect 17 selected candidates. Agreed to appoint Mr. —. Berry of Leeds, or Taylor of Lincoln if reports should be favourable, and if otherwise, to make enquiry about Bartholomew Binns of Dewsbury.

Later, a letter from the Undersheriff of London arrived saying that neither Berry nor Taylor was satisfactory, and that Binns had been sent for from Dewsbury. By the same post came another letter from the Home Office announcing that the execution of Gouldstone was respited from 1 October to 8 October to give an opportunity for an examination as to his sanity. There is no further mention of the murderer, who may have been found insane. Thus the High Sheriff was relieved of a most unpleasant duty.

The most surprising part of this affair is not recorded in the diary. The murderer was condemned to death at the Assizes, and it was then learnt that the hangman had recently died. Thus J.O.P. had to advertise for a hangman. In response to the advertisement there were some 2000 applications for the job. Preparing the 'short list' must have been laborious as well as difficult.

The year had other and keener sorrows, for on 7 March he lost his second daughter Elizabeth at the age of thirty-two years. she was interred at a quiet family funeral in Woodham Mortimer Churchyard on the 12th. After the gruelling year of public duty and private sorrow he took his notable continental holiday.

I hear [wrote his friend Sir Charles Smith] that our High Sheriff intends to adminster Essex affairs from the French Metropolis, which looks as if he did not intend to honour Essex with much of his presence.

Since the diaries concern mainly business matters, there is not a great deal in them dealing with Church affairs. C.C.P. hardly ever alludes to the church at all. In fact, it was so much a part of family life that it needed no special mention. Attendance at church was so regular that only at times of sickness is a journey there by chaise or brougham noted. On 31 December 1871, in spite of a painful inflammation in the veins of his left leg, J.O.P. attended church twice. A similar attack at the time of his sixty-eighth birthday made him lame for about eight weeks:

25th January, 1880. Sunday. Lame. Church in a pony chaise.

15th February, 1880. Sunday. Church twice in Brougham with Louisa. Cold bath—lameness not so well.

7th March, 1880. Sunday. Church twice in pony chaise.

14th March, 1880. Sunday. Church twice in pony chaise.

21st March, 1880. Sunday. Walked twice to church.

28th March, 1880. Easter Sunday. Church nicely decorated, but almost a scarcity of primroses in consequence of the cold weather. Psalms chanted and singing good at both services.

When a new church was consecrated near to his home, he was there:

18th December, 1855. At consecration of new Church at Norton, erected at Mr. Holland's expense.

14th November, 1856. Home, and to consecration of new Church at Latchingdon.

16th June, 1885. Brilliant warm day. With Louisa and Frances to consecration of new Church at East Hanningfield. Large congregation. Service performed and sermon by Bishop of St. Albans. £204 collected at offertory. Luncheon at the School. Afterwards dinner to the poor and sports for the children.

On 8 June 1872 the Rev. R. P. Morrell died, having been Rector of Woodham Mortimer for thirty-seven years. He had done much for the parish. When C.C.P. was alive, he had raised over £250 for the enlargement of the church from the leading parishioners. (11 May 1841.) Mr. Morrell was a friend of the family. A letter to his brother from J.O.P., on 6 April 1873, when the late Rector's affairs were being settled, shows that much of the cost of improvements in Woodham Mortimer Church had been met by J.O.P. He seems also to have had much to do with the induction of a new Rector.

22nd June, 1872. Home. Morning with Mr. and Mrs. Hichens, who came over to see the Rectory and Parish, with the view to deciding as to taking the living. Gave him all the particulars of Tithe etc., and drove him round the parish, church etc.

13th October, 1872. Revd Richard Hichens, the newly-appointed Rector of Wood^m Mortimer, did the duty for the first time.

Some fourteen years later there are interesting entries concerning the preferment of the Rector of Woodham Mortimer, Mr. C. F. Maude. Over the business entries in the diary is scrawled diagonally:

May 4th, 1886. Berkeley told me that he had written to the Bishop that he thought Maude would like the offer of St. James's, Colchester. Told him I wished he had minded his own business.

It is plain that J.O.P. liked and admired the Rector and did not want to lose him. But six days later:

Met C. F. Maude and his brother at Liverpool Street, the former going to Cheraton. Felt sure that he had had the offer of St. James's, Colchester and was going down to consult his friends.

It was very true. Within a month we have the following:

June 9th, 1886. At home morning. Rev. Proctor Benwell brought letter from Mr. Norman that J. T. Round had offered him the living of Woodham Mortimer. Walked with him to the Rectory and in Mr. Maude's absence took him over the House, gardens etc., and to the Church, and gave him information as to income etc.

On 22 August the departing Rector preached his farewell sermon, and the detail with which J.O.P. treated the occasion gives an idea of his disappointment at losing Maude:

Mr. Maude's last Sunday at Woodham. Clear, bright and sunny with east wind. Farewell sermon in afternoon service and afterwards a crowded meeting in the school room to present a Testimonial from the Parishioners to Mr. Maude on his quitting the parish. The subscriptions amounted to over £30, and the objects presented were 4 silver fluted candlesticks, sugar basin and cream jug, and bag to carry canonicals, selected by Chris and all thoroughly approved by the subscribers. Had tea for the last time in the Rectory Garden, and Mr. Maude and his nephew Tom Maude and Lil^n Barlow dined.

The new Rector, the Rev. J. Kemp, 'read himself in' on the morning of Sunday, 26 September. On 15 April of the following year J.O.P. records his appointment as a Churchwarden. He died in office.

Christopher Comyns Parker had had great satisfaction from the reconstruction of Danbury Place and the preservation of a lovely hill site to posterity (see his letter to Elizabeth quoted above). His son had still greater satisfaction at being able to negotiate the sale of the mansion and land to the Church, for, many times after the sale he went to Danbury Palace to dine, to measure timber, or to a church function. During the latter years of his life he gave more time to Church work, attending diocesan conferences more and more frequently:

December 15th, 1861. Conference of clergy and laity at Maldon. Introduced the morning discussion to the meeting. Subject—The

Condition of the Labouring Classes, their present temptations, habits and moral and religious condition, and ordinary recreations etc etc, the means of bettering etc. Afternoon subject, 'Missions', introduced by Mr. Bramston.

Other conferences which he attended were the Stratford Conference of 1870, on 'Education and the Government Bill now before Parliament', and 'Churchwardens' Liabilities', the Chelmsford Conference of 1879 on 'The Cathedral and its Functions for Teaching and Worship in the Diocese', and 'The Whole Question of Sunday Schools', the St. Albans Conference of 1880, the Hertford Conference of 1882 on 'Middle Class Schools', and 'The Salvation Army and how to treat it', and the Brentwood Conference of 1883 on 'Tithe Rent Charge', 'Dwelling of the Poor', 'Purity of Life and the Prevention of Degradation of Women and Children', 'Elementary Education', and 'Marriage with Deceased Wife's Sister'.

*   *   *

There has never been a country in which so many people have done so much voluntary public service as is done in Great Britain today. Week by week our neighbours meet, in village halls, in council chambers, in schoolrooms, in churches, and in the open air, to organise entertainment, to provide recreation, to educate, to furnish material well-being and friendship for the old and helpless, to dispense justice in the courts and to govern our parishes and townships.

This tradition of service has grown into the warp and woof of our lives, from the days when a close-fisted and shrewd dynasty of monarchs turned their Justices of the Peace into the mainstays of county organisation, their Quarter Sessions into the fount of County Government, and their hundreds of parishes into small self-governing communities in which every man who contributed materially to the common weal was entitled to have his say in public affairs.

These monarchs could not have known the profound effect

the creation of this national scheme of unpaid civil servants would ultimately have on the people's life and attitude to life. Centuries of relative freedom from outside interference, and the power to hold its own in world affairs, created a proud and self-reliant nation whose members valued their right to express themselves freely. Agricultural unrest, industrial upheaval, starvation wages, child labour, the nineteenth-century squalor of town and countryside—none of these took from the British labourer the sense of belonging, and the well-being of the whole nation is the framework in which the lives and writings of capitalist and chartist, statesman and agitator, landowner and labourer, are all set.

It is this sense of belonging that lies behind the letters and the diaries of Christopher Comyns and John Oxley Parker. In the midst of pressing business concerns, their lives were lived in this atmosphere of public service, and they shared in full measure the fears, perplexities, and hopes of greater and lesser men. They lived at a time when the British working-classes passed from a vocal but only indirectly effective influence on government, to full citizenship, and in their interest in public affairs, at the rural fête and on the cricket-field as well as on the bench and in County Committee, they contributed to the good health and solidity of the society they lived in, and they helped to prepare for the middle-class state as we know it.

The work which they, and thousands of others like them did, has lasted; even the modern anti-social inventions such as the television-set which is in danger of making a man's home his prison as well as his castle, or the more sinister aspects of the 'Welfare State' which provide a convenient excuse for the self-indulgent citizen to do nothing for his neighbour, has not destroyed, and probably will not destroy, this vitality which was infused into society during Georgian and Victorian times, nor will it take away the grace which was given to our social life by men and women who knew how to live fully and graciously.

CHAPTER XVII

BANKING

WHEN WE SPEAK of banking today we are apt to think of the rock-like solidity of the Big Five, and forget how different circumstances were in the nineteenth century, even in its later years, for it was 1891 that the firm of Mills, Bawtree & Co., with branches at Witham, Clacton, and elsewhere, closed its doors.

Again, an inadequate supply of notes or bullion is a condition unknown today. But in 1819 we find the Epping Quaker, Henry Doubleday, writing: 'Scarce any gold in circulation owing to the restrictions of the Bank of England, which is prevented by the Government from issuing any gold in exchange for their notes, which are as low as 20/–.'* A further currency trouble at this time was the alarming extent of forgery that existed, and in 1821 a petition was presented by an unhappy tradesman who had twenty-five forged notes planted on him in one week. Thus the public were reluctant to accept Bank of England notes, and gold was in short supply, and this no doubt is the explanation of a plan devised by C. C. Parker to solve the difficulty.

He had printed on flimsy paper some notes (*illustrated opposite*).

These he signed and used for paying wages and accounts, and being so well known they probably circulated quite freely in the immediate neighbourhood and were preferred to Bank of England notes, for no one would bother to forge them. It was, too, a good way of borrowing money on the cheap, and there was always the chance they would get lost and not be presented for payment!

A bundle of 650 unsigned were found, and one was numbered

* There seems little doubt that this means a £5 note was valued locally at 20s.

1351, so it seems safe to assume that 2000 were printed, and as the paper on which they are printed has a watermark 1821, the date when they were current can be fixed fairly accurately. Perhaps it should be mentioned that he had no special connection with Sparrow & Co. and the identity of Edward Salmon is uncertain, but was probably his bailiff and as well known in the immediate neighbourhood as C.C.P. himself.

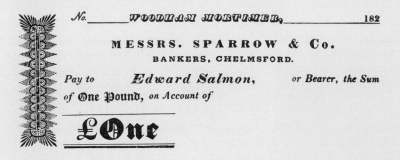

It is worth recording too that the years 1825–6 were anxious years for then occurred the great panic when some seventy or eighty English country banks crashed. The memories of country folk are long, and important events are handed down verbally from father to son, and this may explain the reluctance that still exists amongst the humbler country folk to entrust their money to a bank.

Crickett & Co. of Chelmsford was one of the banks that failed, and on 15 February 1826 the Provost of Oriel College, Oxford, wrote to C.C.P., who looked after some College property in Essex, expressing the hope

that you have escaped pretty well from the calamity which has affected so many in your neighbourhood. Is Cricketts Bank likely to pay a large dividend? From some rumours that have reached me I fear the reverse. It would however be some satisfaction to know which of my own farmers, and to what extent, they are involved in this failure.

A most interesting reply from C.C.P. followed on 6 March.

I fully intended, after making particular enquiry on Friday the 24th respecting the losses sustained by your Purleigh parishioners to have written to you, but to my surprise I found Chelmsford in great confusion and anxiety by a very severe run on the bank of Messrs. Sparrow & Co. A meeting was immediately called and every endeavour made to restore confidence. The result of Thursday last proved that it could not be effected. One of the partners informed me that since the failure of Crickett & Co. their house had paid more than £170,000 in withdrawn deposits and contracted circulation of notes. There was another meeting Saturday when it was made known that the partners have more that £180,000 landed property available besides their Personal Property and that in the Banking Concern there is a surplus of more than £18,000. Cricketts concern was considered one of the best managed Country Banks in the Kingdom and except for the default occasioned by Mr. Crickett's own debts the creditors would have no loss. Ten shillings in the £. will be paid as soon as the law allows a dividend, and by the Books, which are most clearly kept, there appear assets amounting to full 5/–, more from which the expenses of the Commission etc. are to be deducted. Although I intended on the 24th to have ordered your balance to have been remitted, I could not act contrary to what I was urging others to adopt, fully expecting confidence would have been restored. As soon as any balances are at liberty I will as usual pay Messrs. Child the amount, but at present I must keep prepared for weekly expenses and tradesmen's accounts, which do not average with me less than £100 a week. It took me on Friday at least 3 hours to get large notes changed into small and those into cash, only to procure £50 for Saturday night.

The opening sentence of this extract is of interest, for either bankers were not so secretive about their clients' affairs as they are today, or C.C.P. was on specially intimate terms with the partners of the bank.

In 1844 J.O.P. was involved in the crash of another bank, Messrs. Thomas Johnson & Co. of Romford. The last cheque which he drew was dated 27 May 1844 and the counterfoil is marked 'Self (at Sparrow & Co.) £250.' and was clearly an attempt to save his balances. Whether he was successful seems highly problematic.

It was in 1859 that J.O.P. was offered a partnership in

Sparrow, Tufnell & Co. of Chelmsford, a bank with several branches, which had weathered the stresses of the earlier years of the century—years which had proved fatal to so many of the private banks. No doubt it was felt that his intimate knowledge of the farmers of Essex would be of material assistance to the Bank.

The correspondence on behalf of the bank was conducted by William Michael Tufnell, and it could not have been more friendly and sympathetic. The first letter on the subject that we have is

Do not give up your day's shooting tomorrow as I can see you on Friday, though we cannot go into many details on that day [it was market day at Chelmsford] owing to the amount of business and the frequency of interruptions.

There is a light-hearted letter from his brother-in-law, Richard Durant, suggesting that £2000 a year would be a pleasant addition to the income but that it is important to ascertain 'the solidity of the Bank . . . for old Banks in the country are sometimes like banks in the fields, not quite sound'.

On 28 November Mr. Tufnell writes from the Bank

as time presses [a decision was wanted by the end of the year] I think the day you mentioned for going a little more into details upon matters should be fixed soon. I don't see that it must necessarily be here. How would it suit you if I were to call upon you next Thursday morning, say half past eleven on my way to Maldon. An hour and a half would I think suffice for all that need be discussed. I should propose to bring over a copy of our present Articles of Partnership and such abstract of accounts as might appear necessary.

But it was to his father-in-law, Richard Durant Snr., to whom he at once went for advice. It is interesting to find that throughout his life J.O.P. attached the utmost importance to the views of the wealthy silk merchants who were his in-laws. His was the respect of the simple country squire for City folk with their office in Copthall Court. Moreover, J.O.P. was not in a position at short notice to provide the cash needed, and had to borrow most of it from Durant & Co.

It seems quite clear that J.O.P. was anxious to accept, but after his visit to Devonshire to discuss the proposal with his father-in-law, he wrote to Mr. Tufnell raising numerous points about the terms of the partnership. His letter evoked the friendliest possible of replies, and an explanation that the eventualities he feared were unlikely to arise, and mentioned that his partner R. Woodhouse was anxious to increase his share of the business, and that he, W. M. Tufnell, was equally willing to increase his.

By 16 December all had been settled, J.O.P. had accepted the partnership and was to meet the other partners at dinner. A letter of this date from Mr. Tufnell gives further evidence of his thoughtfulness. 'Will you dress at Boreham on Tuesday as I should think it would be more agreeable to make the new Partner's acquaintance on the hearthrug in the hall than in the more formal atmosphere of the Drawing room before dinner.'

The decision was one of the greatest importance to the family for the association with the bank as partner or local director has continued unbroken for 100 years, and it would be a matter of great regret to the family if anything occurred to cause a severance.

Of his work at the bank little is known. The diaries maintain a silence which is disappointing. They tell merely of the meetings of the partners each half-year to consider the accounts, occasional reference to work there on Fridays, which was market day, and to *frequent checking of ledgers* (whatever this may have meant) *at Maldon*, the town near his home at Woodham Mortimer Place.

INDEX

Abbott, Jonathan, 1
Abdy, Sir Thomas, 272
Absentee landlords, 168-73
Agnis, Mrs., 13
Agricultural depression of the 1820s
  and 1830s, 50, 66, 70-3, 136-40
Agricultural depression of the 1870s
  and 1880s, 128, 148-65, 167, 168
Agriculture in Essex in the nineteenth
  century, 135-54
Albert Life Assurance Company, 229,
  230
Anti-Corn Law League, 140, 142
Appleyard, Robert L., 4

Bank failures, 68, 290-3
Bank of England, 290
Banking in the nineteenth century, 68,
  290-4
Batty & Whitehouse, 219
Beadel, William, 180-2, 190, 191, 195
Beefsteak Club, Chelmsford, 53, 254
Benwell, Rev. Proctor, 287
Bermondsey property, 1, 53, 89
Berney, Trench, 21, 24, 25
Bonaparte, Napoleon, 15-17
Boodé, J. C., 166
Bound, Maplesdon, 2
Bourchier, Captain Charles, 92, 169
Bourchier, Colonel (later General),
  89, 92, 138-40, 168, 169, 191, 192
Bovills Marsh Farm, troubles con-
  nected with, 174-83
Bowyer-Smijth, 271
Bradwell, family properties at, 5, 7, 13
Bramston, Thomas, 84, 166, 267, 271
Brentwood Asylum Committee, 278
Bridges, B., 20
Bridges, John, 20, 28, 29-32, 36-8

Brooke-Pechell, Sir George, 92,
  155-65, 250
Brooke-Pechell, Sir George Richard,
  155
Burney, Dr. J. C., 42, 43, 54
Buxton, Sir Edward North, 271

Caswall, George, 92
Cattle Plague Insurance Society, 145,
  146
Cecil, Lord Eustace, 272
Chadwick, Edwin, 267
Chancellor, F., 180, 181
Chapman, 21, 23, 25, 26, 29-31
Charterhouse, 166
Chelmsford-Blackwater Scheme, 193
Chelmsford Grammar School, 166,
  206
Clarke, T. T., 141, 206
Colchester Show, 146, 147
Commissioners of Sewers, 206
Comyns, Dr., 55, 56
Comyns, Emily, 55-60
Comyns, Sir John, 2, 3
Conferences attended by J.O.P., 287,
  288
Constabulary and Highway
  Committees, 278
Copleston, Dr., 68, 69, 82
Corn Laws, 50, 82, 136, 140; repeal
  of, 140-2
County Rate Committee, 278
Crespigny, Sir Claude de, 116, 253
Crickett & Co., Chelmsford, 68, 291,
  292
Crimean War, 280

Danbury, family property at, 5-7, 13
Dawnay, the Hon. Payan, 193, 206

U   295